Advocate
of Understanding

**SIDNEY GULICK AND THE SEARCH FOR
PEACE WITH JAPAN**

Sandra C. Taylor

THE KENT STATE UNIVERSITY PRESS

Frontispiece: Sidney Gulick at retirement, 1934.

Library of Congress Cataloging in Publication Data

Taylor, Sandra C.
    Advocate of understanding.

    Bibliography: p.
    Includes index.
    1. Gulick, Sidney Lewis, 1860–1945. 2. Missionaries—Japan—Biography.
3. Missionaries—United States—Biography. 4. United States—Relations—
Japan. 5. Japan—Relations—United States. 6. Church and international
organization. I. Title.
BV3457.G83T38 1984   261.8′7 [B]   84-12272
ISBN 0-87338-307-9

To my mother, Carol Clark Mortier, for her encouragement and love

CONTENTS

PREFACE

I first became interested in the life and works of Sidney L. Gulick during a year spent in Hawaii, 1972–73, when I began doing research on the phenomenon of the yellow peril and the immigration of Japanese to the territory of Hawaii and then to the mainland of the United States. Preliminary work on the yellow peril led to a paper I presented on the subject at the June 1972 meeting of ASPAC, the Pacific Coast Branch of the Association for Asian Studies. A sabbatical leave at Houghton Library, Harvard University, in the spring and summer of 1975 whetted my interest in Congregational missionaries, and I became further acquainted with the various members of the Gulick family who served the faith prodigiously in the nineteenth century. My first work on Sidney himself began in 1978, when I prepared and presented in San Francisco a paper for the Pacific Coast Branch of the American Historical Association.

That paper, which dealt with Gulick's work from 1900 to 1935, spurred me on to greater efforts when Professor Gerald E. Wheeler asked me a question I could not answer regarding the charge that Gulick had been an agent of Japan. He not only piqued my curiosity, he also told me that Gulick's youngest son, Sidney, Jr., had been a dean at San Diego State University, and was retired in San Diego. Then my work began in earnest, leading me through the National Archives, where Milton O. Gustafson's staff was most helpful, to the Houghton Library again for an extended perusal of the Gulick family papers, to New York City for a delightful interview with Luther H. Gulick, Sidney's eldest son, and to San Diego where Sidney, Jr., and his wife Eve were most gracious hosts and eager informants. Further research in the Swarthmore College Peace Collection was stimulated by conversations with Professor Charles DeBenedetti and Warren F. Kuehl. I found random material in the Bancroft Library at the University of California, and in the Hoover Institution for War, Revolution, and Peace. A preliminary article on Gulick, which I published with Warren I. Cohen's encouragement and guidance, led to correspondence with Richard D. Glasow, who had done a paper on Gulick at the University of Santa Clara in 1971. And finally I returned to New York to work in Council on Religion in International Affairs Papers, at the Rare Book and Manuscript Library at the Butler Library, where much of the material on Gulick's years with the Federal Council of Churches was to be found.

I have quoted from the Gulick papers at Houghton Library, from the Gulick materials at Swarthmore and at Butler Library, and from various collections by permission of the Bancroft Library. The assistance of the librarians and their permission to quote is gratefully acknowledged.

Finally, I owe a debt to the many scholars and friends who critiqued both the style and content of this manuscript through several drafts. Professor Sidney L. Gulick, Jr. not only provided encouragement and information but helped me to understand his father's personality, his faith, and to admire his many accomplishments. Professor Geoffrey S. Smith was unstinting in his admonitions to me to perservere, and he wielded a mean blue pencil in cleaning up my style. Warren F. Kuehl not only helped with style, but was an invaluable friend and mentor in clearing up my confusion on the peace movement. Professors DeBenedetti, Paul A. Varg, and Sharon Nolte also made many helpful suggestions. I owe a special debt of thanks to Professor Akira Iriye, who provided invaluable editorial services and inspiration, and to Professor Roger Daniels, who helped me clean up the final copy for the press and found many "nits" to pick. And last, I must thank Professor Lawrence S. Kaplan who encouraged me to submit this manuscript to The Kent State University Press, and to Tony Scott, Roxann Dickson, and Karen Lauridsen for typing. Karen Lauridsen and my husband, Russell Wilhelmsen, helped with proofreading the galleys. Needless to say, any remaining errors in this text escaped many watchful eyes and are mine alone.

The University of Utah
July 18, 1984

INTRODUCTION

Sidney Lewis Gulick was well known to his contemporaries but—like many writers on pressing but ephemeral concerns—he is all but unknown today. Missionary and publicist, author of more than twenty books and dozens of articles, he championed for thirty years the cause of the Japanese in this country and advocated reform of the nation's immigration laws. From his position with the Federal Council of Churches he promoted goodwill and understanding between the United States and Japan. He represented the best strains of Christian internationalism. Because the causes he advocated ultimately failed, memory of him has faded. Yet history's "losers" ought not be ignored, particularly where time has proven the wisdom of the policies they sought, for their attempts can help us in charting our course for the future.

Gulick was an unusual man from an unusual family. His grandfather accompanied the second group of Congregationalist missionaries to the Hawaiian Islands, and his father was a missionary to Hawaii and Micronesia. The family members had a deep sense of their historic roots and preserved their papers from the early 1820s to the 1950s. Sidney's father's generation included seven missionaries; his own family produced three, and two of his children returned to Japan. His son Luther is even better known as a public administrator and government official in New York. A sense of duty, dedication, and service motivated them all.

Gulick's life is significant for other reasons. It illuminates several aspects of Japanese-American relations heretofore obscure. First, his odyssey sheds light on the roles of American missionaries to Japan and their influence on American foreign policy, which contrasted sharply with the roles played by the better-known "China hands" with similar religious roots. Gulick was the most influential of the Japan missionaries, and yet his ties with that land served to lessen his impact rather than increase it, as friends of Japan became increasingly suspect in the interwar years.

Gulick was not only a missionary but also a "Japan expert" who served from 1887 to 1913 with the American Board of Commissioners for Foreign Missions. He exemplified the New England reform tradition, but brought a liberal approach to Christianity to Japan. A follower of the social gospel, he was concerned with improving the lives and minds of his students, and not just with saving their souls. Hence he became a proponent of the theory of evolution, seeking to convince his students that modern science was not incompatible with Christianity. He also sought to understand and interpret the rapidly changing Japanese culture to the West. He recognized that Japan's emergence as a world power had transformed the island kingdom from an exotic but obscure land to a competitor that could become either friend or foe. By the time he left Japan, his scholarship had made him a recognized authority on the country. His knowledge was so extensive that renowned historian Kenneth Scott Latourette requested his criticisms before publishing the first of his well-known works on the Far East.

Following his missionary service, Gulick spent twenty years with the Federal Council of Churches. Although in its infancy when Gulick joined the staff in 1914, the council quickly achieved considerable importance, speaking for twenty-four million American Protestants. It constituted a pressure group no government could afford to ignore. Under the leadership of Gulick and other internationalists, the organization formed commissions to study problems ranging from relations with the Orient and other world trouble spots, to disarmament, the outlawry of war, and the need for a Christian foreign policy. The council's educational programs were extensive; it had a comprehensive agenda of domestic concerns but sought, above all, to awaken Christian Americans to their duty as citizens in an interdependent world. Gulick and the council were fervent Wilsonians, supporting America's entry into

World War I and believing in Wilson's dream of collective security to prevent a recurrence of the cataclysm. However, shaken by the effects of the war, the Christian internationalists moved from supporting wars with supposedly "moral" aims to opposing armaments and conscription and advocating international cooperation. Gulick's work paralleled in important ways the evolving peace movement. His Christian internationalism was occasionally inconsistent, sometimes contradictory, and irrepressibly idealistic. He conceived of a harmonious world order maintained by reasonable men and reinforced by the Christian spirit. The problem that he identified was of fundamental importance in the interwar decades, and he exemplified the evolution of the liberal Christian approach to international politics.

That the domestic context was inextricably intertwined with the nation's foreign policy was Gulick's basic assumption. He was acutely aware of the sensitive nature of the immigration question, a political issue between the 1890s and 1924 with wide ramifications not only for domestic tranquility but also for international understanding and, ultimately, war and peace. West Coast discrimination against Japanese aliens and dissatisfaction with the ability of the Gentlemen's Agreement to keep further Japanese out of the country created a crisis in Japanese-American relations that affected even missionary work. As a spokesman for Japan's missionary community, Gulick sought to enlist the Federal Council in working for a new immigration law. Council leaders persuaded him to abandon his missionary career to lead the nation in the fight for an equitable immigration policy.

Gulick identified immigration as his special concern. Accepting the nation's fears of being overwhelmed by a new group of immigrants seeking entry, he believed in restriction, but he felt a fair and nondiscriminatory solution for all persons seeking entry was essential for Japanese-American relations. He publicized the quota system and worked tirelessly for its adoption. But his cherished solution was perverted by politics and racism, and oriental exclusion became the law of the land. Gulick refused to accept the 1924 law as the final word and he continued to work for its repeal. He did not live to see the ban on Japanese immigration finally lifted in 1952, but he saw what the exclusionists did not: that prohibiting oriental entry and denying to those already here the right of naturalization was blatantly racist and discriminatory; it could inflame relations with Japan even to the point of war.

Gulick's advocacy of an unpopular cause brought upon him both the wrath of the Japanophobes and the scrutiny of the Military Intelligence Division and the Bureau of Investigation. He became a quarry of the nascent security state in the days of the Red Scare; he was classed as a Japanese agent by overzealous internal security officials who believed anyone siding with the hated Japanese had to be in that government's pay. Public opinion accepted that notion, confirmed by Military Intelligence on the basis of unsubstantiated evidence and rumor. Because of this, his words reached a large audience in the United States, but were discounted by the policymakers in government.

Gulick labored in vain to educate the nation on the reasons for Japan's expansionist policies, for he felt that only through understanding could war be prevented. He worked to ease Japanese-American friction and promoted a more positive relationship between the two peoples. Although he discounted the prospects of war, in part because he had worked to defuse so many war scares, he was not surprised when war came. His futile battle against the negative image of Japan is an illuminating example of the limits of idealism in countering racism and nativism. A dedicated Christian, Gulick never lost faith in the ultimate triumph of justice, which he defined in terms of equity—equal treatment for all peoples, a fair share of the world's economic resources, and acceptance of racial variation and other cultures. His life underlines again the importance of searching for alternatives to conflict and striving to create a milieu of international and interracial justice and goodwill. Although the search for peace is inherently less dramatic than the alternative, the road to war, as mankind edges ever closer to the brink of oblivion it is an even more important story to tell, for in it may lay clues to our survival.

1

A MISSIONARY CHILD

To be born a Gulick in the 1860s meant a particular heritage and a predisposition to a peculiar destiny as a member of a distinguished, close-knit, and religious American family. Sidney Gulick traced his ancestry to the Netherlands. Two Van Julick brothers came to New Amsterdam in 1653 with their father; one brother died within the year. Sidney's grandfather, Peter Johnson Gulick (the Anglicized version of the name), was born in New Jersey in 1797, descendent of the surviving brother. Educated at Princeton, Peter was a devout Christian who joined the American Board of Commissioners for Foreign Missions (ABCFM) in 1827. He and his young wife Fanny accompanied the second contingent of missionaries to the Hawaiian Islands, where they joined an impressive group of Protestants who successfully converted an entire people, the only such instance in modern times. The first of their eight children, Luther Halsey, was born just three months after their arrival. In those years missionary work meant a permanent commitment to life abroad. The Gulicks worked in Hawaii for almost fifty years without returning to the United States, and they ended their lives in Japan, where they moved in 1875 after that mission field was opened.[1]

Sidney's father Luther was sent to the United States to school at age twelve, the common practice among missionaries living abroad. Missionary work was considered a "calling" and not customarily passed from father to children, especially in the Ha-

1

waiian field, where more lucrative pursuits beckoned. Yet Luther
received the call as an adolescent, and he pursued a medical education to further his usefulness abroad. His seven siblings made
the same choice of vocation, an occasion almost unparalleled in
mission history. Luther married Louisa Lewis, who was "from
childhood's days, marked for her deep religious feeling and a passion for personal benevolence," as her son later described her.[2]
Because the conversion of the Hawaiian Islands, where Luther
and Louisa also settled, was imminent, the American Board decided to open a new field in Micronesia. In 1852 the couple sailed
for that almost unknown land, one that turned out to be far less
congenial than Hawaii. The Micronesians had been mistreated by
foreign sailors; distrusting all foreigners, they did not welcome
missionaries. In addition, the islands were extremely remote and
isolated. Three missionary couples were sent to different locations,
and months often passed with no communication between them.

Living on Ponape, the Gulicks welcomed two daughters before the birth of Sidney in 1860. (One adopted Micronesian child,
Kate, died while they were still in that land.) Both his parents'
health had deteriorated in Micronesia so they sought to return to
Hawaii for Sidney's arrival, but were unable to book passage
there. They did reach the small island of Ebon, populated by less
than one thousand inhabitants, where Sidney made his appearance. Louisa was too ill to nurse the infant, and there were no
milk-giving animals on the island. Because they felt hiring a Micronesian wet nurse for the infant would be unsuitable, Sidney
was raised for nine months on the sap of coconut trees. As Sidney
related, those nine months were "one long wail," and indeed, this
diet contributed to his feeble health as a boy. Sidney believed his
frailty had prevented "the normal childhood's experiences, and
doubtless had a permanent effect on my outlook on life as well as
on my methods of thought."[3] Although life in a missionary family
itself was a contributing influence, his judgment was probably
accurate.

Sidney viewed his early years as unhappy, and that made him
ambivalent about undertaking missionary work as a career. In an
autobiographical essay he listed his ancestors' achievements, but
noted: "These few statements will serve to show the religious

spirit and missionary enthusiasm of my parents and grandparents. Believers in family heredity might make much of these facts. But I think they do not really count for as much as seems to be generally thought."[4] His father's career had been hard on him as a child, and it might well have inclined him in the opposite direction. Although Sidney's upbringing was unusual only in that his parents relocated more often than most missionary families, this deprived him of a sense of place and companionship of peers, especially when coupled with his own frail health and his mother's overprotectiveness. The rigors of life in the field seemed to bear more heavily on the wives and children, as numerous accounts of missionary lives affirm, and as we will see later. Few children followed their parents' calling; it was rather remarkable that two of Luther's offspring were drawn to it. Missionary work required a heavy commitment, but religious devotion and a sense of duty and dedication were in the Gulick blood.

THE NINETEENTH-CENTURY PROTESTANT MISSIONARY EXPERIENCE:

The missionary calling had been an esteemed and honored cause in Protestant America in the late nineteenth century. The ABCFM was founded in 1806 in Andover, Massachusetts, an outgrowth of the revivals of the second Great Awakening and the harbinger of the reforms of the Jacksonian era. The board aimed at nothing less than the conversion of the entire world to Christianity. Born of Congregationalism, the ABCFM was tightly structured and well-organized, and the oldest of the soon-numerous Protestant missionary groups. Beginning its work in the home mission field, it soon took a special interest in Asia and the Pacific and then spread its mission field to India, Ceylon, and China. In 1869 its missionaries entered Japan, laying the groundwork for the regular proselytizing activities that began when the prohibited Christian faith was officially "tolerated" in 1873.[5]

Generations far removed from this "calling" may find it difficult to recapture the intensity and the devotion with which the nineteenth-century missionaries approached their task. Filled with boundless optimism and faith that was as much American as it was Christian, they set out to conquer a world for Christ. R. Pierce Beaver, an authority on missions, has written that the enterprise grew to great magnitude, "impelled by simple obedience to the dominical commandment to go and make disciples of all the world with, perhaps, an admixture of the driving force of American 'manifest destiny.' "[6] Few of these zealous individuals were conscious of how alien their beliefs were to the non-Western world. They were unaware that the culture they promoted along with the Gospel was undeniably American, and they refused to consider that more ancient religions might have equally valid traditions. They faced an often-hostile world fearlessly, and although they did not seek martyrdom, they were prepared to die for their beliefs.

The majority of missionaries were men. Few single women ventured abroad before the Civil War, for the mission boards considered it an impropriety. For men, marriage was a virtual requirement for missionary life. As the secretary of one mission board said, "Woman was made for man, and as a general thing man cannot long be placed where he can do without her assistance." Marriage to a like-minded woman not only removed the temptations of heathen women, but it enabled the couple to establish a Christian household abroad. The mission boards did not consider the hardships this imposed on the wives and children.[7]

Women played an important role, however. Single women, like Julia Gulick, Sidney's aunt, were extremely useful because of their single-minded dedication to their religious duties.[8] Wives also occupied an important role in the mission. As "associate missionaries," their tasks included providing a Christian home (considered essential in promoting the faith in Asia), extending hospitality to visitors, and assisting their husbands in the religious work of the mission. Usually they taught English until they had children. Then these women were supposed to demonstrate by their example their high status as women, wives, and mothers in the Christian home, exemplifying Western, Christian mores for the prospective converts. Products of the nineteenth-century "cult of true womanhood,"[9] they were pious helpmates.

While many women married missionaries to share a lifework they also valued, the dual responsibilities of missionary work and motherhood brought special hardships. Residing among people

who were often primitive by Western standards posed many difficulties, especially since the Protestants, unlike Catholics, sought
to live abroad as much as possible like they lived at home—
modestly, but in a "civilized" fashion. "Native" housing was usually uncomfortable, the food unpalatable, and even clothing
could be a problem for those who sought to retain the appearance
of proper nineteenth-century gentlemen and gentlewomen. Childbirth was frequently a hazardous experience for both mother and
infant, and as the children grew, mothers had to cope with childhood illnesses without a readily available missionary physician,
and had to manage stress as best they could. They also were often
the only teachers available for their offspring, as American missionaries feared "contamination" if they allowed their children to
be educated with those they sought to convert. When the children
reached the age of twelve or fourteen, they were sent to obtain a
formal education at "home" in the United States. Sometimes their
mothers accompanied them, leaving their husbands for several
years; in other cases the children traveled on their own.[10]

Higher education often posed an insurmountable financial
burden on the missionary family. Although the mission board
granted an extra stipend for offspring, it did not cover children
over eighteen. Unless they were extremely frugal, parents could
not without some sacrifice cover the costs of college for their
often numerous progeny.

Life also had it special problems for missionary children. Families stationed in remote outposts suffered from isolation, and the
children were not encouraged to play with native youngsters. If
the missionary family were moved from station to station, the
children could not develop roots. Although they usually had very
deep ties to their own family, they were obviously not socialized
into American culture, and coming "home" to a land they had
never seen before could be a shock. In addition, their education
was usually haphazard, and entering the American system of
higher education presented difficulties.

A MISSIONARY UPBRINGING:

Sidney's life followed a pattern not untypical for missionary
children. His family left Micronesia shortly after his birth, and he

spent his childhood in Hawaii, where his father was secretary to the American Board mission. Sidney and his two elder sisters were soon joined by three more siblings, who did provide each other with some companionship. The red-haired Sidney, a sickly child who was, as his father had been, rather withdrawn and quiet, had few other companions. He lacked the assertiveness to meet other children and his overprotective mother allowed little contact with them anyway.[11]

In 1870, Sidney's life changed dramatically when his father resigned the secretaryship of the Hawaiian Board and sailed for America. The Gulicks spent the winter in New Haven, Connecticut, but Sidney's persistent ill health was not helped by the harsh New England climate, and he was unable to attend school. Before he could make friends the family was reassigned to Spain, where Luther had been asked to open a mission for the American Board. One son, Edward, stayed behind in New Hampshire, "adopted" by Dr. Samuel P. Leeds who had no family and wanted to help with Edward's education. At the end of their eighteen-month stint in Spain, Sidney's youngest brother Peter (called Pierre by the family) was born. Louisa was extremely ill following this birth, and the twelve-year-old Sidney became chief tender of the infant, an experience he later recalled as "quite an education."[12]

In two years the family was transferred to Florence, Italy. With a child's quick ear and facile tongue Sidney picked up Italian as he had Spanish. His parents encouraged him to study German, French, and English, and although his mother supervised, "telling me occasionally what to do," as he later wrote, she had little time to hear him recite or review. In the three years they spent in Italy, Sidney developed many new interests. He consumed Roman history, collected old coins, and read widely on subjects as diverse as the Napoleonic wars and the exploration of Africa. Tales of missionary deeds were especially fascinating. His parents encouraged him to keep a journal, which he soon filled with notes on their travels, his ideas, and less cheerful accounts of his frequent illnesses. But the Italian mission was not particularly successful, and the family moved again.[13]

Sidney continued to be largely self-educated. On their way back to the United States, Louisa and the children remained six months in Switzerland while Luther went ahead, and there Sidney learned to speak French. His experiences in European countries and study of their languages left an indelible mark; he retained a deep interest in Europe throughout his life. The sojourn in Switzerland introduced him to another lifelong passion, hiking. He took "tramps" to the top of the St. Bernard and the Diablerets passes, and with his eldest sister Fanny went to Chamonix and Zermatt. The mountains filled him with exhilaration and a sense of the nearness of God, an experience he described as a kind of mysticism. Throughout his life he found the mountains inspiring, and he later shared with his own sons the joys they could bring to the soul.

Sidney was by this time sixteen, small for his age (he stood about five feet ten inches tall as an adult), shy and red-headed, as were his parents and siblings. He never learned the art of easy sociability that children pick up from friends; a serious youth, he preferred reading. Although he was deeply religious, he never experienced the conversion experience that was so common among teenagers in evangelical households; he simply could never recall a time when he was not a Christian. His faith grew from his family ties and his parents' teachings, and the love of God substituted for the close friendships denied him by the location and nature of his upbringing.

No sooner had the family returned to the United States, via London and New York, than Luther accepted a new position with the American Bible Society in Japan. The family traveled across the country to Oakland, California, where they had friends, and father and Frances (Fanny), the oldest at twenty-two, went on to Japan. Sidney and the other children, Harriett (Hattie), Luther, Jr., and Pierre spent the winter first in Oakland and then Pacific Grove with their mother, and in March of 1877, Louisa and the youngest boys, Luther and Pierre, left for Japan. Orramel (Ollie), who had been "loaned" to Uncle Orramel and Aunt Annie Gulick and separated from his family for six years when they were suddenly sent to Spain, died just two days before the family reached Yokohama. Edward, living with Dr. Leeds of Hanover since his family went to Spain, remained in New Hampshire. Seventeen-year-old Sidney, and Hattie, his next elder sister, were to stay in

Oakland. Yet even there the two were apart, as Hattie boarded with one family while Sidney resided with the Reverend John Knox MacLean, pastor of the First Congregational Church, with whom the Gulicks had become acquainted during their stay in Oakland. Sidney later described the MacLeans as "two kind and loving people" who did not understand him.[14] Withdrawn and shy, he lived alone in a small room, unable to communicate with his revered host.

For a year Hattie and Sidney maintained a lonely existence in Oakland, seeing each other once a week or less. They spent the summer at Monterey sharing a tent, which was, out of deference to propriety, divided by a sheet. In the fall Hattie too sailed for Japan, and Sidney was left to begin his formal education.

Sidney had never had any formal schooling, and what instruction his mother had given him had been sandwiched between missionary work, the chores of caring for her large family, and conserving her own frail health. Through Hattie's interceding with the school principal, Sidney was able to bypass the entrance exams to high school (which he might not have passed), and was admitted to the junior class of Oakland High School. This school was a new and pleasant experience for the lonely youth, who found mathematics and the natural sciences especially interesting. He later reflected that science thrilled him because "I realized that I was thinking God's thoughts after Him." He never recognized any conflict between science and religion but rather felt that they confirmed and supported one another.[15]

Sidney was befriended by two families who took him under their wings. Pastor MacLean provided spiritual guidance, and the family of Galen Merriam Fisher gave him love. The Fishers had become acquainted with the Gulicks when they resided in Oakland, through their mutual involvement with missionary work in Japan. Mrs. Fisher's sister, Eliza Talcott, was one of the first single women sent by the American Board to Japan in 1873, and from her the Fishers had become interested in the Orient. The Fisher children provided companionship for both Hattie and Sidney. The two were often invited to meals, and after Hattie left for Japan, Mrs. Fisher continued to look after Sidney. Soon he felt almost like a member of the family. He would spend Saturday evenings at their home, playing games and talking.

Two of the Fisher children were close to Sidney's age. Leonard, a year his senior, was a good friend. Sidney's health improved dramatically in the California climate; he wrote his mother that now, at age seventeen, he weighed 140 pounds. He and Len went on hikes and enjoyed the mountains in the summer, spending five weeks in Yosemite in 1879. The Fishers' daughter, Cara, also became Sidney's companion, and they walked to school together and often took the same classes, although he was a year older. Sidney occasionally took Cara to a lecture (including one on "Women's Wrights [*sic*] delivered by a manly woman"[16]), and they participated in religious activities. The first year he considered her just a friend, but during his second trip to Yosemite in 1880, when she was studying bookkeeping in Portland, he began to realize his feelings for her were special.

During those years Sidney joined the Oakland Congregational Church, after deciding that he needed a religious home. His faith was sincere, but it did make him a bit of a prig as a young man, as in high school he sometimes used religious values to hide his insecurities. He wrote many years later: "I think I must have been a decidedly bigoted, self-righteous, and dogmatic young fellow looking down with contempt on the loose, irreligious lives and talk of my schoolmates." He recalled how shocked he was at his classmates' swearing, smoking, and "impure jokes," for which his upbringing had not prepared him. He viewed his classmates with disdain, and made no friends among them. Having lacked the opportunity to associate with young people his own age, he was ill-equipped for socializing. Later he castigated himself for defending "his stupid inability by religious hypocrisy," but he was too harsh a judge.[17] As an adult he regretted his inability to mix easily with his contemporaries, and it took many years to overcome the insecurities of his childhood.

Sporting a red moustache, Sidney graduated from high school near the top of his class. He enrolled at the University of California in Berkeley but was soon dissatisfied. The students were even more frivolous and irreligious than his high school classmates, and he also felt the education was inferior.[18] Clearly it was time for a change.

His decision was also influenced by the prospect of closer ties to his family. Sidney's younger brother Luther joined him in

Berkeley in the summer of 1880, and the two, together with Len
Fisher and John Bishop, Sidney's childhood friend from Honolulu, went camping for six weeks in Yosemite before taking the
train east where Luther was to enter school. The Gulick brothers
then traveled to New York where they were met by their brother
Edward, and the three then traveled to Norwich, Connecticut,
where they met Fanny, who was now married and visiting her
in-laws. Sidney's reunion with his brothers and sister was a joyous
one, and partly as a result of conversations there with his sister,
Sidney decided to go with Edward to Hanover, New Hampshire,
to study at Dartmouth.[19]

Although Sidney received a scholarship, entering Dartmouth
raised the problem of housing. Edward lived with his guardian,
Dr. Leeds, who let Sidney stay a few days until the doctor decided
he approved of the shy young man and offered to let him share a
room with his brother. Despite the harsh climate Sidney thrived in
college and liked the small New England town. Ever serious and
proper, he found the "hypocrisies" of his classmates especially
offensive as Dartmouth purported to be a religious school. His
critical eye detected certain unnamed practices "that wouldn't exist under circumstances where the semblance of religion did not
bring some temporal advantage."[20] He took a full load of courses
in a variety of subjects including Greek, Latin, science, and
mathematics, joined a religious fraternity, and placed second in
his class his first semester, one position ahead of his brother.

College pranks did not amuse Sidney. He related to his parents
his considerable indignation when some students blew horns in
the middle of the night to disturb a professor whose examinations
they considered unfair. The offenders were threatened with expulsion by the administration unless the entire class apologized.
The self-righteous Sidney remarked with satisfaction that they
voted not to "hang together" on the matter. His mother, who had
kept him and his siblings away from adolescents their age in Europe to prevent their falling in with "wayward youth," must have
been pleased.[21]

Luther and Louisa kept the widely separated family in touch
with one another by requiring correspondence. Throughout his
college years, Sidney wrote a journal which he periodically sent to

his parents, and he often corresponded with his brothers and sisters, especially his sister Hattie, with whom he was particularly close. His relationship with his parents was formal. His father wrote him on occasion, but almost entirely about financial matters, while his mother's solicititude was mainly about his health. The elder Gulicks were transferred to Spain again while Sidney was in college, although his father did come to his graduation. Time and distance, however, took their toll of the familial relationship; Sidney soon felt far closer to Dr. Leeds than to his own father.[22] Hattie, in an engaging word portrait, described her brothers for her parents in a letter written during a visit to Hanover in February 1882. Edward, she said, was becoming a replica of Dr. Leeds, cautious and as stuffy as the village itself. She described Sidney as purposeful and mature; he showed the effects of six years of independent life. She noted with pleasure that he had learned to control his fiery temper: "All this has made a man, and a strong man, out of the delicate boy who liked to be taken care of." Lest she be accused of too much praise, Hattie noted that he lacked imagination, but then, a "year out of Sleepy Hollow" should wake him up.[23] Clearly Sidney had a fan in his sister Hattie.

Sidney wished he had another one in Cara Fisher. During his last two years in Oakland he realized how much he cared for her, but he found it hard to express his feelings in words, and he was not rewarded when he did so. Cara remained aloof, giving him meager encouragement during his college years. She answered his chatty letters only after much delay, and then very briefly. He proposed to her by mail in 1882, but got a diffident response; his only encouragement was her willingness to let him continue writing. Undaunted, he proposed again the next year, and was rejected more forcefully.[24] He understood her message then; the correspondence ended.

Although Sidney was disappointed in love, college as a whole was an enriching experience. Science was a constant stimulation, and Sidney planned during his second and third years to become a professor of astronomy. He later recalled how during the winter of 1882 to 1883 he would spend the night with the telescope and find the experience uplifting and inspiring.[25] He also benefitted from the relationship with Edward, who, he later recalled,

Dartmouth, 1883: Sidney Gulick at graduation.

"taught me how to play, a thing which I can say I hardly knew how to do."[26] The contact with young men his own age was also beneficial, however much he disdained their sinful ways, since he gradually learned to associate with his peers.

Sidney planned to teach science after graduation, but he believed God would personally guide his choice of career. He expected to receive a clear message if God wished him to become a minister, and later he believed that God would provide him a wife if He (God) desired him to become a missionary. His God was a personal deity whom Sidney felt directed his life. Waiting for a signal, he accepted the principalship of a small Ohio school only to learn that the institution had misrepresented itself and was not financially sound. Bankruptcy, his mother told him, was a clear sign from God that He did not intend Sidney to be an educator. He resigned at once and planned to enter Union Theological Seminary in New York City for the fall term of 1883. Money, always a problem, was acquired by tutoring the five children of the wealthy Robert Lenox Belknap family, and later he superintended a Chinese Sunday school in the city.[27]

Union Theological was not the stimulating experience for Sidney that Dartmouth had been. "I crammed in much information. But no great enthusiasm filled those three years," he reflected later, "I was far too busy."[28] Excitement and inspiration from learning that he desired were thus denied him. Tutoring the Belknap children, the eldest of whom was mentally retarded, paid his bills, and his Sunday school teaching was time-consuming though rewarding. He earned a master's degree in theology, but at the price of blinding headaches.

Another problem he faced at the seminary was his estrangement from Cara. However, she came east that fall to attend a nurses' training school in New Haven, Connecticut, and consented to correspond once again. Sidney enjoyed one of the best weeks of his life when she visited him in New York in May of his first year at Union. Cara stayed with relatives and she and Sidney toured the city, sightseeing, visiting museums, and meeting friends from Oakland. Suddenly life opened up again. Sidney spent the summer at Sea Bright, New Jersey, with the Belknap family, pelting Cara with two letters a week. Buoyed with enthusiasm and longing, he even began to broach to her his career plans. The idea of going to China as a missionary had developed from the enthusiastic accounts his parents, who had just been transferred there, had written him. But, despite Cara's interest in the topic, her reaction was muted, and his own passion blinded him to the coolness of her response. In November he wrote again for her hand with words of love: "It is hardly necessary for me to tell you again how intensely I have loved and still do love you." Cara did not reply for nearly six weeks, and when she did she dashed his hopes. Curtly she replied that she had hoped her feelings for him would change, but they had not. She just did not love him, and that was that.[29]

Sidney had some consolation in the nearness of his family. After Dartmouth, Edward taught school for a year and then joined him at Union. Hattie spent a year in New York in medical school but abandoned her goals when her health faltered. Brothers Luther and Pierre were at Oberlin, where sister Fanny Jewett also lived, and Sidney spent some time with them the following summer.[30]

The last year of seminary passed quickly. Sidney worked at the Sunday school, tutored, and finished his coursework. The idea of missionary work in China was still appealing, and his father encouraged his aspirations, but he believed that position necessitated a wife. He tried to find a substitute for Cara, but did poorly. Charlotte Hall, the young woman he began to see, was clearly fond of him, but her parents did not fancy the idea of her involvement with a future missionary who would take her far from home. They asked him to stop seeing her, and he was shocked when she suggested thwarting their wishes through surreptitious rendezvouses. As he later wrote, "She disappointed me by her failure in sterling character." His reaction was prompted not so much by stuffiness as by his continuing love for Cara Fisher. Ardor suffused a letter he wrote her but did not mail: "I tried to forget you but in vain." Trying to distract his mind from his romantic disappointments, in the summer of 1885 he and a classmate took a bicycle tour of the British Isles.[31]

Sidney was graduated from Union Theological in 1886 with the issue of his future missionary career still undetermined. He investigated the possibility of a post with the ABCFM in Shantung, China, during his courtship of the disappointing Miss Hall, but when that romance faded he decided to postpone applying. The mission board did, by this time, accept applications from an occasional single man, but it was not their preference, and clearly theirs was a position he agreed with. In the meantime he took a position as pastor of the Willoughby Avenue Chapel of the Clinton Avenue Congregational Church in New York City and found the work rewarding and inspiring.[32]

Suddenly his future brightened. Unable to forget Cara, Sidney wrote to Oakland once again asking if she would see him the next year when he expected to pass through on his way to China. Cara replied affirmatively within the month, rather quickly for her, and she also revealed that she was visiting with his sister Hattie, with whom she had had some long talks. The next day he heard from Hattie, who told him she had convinced Cara that the new correspondence she had agreed to entertain could not be merely that of friendship. Hattie, who had been playing matchmaker for several weeks, encouraged Cara to write in terms of love. Within a few months Cara had confessed to Sidney that she had been dating a medical student, but their romance had soured. She begged his forgiveness and asked to see him again.[33]

Sidney responded, but raised another problem: he was unable to leave his position at Willoughby Avenue for a trip, he told her; she would have to accept him on what she knew of him in the past. His words of love were touching: "I fell in love once, and I never got over it. I partly made myself love again, but I got over that with a vengeance." Cara was the woman for him, and he asked if she would join him in the mission field in China or Japan.[34] Her reply was equally touching: "I love you. . . . Whither thou goest, I will go." Whether it be China or Japan did not matter as she was caught in the emotion of the moment. He did not learn for many years that what changed her mind was a combination of parental pressure and her own interest in the missionary life. He wrote her parents the traditional request for her hand two weeks later.[35]

The next few months were full of planning for their future. Cara remained in California until just before the wedding, which was held at her aunt's in New London, Connecticut. Sidney debated the relative merits of China versus Japan with the men of the Prudential Committee of the American Board in Boston. China was appealing, the more so as he had heard it was difficult to recruit for that troubled land. But his uncle Orramel had written him a persuasive letter about the need in Japan. "Isn't Japan the El Dorado of missions?" Sidney asked, fearing he might be choosing the easier post.[36] He also hesitated about working too close to his uncle, a religious fundamentalist, for Sidney's own theological views were quite liberal. For example, he was not sure he could accept the notion of the Virgin Birth, and because of that had almost failed to obtain ordination.[37]

Sidney's choice of the missionary vocation did not come easily. For several years in college he had maintained emphatically that he would not enter that line of work, that two generations of Gulick missionaries was enough. He believed for the rest of his life that God had "called" him and opened the way by providing Cara Fisher as his wife. Not only was she willing to marry him, but also she and her family respected the missionary life. However, Sidney warned the American Board not to accept his application too readily just because his parents and grandparents had been missionaries. With his customary solemnity he cautioned them, "My missionary tendency is I suppose somewhat hereditary and for this reason should be even more closely examined."[38] The board was anxious to obtain so qualified a candidate with such a heritage and accepted him without hesitation. Two weeks later he was assigned to Kumamoto, Japan. That his uncle Orramel and aunt Annie were already in that field was an important consideration for the board; more important was its need for workers in Japan. He and Cara were to be stationed with his sister Hattie, who was marrying Cyrus Clark. As it happened, Cara really preferred Japan to China; her cousin Dwight Learned and aunt Eliza Talcott were already there, and being stationed with Hattie was also clearly appealing.[39]

Cara and Sidney were married September 14, 1887, and sailed the next day for Europe. Their honeymoon in Scotland, England, Paris, Switzerland, and Italy was a final gift from Cara's father and from Sidney's wealthy patron Mr. Belknap.[40]

Japan, their prospective new homeland, appealed to Sidney as much as did China. He later reminisced that he felt no disappointment at not being sent to China, for he had left the decision totally up to the board. Its choice was fortuitous. Had China been their destiny, Sidney and Cara would have been posted to the Shensi mission, which was later destroyed by the Boxers during the Rebellion. The newlyweds spent ten days in China visiting his parents, and then sailed for Japan. After landing in Nagasaki, they traveled with his aunt Julia and another female missionary to Kumamoto, where they were met by Hattie and Cyrus and Uncle Orramel and Aunt Annie. Another Gulick had joined the missionary ranks.[41]

2

THE MAKING OF A MISSIONARY

THE CONGREGATIONAL MISSION TO JAPAN:

Sidney and Cara Gulick arrived at Kumamoto, Japan, on January 1, 1888, their only preparation for the country the accumulated wisdom of their relatives there. It was the American Board's practice to send missionaries to the field on the basis of its need and their availability, with some consideration paid to their wishes, health, and presumed capabilities. Prior education about a country was not considered necessary, for the missionaries were there to impart a new faith, not to partake of its traditional values or culture. It was assumed that all pagan lands were dirty, vice ridden, and decadent, their climates unhealthy and their living conditions poor. The languages were more or less equally difficult but could be learned in time, and the place to do that was at the station. There the missionary could teach English, study the foreign language while helping his or her colleagues with routine tasks, and gradually become a useful and functioning member of the mission team.

For a missionary to become fully functional in Japan took from five to ten years, depending on one's language aptitude. Meiji Japan appeared relatively appealing as a mission field in the late nineteenth century. Its climate was tolerable if not ideal, and the land was physically attractive. The Japanese people were curious about outsiders and usually not overtly hostile to them. In many ways the land appeared "civilized" to the American observer: its people wore modest clothing on most occasions, they

17

were no longer "barbaric" in their treatment of foreigners, and they were extremely curious about Western civilization. Although their language was nearly incomprehensible and difficult to learn, and their food barely palatable, these were hardships expected of the assignment, as was their housing—functional, although not nearly warm enough for Westerners. It was not considered a hardship post, nor did it call forth prospective martyrs.

Japan had not always been that way. During the late sixteenth century Christianity had been propagated in the islands by zealous Jesuits and Franciscans from Portugal and Spain. Conversions were numerous, far exceeding the percentage that the Protestants would later achieve, and the faith prospered until Tokugawa Ieyasu's rise to power in 1603. The allegiance of the missionaries and their converts to a foreign religious pontiff seemed a subversive threat to the stability of the new government, particularly as these foreign connections had exacerbated civil war. Seeking unity and total control, the new shogun proscribed the Christian faith and forced its adherents to recant or be killed. There followed several decades of persecution, and the bloody suppression of the Shimabara rebellion in 1638 almost completely erased Christianity from the land. For more than two hundred years missionaries and traders alike were forbidden access to Japan. Christianity became a hated, feared, and forbidden faith, and all foreigners were driven from the country except for the ostentatiously nonreligious annual visit of Dutch traders to Deshima Island off Nagasaki.[1]

But the very inaccessibility of the island nation made it all the more alluring to the hardy and adventuresome. In the early nineteenth century, proponents of the many varieties of Protestantism sought access, as did scientists and naval officers. To prohibit Christianity seemed as intolerable to missionaries as the exclusion of traders seemed to businessmen. It was both an insult and a challenge, one which Japan was ill-prepared to resist. Nor was America alone in seeking access; opening Japan was a prize coveted by Great Britain and Russia as well. In 1854 Commodore Matthew C. Perry brought the honor to America, wresting from the Tokugawa government the limited Treaty of Kanagawa, which opened the inferior ports of Shimoda and Hakodate to a restricted trade.

Missionaries came later; the shogunate remained obdurately hostile to Christianity, and Perry did not press the case. The first missionaries were workers of the Episcopalian, Presbyterian, and Dutch Reformed Churches, and were allowed entry in 1859 only with the ratification of the more favorable Harris Treaty of 1857 that opened the port of Nagasaki and allowed foreigners residence. Learning the language was the first challenge; a Japanese could be punished with death for teaching it to foreigners. Nonetheless, a famous early missionary, the Presbyterian Dr. James C. Hepburn, dispensed medicine while he worked on romanizing the language and translating the Bible into Japanese, a task not completed until 1888. He and Samuel Browne and James Ballagh, both of the Dutch Reformed Church, were the best-known of those early pioneers, and they were soon followed by the Baptists and Congregationalists. These early missionaries capitalized on the Japanese desire for Western learning to attract an audience, for whom Christianity was distinctly subordinate to practical knowledge.[2]

In 1869 the American Board of Commissioners for Foreign Missions, the missionary arm of the Congregational Church, sent out its first workers, the Reverend Daniel Crosby Greene and his wife. The second American Board missionary was the Reverend Orramel H. Gulick, who arrived in 1871; his sister Julia arrived in 1874, and his brother John Thomas the following year. These offspring of Peter H. Gulick, Sidney's grandfather, confirmed the family's interest in the land. By the time that Sidney and Cara arrived, the board had ninety-four missionaries in the field, stations in eight locations, and had established schools wherever they went.[3] The Congregationalists were building on a quarter century of missionary work in Asia when they entered Japan, which had long captured their imaginations. The churchwomen of Brookline, Massachusetts, had contributed over six hundred dollars for a mission to Japan nearly fifty years earlier, in 1827, and this sum had grown to over four thousand dollars by the time the mission was actually established.[4] Although Roman Catholicism also returned to Japan and Russian Orthodox Christianity secured a foothold in the 1870s, Protestantism dominated the field, and the Congregationalists soon were the most numerous of the Protestants.[5]

Those first missionaries arrived at a particularly turbulent point in Japan's history. The feudalistic Tokugawa shogunate had already experienced severe economic stress before Perry's visits, and the arrival of the foreigners proved an intolerable embarrassment to a government dedicated to subduing barbarians. Technologically incapable of driving the hated foreigners out, the government had to accept their presence, at least temporarily. However, this produced increasing tension as the Westerners continued to arrive with new demands and radical ideas, forcing Japanese acquiescence to unequal treaties. By 1868 the Tokugawa regime could no longer survive the strain, and the almost bloodless Meiji Restoration took place.[6]

The Meiji Restoration, which in the name of the young Emperor Meiji (1868–1912) restored the monarchy and substituted oligarchic for feudal rule in Japan, immediately began the task of modernizing the country. Not ashamed to borrow, the new leaders sought the most successful and useful examples the West had to offer. Aiming in time to end the unequal treaties and eventually to repel the foreigners, they had first to discover the sources of Western strength and adapt new models for Japan. While the most urgent needs lay in revamping the economy and creating modern armed forces, education was also reformed according to Western standards. These changes, coupled with the abolition of feudalism, profoundly affected the entire society.[7]

The question of the religious basis of the state was also important to the new government because belief systems affected people's morale and willingness to serve. Buddhism, the faith of the masses, was too closely associated with the ousted Tokugawa, while Shintō was too vague and amorphous. The Meiji government viewed Christianity with distaste as both illegal and an unwanted foreign intrusion, and the common people regarded it with indifference or suspicion. In fact, when the existence of a band of Christians, whose forefathers had practiced Catholicism secretly for two hundred years, was discovered at Urakami, the government was only dissuaded from executing them by the protests of some Western nations. It then attempted to convert them to Shintō, and exiled them from their native village to other clans who tortured and killed most of them.[8] Western reaction to this incident demonstrated to the Meiji oligarchs that Christianity was more than a domestic issue. The Japanese saw that the Western powers viewed hostility toward the faith as a sign of barbarism. To the West, such persecution provided proof of the dangers of negotiating new treaties that surrendered extraterritoriality.

In 1871, the Reverend Orramel Gulick's language teacher, Ishikawa Einosuke, was arrested by the secret police after he had attended Christian religious services. Although he in fact had gone out of duty to his employer, he and his wife were suspected of having converted. The incident quickly took on international significance. A mission led by Prince Iwakura was at the time in the United States attempting to secure treaty revision and acquire Western knowledge in a variety of areas, from education to technology. When the delegation reached Washington, Secretary of State Hamilton Fish asked the Japanese about the status of Christianity in Japan. The ministers tried to maintain that the edicts prohibiting the faith were no longer enforced, but American Minister to Japan Charles DeLong brought up the story of Ishikawa, who was still in prison then in 1873. An embarrassed silence followed this disclosure. The members of the Iwakura mission had similar discomfiting experiences in England and France regarding Japan's prohibition of Christianity. Clearly, matters of faith were of considerable significance to foreign relations. Prince Iwakura himself cabled the government to release all imprisoned Christians, but Ishikawa died in prison. This incident increased pressure on the Japanese government to reconsider its position on the foreign religion.[9]

A few months after the return of the Iwakura mission to Japan, the government ordered the removal of the edict boards which listed various regulations, including the prohibition of Christianity. The reason given for the removal was patently face-saving: they were unnecessary since everyone knew the laws anyway. While this quasi-recision did not exactly grant religious toleration, which did not come until 1889, it did indicate a considerable change in the official position. Missionaries could now work in the treaty ports, although they needed passports to travel or reside in the interior. Clearly the government's primary motive in this was to win goodwill abroad, without which Japan could not hope for amicable relations and eventual revision of the treaties. The Iwakura mission urged the government to pursue a program to convince the West that Japan was not persecuting Christians.[10]

The Japanese government was also curious about Christianity and its importance to the culture of Western nations. Seeking a state religion which would keep the masses docile and subservient, the Meiji regime tried briefly and unsuccessfully to replace Buddhism with Shintō in order to promote reverence for the emperor. However, despite its popular appeal, Shintō lacked the attributes which would enable it to be successfully transformed into a national religion. Although an office of Shintō worship was established in 1869, it was quickly abolished on the recommendation of the Iwakura mission. There was even some talk of making Christianity the state religion in order to achieve treaty revision. This was not based on any enthusiasm for the faith per se; the government sought merely to use religion for its own ends. Complete religious toleration was an alien concept to the autocratic regime. The Meiji government sought to import Western technology without Western thought and ideology, and it was only later that it recognized the impossibility of this.[11]

The ending of the ban on Christianity did stimulate missionary activity, however, for now the evangelicals could actively promote their faith instead of masking it behind the teaching of English. Language instruction, however, was the only way they could attract an audience. English was rapidly becoming the mark of the educated person in modernizing Japan. Capitalizing on this trend, the missionaries established schools and began teaching the language, using the Bible as a textbook when they felt secure enough with their students. Portions of the New Testament were translated into Japanese in 1870 and published in 1872 and 1873; the translation of the Old Testament was completed in 1880, and the New Testament in 1888. However, the missionaries were always sensitive to charges from home that education was overshadowing evangelism (a problem Sidney would later face), and as soon as they were able they added to their work such tasks as intinerant preaching, Bible study, home visitation, and prayer meetings. The wives and single women did "women's work": teaching women (as Cara would soon do) and singing to children, instructing in Western ways of child care, convening ladies' prayer and study groups, and visiting homes. By 1880 the Congregational mission had established five stations: Kobe, Osaka, Kumamoto, Niigata, and Sendai, and was working to open another at Kyoto.[12]

The decade of work from 1873 to 1883 produced very few converts. The first Protestant church was founded in Yokohama in 1872, the second the following year in Tokyo, but they counted fewer than ten believers between them. Buddhism provided competition by preaching to the common people on the evils of the foreign faith. The missionaries viewed Buddhism as corrupt, but they found Shintō even more unacceptable as it was so much more obviously pagan. Their dislike caused them to discount the indigenous strength of these faiths. Instead, they found Japan to be a "nation in search of a religion" that offered an incredible potential for conversions. Perceptions of this potential caused the mission boards to send more missionaries to Japan: Sidney and Cara were only part of the ABCFM's response. Christianity, as the true faith, could serve a social role, "restraining the evil passions of men," as Shintō and Buddhism had once done,[13] and it could also improve the moral fiber of the land while providing for its converts the key to eternal life.

Although the Japanese masses remained indifferent, Christianity did have certain elements working in its favor. Foremost was the tremendous popularity of Western ideas among the intellectual elite. Orramel Gulick noted in 1871 that the rapidity with which foreign ideas, thoughts, manners, and customs were being adopted was "enough to take one's breath away."[14] Most of those who ultimately converted were samurai, once a privileged class but now in economic distress with the abolition of feudalism in 1876. The reasons for their conversion were complex. Many were alienated from the new regime, cut off from their traditional privileges by the Meiji Restoration. Since they were members of clans associated with the ousted Tokugawa shogunate, they were also excluded from posts in the new government. Some intellectuals sought not only a new livelihood but a new meaning for their existence. For other samurai, Christianity seemed to provide a better way of serving the nation, a way of helping to "participate in the formation of the new Japan."[15] Although the common people identified Christianity as a foreign evil, many samurai felt it was an outgrowth of Confucianism and hence a logical culmination of Japan's cultural tradition. Its emphasis on duty was akin to traditional Bushido, the cult of warrior virtues. They gained from Christianity a sense of purpose, a "consciousness of being elite or 'elected' by god to the service of social reform based upon the love of one's fellow man."[16] If they could identify Christianity as compatible with patriotic citizenship, they could view conversion not as a subversive act, but in line with Japanese tradition, and also creative and useful to the state's needs. That also gave them a source of pride.

This peculiar attraction of Christianity, particularly in its American guise, slowly began to draw converts. The story of the Kumamoto Band demonstrates this appeal. In 1876 a group of young men, some twenty-two students of Captain Leroy L. Janes, a retired army officer teaching at the Yōgakkō, made a public conversion to the faith, the largest mass conversion to that point in the mission's short history. Janes, a remarkable man, became the headmaster of the new school at Kumamoto, and although he did not know Japanese, he inspired his students with his ideals, which tied a belief in Westernization and Christianity to the development of men of strong character. Very strict on admissions requirements, he soon won the trust and loyalty of a group of students, whom he began to instruct secretly in Bible study and prayer at night. After several years of Janes's charismatic influence the young men risked public wrath and openly declared their faith. Their conversion was important not only because of their numbers but also their nature: they were samurai and potential leaders of new Japan.[17]

However, aside from this one remarkable success, conversions came slowly but steadily. The process was hampered by social and political turmoil and apprehensions about the indiscriminate borrowing of foreign concepts. The centuries-old fear of Christianity did not disappear easily, especially among the masses, who viewed the religion with suspicion. Because the Japanese family possessed great power over its members, few individuals were willing to risk being disowned, as they would be if they adopted the alien faith. Only the upper class displayed any genuine curiosity, and its interest was balanced by its espousal of traditional military virtues and growing national consciousness.[18]

Of significance in the history of the Congregational mission in Japan during this period was the founding of Dōshisha University. The American Board tried in vain for three years to obtain official permission to found a Christian college in Kyoto, a stronghold of Buddhism. The successful establishment of the school was made possible through the efforts Niijima Jō (Joseph Hardy Neesima), who left Japan illegally in 1864 to study in America. He became interested in Christianity, acquired an American sponsor, Alpheus Hardy, and attended Phillips Academy, Amherst, and Andover Theological Seminary. While still a student, the remarkable Niijima served with distinction as interpreter for Prince Iwakura during his mission to the United States. After graduating from Andover, he was appointed a corresponding member of the Japan Mission of the American Board, and he convinced the board to contribute five thousand dollars to found a Christian college. Niijima attained enormous prestige in his native land through his work for the Iwakura mission, and this enabled him to secure permission to establish a school in the ancient capital of Kyoto. The first class in 1875 consisted of about forty students, most of them Christian.[19] A number of the Kumamoto Band entered Dōshisha in 1876, and subsequently became leaders of Japanese Christianity.[20]

Beginning in 1882, Protestantism in Japan experienced a period of rapid growth later termed the "Seven Wonderful Years." The Congregational church's membership grew from one thousand to nine thousand converts, while the second most numerous denomination, the Presbyterians, expanded from two thousand to nearly nine thousand.[21] Concentrating their forces in a few key cities, the ABCFM missionaries not only won the most adherents, but also were successful in attracting the largest number of outstanding and able leaders. Their converts were primarily male, upper-middle class, often students—people who had had the opportunity of a Western education and who therefore had courage enough to shake off traditional mores.[22] Government leaders did not attack the faith openly during those years, as their goal was to obtain treaty revision, and to achieve that goal they were willing to make some sacrifices. The converts, on their part, were attract-

ed because Christianity was the faith of the West. Conversion became almost a fad, part of the wave of indiscriminate borrowing
that marked the decade.

The missionaries were pleased with the results, although they
questioned the motives. They showered praise on the Japanese
people, "attractive for what they are, attractive for what they
need and for their willingness to receive, and attractive for their
possibilities as a people."[23] They also praised the Meiji government, claiming that it knew "the highest civilization is impossible
without religion, and, quick-witted, keen-sighted, . . . they recognize Christianity as the best religion, indeed as the only possible
religion for the new Japan."[24] Other missionaries did suspect that
its popularity perhaps stemmed from the wrong reasons: "To win
acceptance for Japan in the West, to obtain treaty revision."[25] The
Congregationalist Reverend James H. Pettee feared this conversion out of expediency, and urged the "so-called Christian nations
[to] deal justly by Japan, and revise the treaties so that this reason
for a nominal adoption of Christianity may be removed."[26] This
was the first attempt to urge the State Department to modify its
foreign policy toward Japan, and its missionary origins are
significant.

Despite these notes of caution, the missionaries could not help
but rejoice that so many souls were being won for the Lord. They
praised the converts, finding in them many admirable traits. They
were "a people intensely patriotic, not ready to admit the rule of
foreigners, but in general quick to learn and easily influenced by
sincere love. They are not savages or barbarians, but a high, intellectual race . . . a vigorous and independent nation which is sure
to have an important part to play in history," said the Reverend
Dwight Learned, Cara's cousin.[27] While the Congregationalists
urged the sending of more missionaries to capitalize on this surge
of interest, they cautioned that only the best candidates be sent.
The Japanese ministers of the Kumiai (Congregational) churches
were themselves very competent and quite independent, and the
new American missionaries would ideally be their helpers, not
their leaders. Both these pastors and their congregations were too
intelligent to be patronized, too bright to accept superficial explanations. As one journal noted, "Too many of the Japanese are

thinkers for any foreigner to have a lasting influence over them except he be a man of exceptional intellectual as well as spiritual power." The new missionaries would also need a high language aptitude, to be able to learn this most difficult tongue.[28]

The successes of the "Seven Wonderful Years" made the missionaries unduly optimistic about the future. They confidently expected that Japan would be converted by the end of the century, and believed that if the mission boards would only send them enough assistance, the task could be turned over to the Japanese Christians themselves in short order. "Protestant Christianity has the opportunity of saving a nation almost in a day, of giving a grand object lesson in missions," wrote the Reverend Pettee. "Save Japan and you have saved the Orient."[29] Such was the situation when Cara and Sidney Gulick sailed for Japan as part of the increased forces dispatched by the Congregationalists to capitalize on this great opportunity.

THE KUMAMOTO YEARS:

The ABCFM had decided to open a mission station in Kumamoto as a result of the interest in that city sparked by the conversion of the Kumamoto Band. To establish the new post they selected the veteran Reverend Orramel H. Gulick and his wife Annie, transferring them from Niigata, where the northerly climate had become too severe for the elderly couple. Reverend Gulick immediately set about recruiting family members to join him, and he soon convinced his sister Julia to come to the city. Julia was already a successful missionary: she had learned the language well, and like many single women, dedicated virtually all her waking hours to the cause, not only doing "women's work" but also working as an itinerant evangelist.[30]

In addition, Orramel persuaded the board in Boston to send him his nephew Sidney and niece Hattie and their spouses. The two couples arrived in Kumamoto within a few months of each other, and Orramel established a school where they taught English. The post was rugged and remote, and a center of antiforeign agitation. Within the first year the missionaries experienced an earthquake and suffered considerable ill health, exacerbated by the lack of a Western-trained physician in the city. Sidney and

Cara were forced to spend some time in Osaka, and they traveled to Kobe and Kyoto frequently to see physicians. Both Cara and Hattie became pregnant within a year after their arrival, and they and their babies suffered from the lack of a doctor. In addition both families complained of the drafty Japanese houses in which they lived and their inability to secure permission to construct their own.[31] But the greatest hardship was the indifference, if not outright hostility, of the people.

For the men the main task was learning Japanese. Sidney found the routine a time-consuming one, studying all morning, then teaching English at the boys' school in the afternoon. He was shocked to learn that there were only about a dozen missionaries out of all the denominations who had achieved true fluency in Japanese, and none who had totally mastered the language and could work without a teacher or translator. As he wrote his friends, "In China a man is considered ready to preach publicly in three years, but here five is the norm." Those few who could translate characters could not handle the spoken tongue, he noted. Since most opted for verbal fluency, this meant they were cut off from all local news since they could not read the newspapers, and they were denied access to the country's great literature—more of a deprivation for Sidney than for the others. The lack of suitable grammars and dictionaries complicated their task. Sidney resolved to be able to preach in Japanese in five years, and to be able to read the language—an accomplishment he viewed as almost impossible—in fifteen to twenty years.[32] Because of the language barrier, he was not optimistic either for the mission or for himself as a missionary.

Sidney no sooner entered in the field than he found himself at odds with his colleagues. The issue concerned a proposed merger of the Congregational and Presbyterian churches in Japan. (The two creeds had once merged in the ABCFM itself, where they cooperated until separating in the 1860s.) Sidney opposed the plan because he felt that the Presbyterian creed was too elaborate and detailed. This position was supported by the principal of his school, Kumamoto Band graduate Ebina Danjō, by the well-known Niijima, and by fellow missionary Jerome Davis, but most colleagues longer in the field opposed him. The issue was complex; the American Board was split over the matter and, due to the loose organization of Congregationalism, the board was unable to speak for the Kumiai churches, which were generally opposed. At the Japan missionaries' annual meeting in May 1889, strong reservations were voiced against the proposed merger, and effectively killed it. Sidney felt later that he had paid a high price for his all-too-vocal opposition. His colleagues considered his actions presumptuous and brash for one with such a short time in the field. Reflecting on the episode much later, he concluded that the outcome was worth the conflict, because the Kumiai church was more liberal than other Japanese churches and better able to withstand the hard times that beset Japanese Christianity in the 1890s.[33] His conclusion was correct but his reasoning probably faulty. The Kumiai churches remained strong because they pioneered in transferring leadership to the Japanese ministers and in becoming self-supporting.[34]

The first few years of Sidney and Cara's service passed swiftly. Their first child, Susan Fisher, was born in December 1888, and Sidney and Cara went to Kyoto for six months during the pregnancy and childbirth. Mother and child were cared for there by Cara's aunt Eliza Talcott. Their second child, Luther Halsey, arrived in January of 1892. In the summer the mission force traditionally went to Mt. Hieizan above Kyoto, to gain relief from the heat and humidity and to regain their strength. Wherever he was, Sidney studied Japanese six to eight hours a day, in addition to his mission work and teaching.

The station, however, did not fare well; it became even smaller when, in 1892, the Orramel Gulicks went on furlough to Honolulu and the Clarks were transferred to Miyazaki on southern Kyushu. Aunt Julia noted with some dismay that this made Sidney the only man in the station, hence in the eyes of the Japanese the only responsible party, "no matter how many women there are, sharing in and influencing his decisions."[35] Although the Kumamoto missionaries urged the board to send replacements, it was anxious to expand and had insufficient candidates to meet all requests. Fortunately, Sidney and Cara's health was good and the children strong, and they coped, but at the price of loneliness and overwork.

Some problems were alleviated with time. For a short while Cara taught nursing and care of the sick in the Kumamoto girls' school, which enabled her to obtain a five-year passport; Sidney just held a temporary passport for the interior, which required his returning to a port once every three months.[36] Finally, after much delay, they were able to build a Western-style house, a great improvement over the cold Japanese dwelling. Sidney described their first house to the board, noting that it was not too bad, not as cold as the homes of the other foreign families, although his study was sometimes thirty degrees Fahrenheit and the light so poor his eyes suffered.[37] Such were the tribulations of the career he had chosen.

Sidney gradually increased his missionary activity as his understanding of the language improved. In 1892 he noted with pride that he had preached his first sermon in "this dreadful language."[38] He later recounted the method he used to convert his students. He would begin by teaching the Sermon on the Mount and the Parables, and then the life of Christ, to those desiring English instruction. His theology was liberal; he stressed the ethical teachings of Jesus rather than the miracles. He took pains never to attack or criticize the indigenous religions, as earlier missionaries had done and some of his colleagues still did. As he wrote some fifty years later, "I think I sometimes stressed more than I now would the excellencies of Christian civilization."[39] But at that time he still believed in them; the ethnocentric missionaries generally had a difficult time separating their faith from the American, or Western, way of life. Gulick in fact was exceptional, and he preached a liberal humanistic doctrine which did not disparage the Japanese traditions.

Meanwhile, political changes in 1889 and 1890 had a significant impact on missionary work. For the previous five years the oligarchs had been working to devise a constitution which would reflect their conservative political philosophy, establishing a limited constitutional monarchy in which the emperor would be the center of the state and a living god. Drafted by Ito Hirobumi, the document was discussed only by the Privy Council in the presence of the Emperor Meiji, and was proclaimed by him in February 1889. Although the government consisted of three branches, the executive was made supreme and the military gained direct access to the throne. The document established freedom of religion along with freedom of thought and speech, but these were subject to the limits of the law.[40] Christianity was thus publicly recognized for the first time, although it would not be encouraged by a government that proclaimed its head, the emperor, sacred and inviolable.

This latter point was made clear the following year with the promulgation on October 30, 1890, of the Imperial Rescript on Education. This vague document set forth ethical principles to govern the thought of the nation and the actions of teachers and pupils. It ended nearly twenty years of experimenting with educational policy, during which time the government had tried both a French-modeled centralized system and an American-style, decentralized one.[41] The rescript marked a shift from Western values back to traditional Japanese wisdom, the notions of righteousness, loyalty, and filial piety. Education would indoctrinate youth according to the authoritarian principles of the government, rather than in independent thinking. The document became a formidable weapon to use against liberal thinkers and Christian believers alike, as it signalled a resurgence of conservatism and the rejection of the notion of unlimited borrowing, of pragmatic and utilitarian ethics. In an effort to reassert traditional values in education, it also marked a reaffirmation of the "kokutai," the national essence of Japan, and thus it set the course of Japanese education until the end of World War II.[42]

The impact of the rescript upon the missionaries was both immediate and long-term. In the short run, xenophobes used the document to assert that Western nations knew nothing of the true principles of loyalty and filial piety, and to point out that many Christian teachings were opposed to the emperor's desires. The rescript changed the relationship between the missionary teachers and the Japanese educators who ran the schools in which they taught, producing considerable tension and conflict in some institutions, particularly the one at Kumamoto. In the long run, the document signified the end of the "Seven Wonderful Years" and marked the beginning of a period of hostility toward the further expansion of Christianity, which again found itself a revolutionary faith trying to operate in an absolutist state.[43]

The Rescript on Education and the Meiji Constitution precipitated a wave of antiforeign nationalism that had been in Japan throughout the 1880s. Railing against too rapid Westernization with its indiscriminate borrowing, nationalists questioned the value of replacing indigenous Japanese culture with Western importations. Treaty revision was a sore point among those who found the unequal treaties imposed by the Western powers humiliating, and who had already failed once to renegotiate them. Widespread opposition raged throughout the land when rumors spread that the government was making too many concessions merely to gain a better position in negotiations.[44] Nationalism replaced the earlier mania for Westernization. Borrowing foreign culture or a foreign religion was now viewed as unnecessary, since both lacked the practical utility that made the adoption of Western technology essential. In addition, Christianity was charged with "denationalizing" Japan, a dangerous charge in those highly nationalistic times.[45]

Christianity also suffered from two forms of competition. First, indigenous Japanese faiths revived with the nationalistic resurgence, and Restoration Shintō became the state religion. The revitalized cult adopted the belief in an afterlife, possibly from Christianity, but more importantly, it taught respect for the emperor, adding a religious fervor to the Confucian notion of respect. Shintō fit in much more harmoniously with the new nationalism than Christianity with all its Western trappings could ever hope to do.[46]

Certain Western ideas and liberal doctrines also challenged orthodox belief. The Reverend John T. Gulick, Sidney's uncle, felt that the greatest danger to Christianity in Japan came not from Buddhism but from materialism, not from the religions and superstitions of the old Japan but from the skepticism of modern Europe. "It becomes every day more apparent that the natural heart of progressive Japan is the eager disciple of rationalistic and materialistic Europe," he wrote.[47] Japanese travelers and students abroad brought home tales that refuted the notion that Christian civilizations were morally superior to the East, and they also told of the widespread popularity of atheism. They learned of the "higher criticism" of the Bible, and found its claims intriguing. The missionaries were not only foreign, but it appeared their doctrine was obsolete. Alert Japanese observers perceived that many Westerners even viewed missionaries themselves as rather parochial and simplistic salesmen who confused the culture of Western civilization with the teaching of Christianity. Religious liberals also discredited the more fundamentalist denominations. For example, the Unitarians, who came to Japan in 1887 to teach but not to convert, were highly popular with Japanese intellectuals, and they put the other churches on the defensive.[48] Moreover, current scientific inquiry seemed to suggest that agnosticism, if not atheism, was the "modern" approach, a telling point in a society as enamoured of science and technology as Japan.[49]

The missionaries had enough trouble within the ranks of their own converts without these outside threats. Most missionaries tended to see themselves as the principal workers, the leaders, and their Japanese colleagues as the helpers, the "native agents." They could not recognize that they were patronizing their converts, that in Christianity as in technology, as soon as the Japanese had acquired the skills to do the job themselves, they would do so. The Japanese chafed at the "religious extraterritorial atmosphere" in which the missionaries lived, culturally isolated from their surroundings in individual replicas of American homes.[50] And they wanted their adopted faith to become indigenously Japanese.

There was also conflict over church organization and religious beliefs. In 1890 Yokoi Tokio, a prominent Kumiai Christian, published an article in a Japanese paper which was reprinted in the English-language *Japan Weekly Mail*, lamenting that Japanese Christianity was a pale imitation of that practiced in England and America. As the Western faith was based on Greek literature and Roman law, Japanese theology should be Japanese, with rites and ceremonies based on their own traditions, according to this article. The reliance on foreign models had to end.[51] Yokoi's article was to the missionaries evidence of a "morbid nationalism."[52] Other converts did not go that far, but they did advocate self-sufficiency and a separation between the Kumiai churches and the mission board. They also disagreed over the proper stance to take in this time of religious crises. The missionaries favored more open expressions of faith, while the converts wished to stress inner spiritual development and emphasize their place within Japanese tradition.[53] Quarrels over finances also assumed nasty proportions when the more outspoken Japanese Christians demanded not only control over their own government, creed, and expenditures, but over the money allocated to the missionaries as well.[54] As one missionary wrote, "how much money and how little missionary" was the question.[55] Although this trend had its counterpart in the opposition to foreign advisors and teachers throughout the government and economy, the missionaries, often isolated from the rest of the foreign community, had no wider context into which to put their own distresses. They persisted and were able to hold their own throughout the decade, but it was clear that the wonderful years had ended. They recognized that their earlier optimism had been misplaced, and that Japan would not become Christian by the beginning of the twentieth century.

Inevitably these larger currents had their impact on the little mission at Kumamoto. The government's department of education made life difficult in many ways for Christian schools as it sought to increase the prestige of government schools and diminish support for the alien faith. Graduates of Christian schools encountered difficulty entering governmental institutions of secondary or higher education, and the way was often barred for them to enter the army or higher levels of government service.[56] The more immediate problem at Kumamoto, however, involved control of the school itself. Because foreigners could not own land in Japan, the schools and residences that they built were registered in the name of a Japanese Christian or a board of trustees.[57] As long as the Japanese owner who controlled the institution agreed with the missionaries' policies towards its use, this system was satisfactory. However, with the promulgation of the Imperial Rescript and the resurgence of nationalism, the government became more insistent that schools not be used to promote Christianity.

There had been no problem during Sidney and Cara's first two years at Kumamoto. The principal of the missionary-run boys' school, the Eigakkō, was Ebina Danjō who later as president of Dōshisha attempted to harmonize Christianity, Shintō, and Japanese ethical morality,[58] and who was supportive of the missionary teachers of English at Kumamoto. In 1893, however, a man named Kurahara took over as principal and pastor, and trouble began. First a charge was made that one of the teachers had uttered unspecified "treasonable words." A wave of ill feeling and strained relations quickly spread throughout the Japanese Christian community, threatening its very existence. Kurahara then demanded the severing of all relations between the ABCFM mission and the school. The school itself was entirely self-supporting except for the English program, which the board subsidized.[59] The situation grew tense.

Sidney responded to this attack with indignation and outrage. The problem was Kurahara and the Kumamoto Band, he charged. Since Kurahara became principal there had been no conversions and the Japanese Christian teachers in the school had been discharged.[60] Although Ebina had been supportive, others of the Kumamoto Band were strong nationalists and unwilling to take second place to the missionaries. Although they had been dramatically converted, they could only accept Christianity if it were sufficiently "Japanized." Several of the group ultimately rejected the faith entirely. Gulick complained to the American Board that the dissension at the school ran so high that Japanese members felt demeaned even to ask the missionaries for help in teaching English. As sentiment in the board inclined more and more toward abandoning the mission for greener fields, Sidney grew more adamant. To leave would be either like "commiting harakiri," or running away. This trait was to him a great failing in the Japanese character, that they would give up rather than fight. The very idea that Americans would also adopt such a posture outraged him, for he felt the Kumiai church was not strong enough to survive alone. Its samurai members, "proverbial in their disregard and ignorance of the value of money," would squander the board's resources.[61] He also criticized the senior members of the mission, John Hyde DeForest and Daniel Crosby Greene, for advocating self-governance for the Kumiai Christians.[62]

The board chose not to fight. It withdrew the missionaries temporarily to Osaka and dispatched a delegation to decide the station's fate. Sidney beseeched the delegation not to be misled or swayed by the eloquent Kumamoto Band, but to support the mis-

sionaries' returning to the station and working independently of
the Kumiai churches. He was alone in his protests; the other young
missionaries lacked the courage necessary to challenge their
elders in the field, and (perhaps because they lacked the Gulick
name) did not presume to tell the ABCFM what to do. Sidney
continued to advocate giving the missionaries more independence from the Kumiai churches, but in vain.[63] The board knew
better than he that the church could not exist if it antagonized its
offspring, the Kumiai Christians, especially when the times were
not auspicious for the work. Kumamoto was not the place to stand
and fight.

The Kumamoto school was not the only educational institution
to suffer in the dark days of the 1890s. In fact, the whole Japan
mission underwent a decline. Church services were poorly attended, friction rife, and controversy between converts and missionaries spread. The Dōshisha, founded by Niijima and the
board, slowly lost its Christian character after the former's death
in 1890, and it was beset by the same problems with its trustees as
befell the school at Kumamoto. According to Gulick, the Kumamoto Band was at fault in both cases.[64] The board evinced alarm
when the trustees decided to restrict the teaching of Christian ethics to the theology department to gain government support. The
mission chose gradually to reduce its subsidy to the school and
terminate it in 1898, and even threatened to sue the trustees. This
controversy ultimately ended in the board's favor when the old
trustees resigned under pressure from angered alumni. New ones
were elected, and a new constitution reaffirming the Christian
character of the school was adopted.[65] But a little coercion accompanied by compromise was essential to survival, and often
fighting had to be measured in terms of the worth of the object.
Dōshisha was worth it, Kumamoto Eigakkō was not. The red-
haired, red-bearded, short-tempered Sidney Gulick could not see
this.

INTERMISSION— THE FIRST FURLOUGH:

The expulsion of the mission from Kumamoto provided more of a
break than Gulick foresaw. The family, with a new baby, Pierre
Leeds (called Leeds after Sidney's Hanover mentor), relocated

temporarily in Osaka, hoping to return to Kumamoto in the fall of 1894. Sidney spent part of the time in itinerant evangelism in Kyushu and devoted himself to intense language study. He was convinced that only truly able, well-educated missionaries, skilled in the language, could succeed. "We must be able to speak in sophisticated language to counter rationalism and Unitarianism," he wrote the board in Boston, to assure that "young Japanese educated abroad don't go astray in their thoughts."[66] His goal was to publish in Japanese, to counter what he regarded as "ultra-liberalism" by providing converts with theological works explaining and justifying the faith. He also began work on a study, *The Growth of the Kingdom of God*, which would provide them with a history of Western Christianity.

At the end of October 1895, Gulick departed suddenly for the United States. This abrupt leave-taking—he had given only three days' notice—was occasioned by his sister Hattie's mental breakdown. Burdened with small children and more susceptible to the rigors of missionary life, Hattie collapsed, and as her husband was also unwell, Sidney was delegated by the mission to take the family home. He accompanied them all the way to New Jersey to his brother Edward's, where he was joined six months later by Cara and the children, in June 1896, for the board had decided that he too should go on furlough.[67]

The culmination of this first phase of missionary work provided Sidney with some opportunity for reflection. His own assessment was rather dismal, the product of his persistent sense of inferiority and feeling of being an outsider both in Japan and in the mission community. He wrote Cara from the East Coast in December of 1895, comparing himself with his brothers Luther and Edward. Luther was establishing himself as an authority in physical education, and Edward was a successful pastor. Next to them he felt a failure. "I suppose I ought not to care what I am and accomplish and what I am thought, so long as I do my best and am true. But somehow I do wish I had something like the ability and success attained by my brothers."[68]

In part his pessimism was situational; he had given his all in the Kumamoto fight, and in vain. He had also antagonized his senior colleagues in disputes over mission policy, and had tangled with Japanese Christian leaders over the issue of control of the Kumiai churches. His advocacy of a stronger role for the missionaries in Japan ran counter to the prevailing trend, for Japanese leaders demanded more independence and authority over their own churches, and the older missionaries realized it was wisest to accede and let them make their own mistakes. In fact, Japanese control of the largely self-sufficient Kumiai churches was their great strength, not a weakness. Gulick saw the forty million unconverted souls crying for help, needing more missionaries, while the Japanese leadership viewed the missionaries as foreign intruders hanging on to their positions as teachers, unwilling to let their students take control. To Japanese Christians the missionaries were paternalistic and limiting.[69] Sidney was still too culture-bound, unable to dissociate Christianity from its Western context and its specifically American accoutrements. He concluded that the greatest personal contribution he could make to the Japan mission was to become truly proficient in the language; he could at this point speak well and could read two thousand characters. He also determined to pursue advanced theological training in order to be able to better persuade intellectual Japanese that Christianity was the wave of the future, not an ebbing tide. He felt his own training woefully inadequate to accomplish this mission: "If I had known when I came to Japan of the special need for academic training in such areas, I wouldn't have applied to come."[70] He blamed his failures on himself rather than upon external factors, and he carefully planned his furlough to correct what he perceived as personal shortcomings.

3

THE MAKING OF A JAPAN EXPERT

ON FURLOUGH:

When Sidney Gulick arrived on the East Coast with his sister in the winter of 1895 he expected to return promptly to Japan. But the board had granted him a furlough so that he could receive the additional theological training he had requested. After summering in New England, Sidney sailed for England in October 1896, while his family returned to California. The separation, the first of many, lasted nearly a year.[1]

The years from 1896 to 1913 would be productive ones for Gulick. He not only mastered the skills of a missionary but went on to become a scholar of international reputation, a writer, a theologian, and a recognized authority on Japan.

While at Oxford Gulick finished a book he had begun writing during his Osaka exile. Entitled *The Growth of the Kingdom of God* (1896), it originated from a series of lectures he had given to Japanese youth to convince them of Christianity's truths through an examination of its history. Although missionary writings were generally restricted to brief journal accounts of labors in the field, Gulick persuaded the board of the need to translate and publish theological works for his students; his colleagues subsequently persuaded him to publish this book for a wider audience.[2] His work traced the history of Christianity in the United States and England, explaining its beneficial influence in the world and the transformations it had wrought in the Western nations. In addition, the project helped Gulick to clarify his own understanding of the role of a missionary and to explore the meaning the faith had in his life.

Gulick's interpretation of Protestantism, which he saw as the most vigorous and dominant form of Christianity, stressed its social conscience. His ideas foreshadowed those of the Baptist Walter Rauschenbusch, whose social gospel message, developed in *Christianity and the Social Crisis* (1907), had wide influence. Gulick believed that while saving individual souls for Christ was important, Christianity's social message was equally valuable.[3] Liberal Christianity advocated marriage based on the equal status of both partners, promoted prison reform and the improvement of public education, and crusaded against vice. Gulick expressed his liberal outlook in his book when he denied that adherents of non-Christian faiths would suffer everlasting punishment. "God, being a loving Father, can do nothing unjust," he wrote. Although he was willing to concede that all great religions contain elements of truth, Christianity was the most all-encompassing. He justified the missionary movement as a way to fulfill God's command to publish the gospel of love, justice, and mercy so that it might be of benefit to all regardless of their baptism and church membership.[4]

In *Growth of the Kingdom* Gulick tackled an issue that would plague him throughout the rest of his life, that of reconciling the behavior of the so-called Christian nations with the tenets of the faith. Western nations often acted in non-Christian ways, sometimes grasping, ruthless, and overreaching, ignoring in practice what they espoused in theory. Gulick, however, denied that the West was able to achieve world domination precisely because it had ignored Christian precepts in favor of power politics. Such behavior hindered rather than helped the West achieve power, he maintained. Although that contention was perhaps idealistic, his conclusion was not: the governments of Christendom were in fact not Christian, nor did they profess to be. According to Gulick, they were instead "armed camps with machinery in preparation for mutual slaughter." Religious rule was no answer, as it had not worked in the past, and he preferred striving to transform the behavior of Western nations to a more Christian standard.[5]

In England Gulick added a chapter on the growth of the church in that country and was delighted when the book was accepted for publication in 1896 by the religious publishing house Fleming H. Revell in New York; it would add a little money to the family's thin coffers. Gulick completed his studies at Oxford in March 1897 and then traveled to the continent to visit missionary relatives and to study German. He returned to the United States in the late spring, and the family journeyed to Japan in September via Hawaii. They reentered the mission field refreshed and full of enthusiasm for the work that lay ahead.[6]

THE MATSUYAMA YEARS:

A new atmosphere greeted the Gulicks on their return to Japan October 24, 1897. The overtly antiforeign attitudes of the people had dissipated as the country adjusted to life under the Meiji constitution, and the particular antagonism toward missionaries had abated. The Committee ad Interim of the American Board's Japan mission reassigned the family to the old castle town of Matsuyama, which was not as remote as Kumamoto had been. Stationed with another family, the Gulicks would not again suffer the loneliness of the Kumamoto years.[7]

Matsuyama, on the Inland Sea, was a beautiful city whose people received them cordially, and the years there were happy ones. Cara was busy as their family increased to five children with the birth of Ethel in December 1898, and Sidney Lewis, Jr., in August 1902, and Gulick immersed himself in scholarship, reading and writing extensively in addition to performing his mission work. Drawing on his broad knowledge and interest, he also lectured on science and attracted a diverse audience, with discussions of the timely and intriguing subject, evolution. He believed in the importance of instructing students in modern scientific theories and in demonstrating to them that it was possible to be both a Christian and a scientist. To whet their interest he organized a "University Extension Club," as he called it, that met evenings in a special building of the mission's night school. Cara and two single women missionaries at the station taught English; then a Bible class was offered, sandwiched neatly in between the two more popular offerings (English and science), after which Gulick would talk on such subjects as astronomy, geology, physics, biology, psychology, and sociology to about one hundred people. In addition, Christian Japanese professors taught the history and constitution of Japan to the students. Although Gulick in his "Reminiscences" stressed that his "main work was touring," even as he traveled he took along a half-dozen books on a wide range of topics.[8] His reputation as a scientist began to spread as his career as a scholar developed.

Gulick's interest in evolution stemmed from a liberal concept of Christianity; like the well-known Congregational minister Washington Gladden, they saw in evolution proof of the far-reaching and comprehensive purposes of the Divine Creator. Sidney's academic curiosity was whetted by his uncle, John Thomas Gulick, who was a noted student of evolution. During his early years in Hawaii, Uncle John had amassed an extensive collection of fossil snails, which he studied while at his later posts in Micronesia, China, and Japan. He used the resulting data to test and rework the concepts on which Charles Darwin's ideas were based.[9] He had met and corresponded with the famous evolutionist, and he discussed Darwin's theories extensively with Sidney. John Gulick's beliefs were not so exclusively based on natural selection as Darwin's; the former believed it important to give weight to teleology in the nature of the evolving organism. These ideas seemed compatible with Christianity, for he believed man of all creatures possessed superior intelligence and a "partial apprehension of the Purpose of the Creator in producing all and in placing him over it." Man therefore owed a special obligation to God. Each individual was responsible for his own life and for influencing others. Human societies, if provided with sufficient options, could evolve through conscious choice. This made the missionary's work dispensing the truth doubly important, for their converts could then choose the better way, Christianity, and progress to a higher level of civilization.[10]

Sidney grappled with the concept of evolution for many years, attempting to reconcile it with Christianity. He finally concluded that creation had to be initiated by a mind, a spirit—the Christian God. The force that created the universe had devised laws according to which species evolved. Instead of creating animals one by one, this "mind" established a set of principles which explained the many species of animal and plant life. Gulick felt the purpose of evolution was the production of "children of

Kobe, 1902: Aunt Julia Gulick joined in a family portrait. The children are (from left), Luther, Leeds, Ethel, and Sue; Cara is holding Sidney, Jr. Gulick is in the center back.

God—at once free and holy. The evolution of plant and animal life is to produce an environment for one favored line—man."[11] From simpler forms came this highest order with a special purpose in the total scheme of things.

Such ideas led to opposition from his more conservative colleagues. His sons later recalled that the Japan Mission Board attempted to try Gulick for heresy and to excommunicate him for his beliefs. However, when the Boston Board learned of this the secretary told the mission that it had no jurisdiction in such matters and to drop the case, which it did.[12]

Gulick believed that evolution was too significant a theory to be dismissed or ignored, and that Christianity had to respond to it or be considered outmoded by the Japanese. The latter, with their intense curiosity about new ideas, would use that reply as a test of the faith's relevance to the contemporary world. Bright students were quick to detect intellectual falsehood, and many Western speakers had already popularized the evolution theory by the time Gulick began lecturing on it. Edward S. Morse, a distinguished naturalist from Salem, Massachusetts, who became the first professor of zoology at Tokyo University, lectured on evolution in the fall of 1877. Other well-known lecturers also promoted it, such as the philosopher Ernest Fenellosa who advocated evolution as superior to the Christian account of creation, as did other speakers hostile to religion. The liberal Christians counterattacked, maintaining that science and faith were different aspects of knowledge and necessary adjuncts to each other.[13] But many conservatives could not accept such an accommodation, and the debate wracked the community of the faithful and provided a stimulating and enlightening spectacle for the Japanese.

During the Matsuyama years Gulick turned increasingly to writing. He had penned the usual brief articles about his work for missionary journals since his arrival, but after his furlough and after having completed his first book, he began work on a massive study, *The Evolution of the Japanese.* His goal was ambitious: to produce both a publishable book and a dissertation that he hoped Dartmouth would accept for a doctorate in sociology. Since residency in Hanover was impossible, he requested the college to allow additional reading and an examination in its stead. Gulick's goal was congruent with his desire to "reach the thinking men of this land" who would be impressed by the advanced degree.[14] He recognized that Christianity was making little progress among the common people, for, as he wrote pessimistically to the board, he had labored long among them and had little to show for it. The people had heard the Christian message and, their curiosity sated, had no desire to hear more. Although they now tolerated the faith, they were indifferent to its message and were as "heathen" as ever. Matsuyama was full of temples and immorality, geisha were abundant, and society there as he perceived it was "generally rotten."[15] Only the intellectual elite had any interest in the foreign religion at all, and he hoped to capitalize on that.

While the book was written to be a dissertation, Gulick did have to justify its contents to the ABCFM. He advised the members that the work dealt with two topics of wide current interest, social evolution and the origins of the new Japan. He aimed also, he said, to "show the rationality and necessity of missionary work on the most thoroughgoing principles of social evolution."[16] With such arguments he succeeded in gaining the board's approval for his project, but his other purpose did not reach fruition, and his dreams of acquiring a doctorate were soon dashed. Dartmouth had instituted a residency requirement and deemed him ineligible for an earned doctorate, although the school did award him an honorary doctorate of divinity in 1903. (Yale and Oberlin followed suit in 1914.) However, by the time he learned of his ineligibility in 1899, he had completed the book. His sister Fanny Jewett helped him revise it, and it was accepted for publication. As he later recalled, "It was this book that established my reputation as a scholar and a writer."[17]

The Evolution of the Japanese (1903) was an attempt to interpret modern Japan in the light of social science and to understand the national character. Gulick desired to be objective, even if that meant being critical, but he assured his readers of his love for the Japanese people.[18] The book covered an array of topics, beginning with an historical sketch of the modernization of Japan. Gulick sought to explain a phenomenon that had excited the world, the transformation of Japan in thirty years from a traditional society to a modern state. Basing his historical analysis on ideas of social evolution as he and his uncle understood it, Gulick concluded that Japan's progress had resulted from a change in the social order. The nation's fantastic development was apparent after its surprising victory over China in 1895, an event of which Gulick apparently approved. But he maintained that Japan had undergone evolutionary changes that were developmental in nature, rather than revolutionary; they were incremental, not the product of dramatic upheaval. As he claimed, "The true explanation of Japan's rise is to be found in inherited mental and temperamental characteristics reacting on the new and stimulating environment and working along the line of true evolution." In other words, the Japanese progressed because they were supremely able to adapt to new circumstances and desired to conform to the customs of their Western models.[19]

Gulick then moved in his discussion to an analysis of Japanese character. He praised what he found admirable, such as the ability to be discriminating borrowers. According to Gulick, the Japanese were cheerful, industrious, ambitious, and full of self-confidence, but he disliked their tendency toward jealousy, their revengeful natures, and he deplored their treatment of women. Although they appeared irreligious and had almost no sense of sin, he maintained "the apparent irreligion of today is the groundwork of the purer religion of tomorrow."[20]

Gulick concluded his work by tying the Japanese case to his general beliefs about evolution and the nature of Asian civilization. In its earliest stages of development, all mankind "must have been little removed from the ape." He believed that the Japanese had developed a unique culture through their social evolution, and not because they possessed any inherently different capabilities or characteristics. According to Gulick, there were two types of evolution: biological, through which innate characteristics were passed on; and social, by which acquired characteristics or habits such as dress, diet, and other aspects of culture were transmitted and transformed over time. The Japanese culture was distinctive, but biologically their innate abilities were the same as those of any other race. As their society was impacted by modernization, the Japanese people would continue to change—for the better, he implied.[21]

Gulick's work attracted international attention, coming as it did after the works of Lafcadio Hearn and Percival Lowell had already established a market in the United States for Japanese exotica. Hearn, who moved to Japan in 1890 and married a Japanese woman, was the best-known writer on Japan in the 1890s. His stories and sketches of life in the small town of Matsue were delightful depictions of old Japan, and in his two major works, *Glimpses of Unfamiliar Japan* (1893) and *Japan: An Attempt at Interpretation* (1904), he attempted to synthesize his experiences with the land and its people. Although he was both sensitive and sympathetic to his adopted people, his works became equated with the notion of the romantic, exotic, and almost "otherworldly" Japanese. Lowell, scion of a well-known Boston family, traveled as a businessman to East Asia. He wrote several books, the first of which, *The Soul of the Far East*, was published in 1888. Another work, *Occult Japan* (1895), stressed the bizarre aspects of the Japanese personality and in particular the esoteric rituals of the Shintō faith. Neither Hearn nor Lowell learned the Japanese language, however, and neither spent the amount of time in Japan that Gulick did. While Hearn did read voraciously about its culture, Gulick's studies were more systematic and scholarly.[22]

Readers found in Gulick's work something different from the studies of Lowell and Hearn, something more perceptive, scholarly, and scientific, and not rooted in a study of the quaint. Reviewers responded with praise. *The Nation* was "delighted." The *New York Times* noted how much more critically perceptive Gulick was than Hearn had been. The *American Journal of Sociology* called the book "the best description and the most searching analysis yet of that unique phenomenon, the modern reconstruction of Japan." *The Outlook* described it as "observant and clear-headed," and missionary and Christian journals also praised the work.[23] No doubt the tribute that thrilled Gulick the most was contained in a letter from the philosopher William James, who told him, "It makes me understand them as I never did before . . . you have done a genuine work of interpretation and set a model for future studies in ethnic character."[24] One sour note came from a Japanese student at Yale, who charged him with ridiculing the imperial family and the Japanese people and accused him personally of immorality. The missionary community investigated and found the man mentally disturbed, but his charges resounded for a year.[25] While Ebina Danjō did criticize the work for its Christian, Anglo-Saxon bias, on the whole he lauded Gulick, as did other Japanese Christian leaders.[26] The enthusiastic acceptance of the book—it went to five editions and was the only one of Gulick's works to pay substantial royalties—was highly gratifying to its author, and it launched his scholarly career.[27]

After this project Gulick continued to immerse himself in writing, although he did not neglect speaking, for he was now fluent in Japanese. He found the two subjects on which he was most prepared to write precisely topics that excited current interest. America was fascinated and at the same time somewhat horrified by the specter of an emergent Japan, and anxious for observant accounts. In addition, Japanese intellectuals were intrigued by the

challenge of the theory of evolution, which seemed to them not
only plausible but also threatening to the very basis of traditional
Christianity. In his last years in Matsuyama Gulick addressed both
topics.

In January of 1903 Gulick was invited to give a series of five
lectures on evolution and religious thought at Dōshisha University. The Kumiai church in Japan faced a crisis, for the controversy between science and religion was discrediting the latter,
especially the supernaturally-based, fundamentalist faith preached
by the majority of missionaries.[28] While most of these adherents
denounced evolution or ignored the topic altogether, Gulick did
not. As he wrote a friend, "I hope to stem the tide of bald materialistic evolution and to let the public know that evolution is not
necessarily anti-Christian"; he also sought to reverse the belief
that the theory was "almost synonymous with materialism and
irreligion."[29] The lengthy preparation of the lectures forced him
to drop his pastorship, although he continued his teaching. But the
effort proved worthwhile: the lectures were well-received, and
he was pleased that even the most conservative members of his
own denomination, the Reverends Jerome D. Davis and Dwight
Learned, approved of them. He then decided to publish his ideas
in Japanese, hiring a Japanese assistant several hours a week to
translate. His uncle John helped develop his ideas, and the project
extended over several years.[30]

Gulick's lectures and writing did little to stem the inroads that
evolutionary theory made into the growth of the Christian faith,
particularly among the educated. His was a lonely voice among
the theologically conservative missionary community. While
Congregationalists were generally more accepting of evolution
than other major Protestant denominations, their missionaries in
Japan were suspicious while the more fundamentalist groups
were quite opposed. But Gulick's efforts were on the right track, if
Christianity were to maintain its hold among the intellectual
community that had found the faith so appealing at the outset.

FROM MISSIONARY TO THEOLOGIAN:

Early in 1904 Sidney received an offer that both surprised and
excited him. George Albrecht, a German-born missionary who

had served as professor of systematic theology at the Dōshisha for some years, had been discovered by his students in a compromising situation and forced to resign. Although Gulick was quite willing to forgive him his sexual indiscretion, his other colleagues were not, and they decided to ask Gulick to join the faculty. His initial reaction was mixed; he appreciated the honor, but he wrote Dwight Learned that the offer filled him with dismay and ambivalence. Not only did he lack credentials for the work, but he had previously evinced no particular interest in theology either. In addition, Gulick had been arrested the previous year for taking photographs of his family at the beach in what turned out to be a prohibited military zone, and he feared his rather ludicrous "criminal record" would enable the government to invalidate the appointment. Hoping they would select someone else, he listed a series of demands to be met before he would consider the position: permitting him to finish the book on evolution, which entailed giving him free time at the Dōshisha in the fall, sending his family home so his children could begin regular schooling, and allowing him to embark on a year-long course of study in the United States, Great Britain, and Germany to prepare himself as a theologian. But they were insufficient deterrents. When his colleagues in Japan conferred, the only theologian among the missionaries, Jerome Davis, was critically ill; he was the most qualified for the post, but his unavailability made Gulick the obvious choice.[31]

Gulick was, however, concerned about the acceptability of his views. He reminded his colleagues and the board in Boston that they would be selecting a man with "liberalistic tendencies" if they chose him. The post at Dōshisha would put him in the crossfire between conservative and liberal Christians from both the missionary circles and the converts. He wrote his aunt Julia that he wanted the mission united on his appointment and appreciative of his views, for he believed that anyone teaching theology who did not attempt to integrate it with the study of evolution would lack influence with the students. Although this might upset the more conservative missionaries, he would not change his position.[32]

After debating this issue all spring, Gulick accepted the position in May when the board agreed to his conditions and secured

the Japanese government's concurrence as well. Preparations to
leave Matsuyama and to send his wife and children home were
speedily taken.[33] The missionary would become a theology
professor.

THE GULICK FAMILY LIFE:

When the family returned to the United States in 1904 it was a
relief to Cara Gulick, for her own work and family cares had
brought her to the point of exhaustion. Although her husband was
about to embark on a new and more settled career as professor of
theology, her life as missionary, wife, and mother had become
increasingly hectic as her family grew. In part this was the result
of the vicissitudes of missionary life and the normal cares inherent
in raising five children, and in part the result of the nature of her
relationship with Sidney and his way of life.

His marriage in 1887 had fulfilled Gulick's dreams. He loved
Cara then, and his devotion never wavered over the fifty-three
years of their married life. But for her the situation was different.
Cara was ambivalent, uncertain for many years that she had made
the right choice. Her family wanted her to marry a missionary,
and their wishes probably influenced her decision to drop her
resistance to Gulick's entreaties, yet she did not kiss him until they
were married. Years later when she found out about his brief
courtship of Charlotte Hall she wrote in anguish: "But why, oh
why, did you let me do it? I have often felt I wronged you in
marrying you—that you would have been happier and gone
further with someone else and now I know it."[34] Gulick, who had
told her of the episode in 1934 in the course of writing and circulat-
ing his reminiscences, overcame her doubts with continued reas-
surances of his love, which had been steadfast for over forty
years, but the episode illuminated their relationship and personal-
ities. He was the one who loved the most, although he was apparently shy about demonstrating it, while she was hesitant and harbored deep feelings of self-doubt.

Despite Cara's hesitation, their marriage appeared to be a
happy one. Gulick treated her with great consideration on their
honeymoon, for he soon realized that he had to win her love, and
that it would be a long, slow process. They both liked Japan and

immersed themselves in the work there, although Cara's religious devotion never matched Sidney's zeal. She gradually was able to express her feelings for him, while he, the more diligent writer, wrote of his for her whenever they were apart. They decided not to have children until they were "ready," and both later recalled with some amusement how that decision postponed the consummation of their marriage. He felt the delay helped win her affection, for it demonstrated to her his patient devotion. The birth of their children deepened their love, for each one was planned and desired. Gulick vividly expressed his sorrow at their separations in these early years, and he clearly missed her advice. As he tried to decide about going to Oxford in 1895, he wrote of his need to discuss it with her "in our customary style, while dropping off to sleep—that is, you dropping off while I keep up my end of the talk!"[35] Theirs had become a warm and comfortable relationship.

Perhaps the most poignant episode in their relationship came in 1889, when they were at Matsuyama. Sidney gave Cara an unsent love letter he had written her twenty years earlier, when he was such a lonely youth in Oakland. The missive described how much she meant to him, and how his devotion had grown. The letter moved her deeply, and she responded, "I thank God for the love which He has given us one for the other, and for our joy and happiness in our work, in our home, our children, and in each other."[36]

Yet even as the children provided joy, they were a source of expense and a complication in their lives, just as children were for most foreign missionaries. Sue and Luther's births had required long separations between Cara and Sidney because of the lack of a physician in Kumamoto, and occasionally missionary duties conflicted with the role of husband and father. In Osaka in 1895 Sidney wrote the board that the three children were recovering from diphtheria and measles, and his wife had just sprained her ankle. It was a poor time to leave, yet he set off on a preaching tour.[37]

The twin problems of raising children in a missionary environment were maintaining their health and educating them. Sue and Luther were reasonably healthy children, but Leeds, born in 1894, was sickly and demanded much care from his mother. The stay in Oakland was terribly hard on Cara, who had the sole care of the three children and an inadequate income. Child care exhausted her, but they could not afford to hire a governess.[38] Missionary salaries were technically merely "living allowances" paid to both spouses with small increments for each child. The Gulicks received a small additional income from Cara's parents. The Congregationalist motto, "Make it do, use it up, do without," was a byword for missionaries. Housing was provided by the mission board, and in Japan, servants, at least a cook, maid and gardener, were both inexpensive and essential in dealing with the local culture. But no mission family lived affluently; only if both partners were extremely careful managers could they survive comfortably.

The Gulick household in Matsuyama finally provided a settled environment for the family. Luther, the second eldest child, remembered their home vividly nearly eighty years later. It was a compound with spacious living quarters for the family, separate servants' quarters, and copious storage areas. The home, built for a previous missionary family, included three guest bedrooms, and the grounds contained a back yard, a tennis court, a vegetable garden, and a lawn, all surrounded by a high adobe wall with a gate which was barred at night. Luther recalled that his father was a very busy man, supervising a school and the staff of the Kumiai church, preparing his own sermons as head pastor, writing reports to Congregational church groups and the board, and working on his books and projects. He maintained an ongoing interest in the phenomenon of "fox possession," people whose spirit was believed possessed by a fox, and he researched cases of it for another book he never published.[39] After conducting prayers for the servants and the family each morning, Gulick and his two secretaries would be sequestered from 8 A.M. to 4 P.M. in the study, breaking only briefly for lunch and an afternoon nap.

This orderly routine was often disrupted by guests, an additional expense. Matsuyama had no hotel for foreigners, and the Gulick home often housed wayfarers, who might be deadbeat travelers, war correspondents, or church visitors. The most famous guest Luther remembered was the explorer-journalist George Kennan (uncle of the well-known George F. Kennan); Luther, in his teens, interpreted for Kennan and showed him the sights.

The home was a busy place, and Cara was in charge of its domestic activities. She raised flowers in a solarium and Luther kept wild birds as pets. With the aid of a full-time Japanese tailor, Cara made all the family's clothes. She raised vegetables to supplement the staples they received yearly from San Francisco and even ran a convict rehabilitation program for a while; that ended suddenly when an ex-convict raped the family's cook.[40]

The education of the children was a continuing dilemma. Sidney and Cara taught Sue to read, and she devoured her father's library at an early age. Luther was more difficult; he did not read until age eight or nine, when his eye trouble was finally diagnosed and corrected in Tokyo. On occasion his father hired a workman to teach the boy carpentry to keep him busy. Since Leeds was an invalid, the two older children's studies were supervised by their father's secretary, who attempted to keep them studying three or four hours a day, but often in vain. Gulick himself taught them geography.[41] All attempts to engage a tutor failed. Sidney's concern about his children's education was expressed later: "This coming of children into the home one by one, and their training in this land where there is so much that we wish them not to see or hear has been an education of head and heart of no little importance."[42] Like other missionary families, they ultimately resolved the problem by sending the older children away. In 1904 Sue was sent to Kobe College to study music, and preparations were made to send Luther to Oakland, for Leeds and the two younger children now demanded attention.

Cara was an innovative and creative missionary wife. She pioneered the raising of tomatoes in Japan and conducted cooking classes for the local women, showing them how to use eggs and milk in their diet and learning how to do Japanese cooking. Since she was a trained nurse, she was often called upon in local medical emergencies. In addition, she performed the usual tasks of a missionary wife, conducting Bible study, making home visitations, and leading ladies' prayer meetings. When two new babies were added to the family her health began to fail. Heart trouble began with the birth of Sidney, Jr., and led to a physical breakdown in Germany two years later.[43]

Sidney could provide little help with domestic concerns. His scientific work brought him many students, and business and education leaders sought his assistance as they attempted to devise religious or ethical solutions to social problems caused by industrialism. Matsuyama was an industrial city, and the plight of the factory girls brought in as cheap labor distressed him. Believing in the social gospel, he felt that religion should act as a social mediator and help to improve conditions of life.[44] The factory girls in Matsuyama were virtual slaves; he and the other members of the mission worked to establish a Christian home for them, for conservative and liberal Christians alike shared a concern for the well-being of the people among whom they worked.

The Gulick home was a warm and loving place. Sidney and Cara were very close, although they maintained a Victorian reserve in front of the children. Their relationship withstood the test of time and the separations that became even more lengthy when they returned to the United States. For nearly ten years, from 1914 to 1924, Cara lived in Oberlin where her children attended school, while Sidney resided in New York, visiting the family whenever his frequent travels took him in that direction. Their children suffered no lasting harm from the lack of early formal education or their Japanese upbringing. While the two elder children learned Japanese well and had many Japanese playmates, the younger children, who spent their childhoods in Matsuyama and Kyoto, associated more with other American children. They did not grow up with that sense of isolation Sidney had felt as a youth. They flourished in their parents' love and care, and developed a strong sense of family identity. The Gulicks were an historic family with deep and strong roots, and their offspring were often reminded of that. They were trained in the family custom of keeping in touch through correspondence when apart, as Sidney had been by his parents. (His father had died in Japan in 1877; his mother had also retired there and lived with his sister Hattie until her death twenty years later.) The result, in both his and his father's families, was a close-knit family with strong ties.

4

FROM MISSIONARY TO THEOLOGIAN: THE KYOTO YEARS

RETRAINING AS A THEOLOGIAN:

In early September 1904, Gulick began his second furlough. It included little rest; he embarked on a crash course in theology that took him to the Pacific School of Religion, to the universities of Chicago and Yale, Oberlin and Dartmouth Colleges, and Andover and Hartford Theological Seminaries. Interspersed with his studies were the usual talks returned missionaries always gave while on leave, talks which not only advanced the cause but also helped raise some money. In addition, the energetic scholar managed to write another book, *The White Peril in the Far East.*

Gulick spent the second year of his furlough in Europe. It took some financial maneuvering to get the entire family abroad, since the two eldest were no longer eligible for the board's support, but he raised the money and sailed in late April of 1905. By early July the entourage was settled in Marburg, Germany, with the children in school.[1] Cara remained there with the children, while Gulick spent the spring semester alone in Berlin and even traveled to England to fill a request for lectures on the issue of opium addiction among the Chinese.[2]

The year was an exciting and difficult one for the family and a stimulating one for Gulick. Everyone suffered from the harsh German weather but adapted well to the new culture, perhaps too well. A stern parent rebuked one Otto Hassenpflug who sought Sue's hand. Gulick complained that their customs were too different, and Otto smoked and drank![3] In addition, Sue was only seventeen.

However, the year was hard on Cara. Suffering from a weak heart, exhausted by the extensive travel and the effort of managing the large household, she suffered a physical breakdown at the end of the year and spent several weeks in Switzerland recuperating.[4]

The summer in Marburg provided time for pleasure hikes in the Alps, and time for a busy father to get to know his children. The family returned to Japan via Italy, the Suez Canal, and Ceylon, and settled into a new home in Kyoto, where Gulick assumed his post at the Dōshisha in January of 1907.[5]

INTERPRETING JAPAN TO THE WEST:

Although the Gulicks had been far from Japan, it was never distant from their thoughts. Japan's expansionism put it often in the news, and in his addresses in America Gulick was often called upon to explain those actions to an interested public. For the first time he faced the two issues he would spend the rest of his life analyzing—the reasons for Japanese expansionism, and the effect of discrimination against Japanese immigrants in the United States on Japanese-American relations. In 1905 he was traveling too much and was too engrossed in his studies to be aware of the latter problem, but the Russo-Japanese War made it impossible for him to ignore the former.

The Gulicks lived in Japan for most of the Meiji era (1868–1912). During that time the Japanese Empire gradually expanded, both to accommodate a growing population and to achieve stature as a world power. Some of this growth was peaceful, accomplished through shrewd diplomatic negotiations that enabled the new regime successfully to reassert old claims to such territories as Southern Sakhalin, the Bonin Islands, and the Ryukyus. But other desirable lands, including Korea and Taiwan, were claimed by China or were nominally independent. China itself was an even greater lure, for as the Meiji oligarchs created a viable economic structure and an effective system of governance, the Manchu regime was falling into hopeless disrepair. The condition of China as the "sick man of Asia" posed an irresistible temptation to Russia, but its rich markets also attracted Great Britain, the outside power with the largest trading interest, in addition to the United States and Japan.

Unaccustomed to the "diplomacy of imperialism" practiced by the Western powers, the Japanese sought first to wrest Korea from China's grasp,[6] and the Sino-Japanese War of 1894 to 1895 accomplished that objective. China relinquished claims of suzerainty and the isolated kingdom was left as prey for Japan or Russia. But Tokyo's attempts to seize the Liaotung peninsula in the treaty settlement of Shimonoseki in 1895 met with failure, for the Triple Intervention of Russia, France, and Germany forced Japan, for anything but altruistic reasons, to disgorge it. Frustrated on one front, Japan did acquire the rich island of Taiwan, however, and proceeded to incorporate it into its empire.

Gulick, like most missionaries in the 1890s, paid little attention to those developments. The war with China was a brief one, China a vital mission field, and the missionaries did not take sides. Of greater concern were Japan's attempts to revise the unequal treaties foisted upon it by the West. On this issue the missionaries were united, for if the West were to give up extraterritoriality and the conventional tariff, the missionaries believed the Japanese would abandon the onerous system of requiring passports for internal travel and restricting foreigners' rights to residence. Foreigners might even be permitted to purchase land. Most of them also felt Japan's cause was just; the nation was adopting the hallmarks of Western civilization as it revised its legal code, expanded educational opportunities, and tolerated the promulgation of Christianity. The missionaries began petitioning the American government to revise the treaties as early as 1871. Every Protestant missionary in southern Japan signed a petition urging treaty revision that was printed in the *Japan Weekly Mail*, May 17, 1884.[7] Pragmatic as well as idealistic reasons motivated them. Japan seemed so close to becoming a Christian nation that the unresolved dispute over treaties appeared a hindrance to conversions; resentment of inequities engendered deep hostility to anything foreign.[8] Even after the "Seven Wonderful Years" passed, the missionaries continued to support treaty revision as beneficial to the Christian cause.

After years of unsuccessful negotiations, the Western treaties were finally revised in 1894, to take effect five years later. The new American treaty allowed its nationals to enter, travel, or reside anywhere in Japan; no longer did they have to be in Japanese employ to reside outside the treaty ports. It provided for freedom of conscience and confirmed present land leases in perpetuity. Land purchase rights were not negotiated, for the United States was considering denying them to Japanese immigrants to America. A tariff was agreed upon, and most-favored-nation status was retained. [9]

When the terms of the new treaty were made public, the American Board's foreign secretary, the Reverend James L. Barton, complained about the provisions regarding religious schools. The Imperial Rescript on Education of 1890 had established that schools seeking government recognition could not teach religion. Barton feared this meant that missionaries would no longer be able to teach, but he was reassured that the provision only applied to schools seeking government recognition—a right that entitled them to certain privileges, but was not a necessity for their existence. The State Department concluded that this clause did not imply an antireligious policy, and it lodged no protest. [10] In fact, the new treaty greatly improved conditions for missionary work.

Gulick was in the United States during most of the Sino-Japanese War and made no comment on it at the time. However, by the 1890s he had formed some strong opinions about the Japanese themselves. Although he decried their "ambitious self-confidence," [11] their avarice and other vices, he did develop a feeling of admiration for them. Their intelligence and willingness to learn evoked his praise, but he also approved of their "spunk." In his "Reminiscences" he recalled an episode from his honeymoon. He had seen a gang of Chinese workmen in Hong Kong ordered to do a task by a white supervisor. When one workman failed to understand, the white man knocked him to the ground. This was his first experience of what Gulick called "the domineering spirit of the white man in the Far East," and it prompted much reflection. He concluded, "When I thought about that event [later] in the light of my experiences in Japan, I am confident that the Japanese would have united in thrashing the man." [12] To Gulick's way of thinking, such would have been an entirely proper response for such arrogance.

This idea of the "white peril," of the Europeans as the real aggressors against the Asians, grew in Gulick's mind. While European and American racists popularized the notion of a "yellow peril," of the Orient as a military and economic threat, Gulick recognized that perspective as narrow and one-sided. The idea of Asians as sneaky, treacherous, and devious captured the Western imagination through the writings of men like press lord William Randolph Hearst or military theorist Homer Lea, who wrote in 1909 *The Valor of Ignorance,* a diatribe against the Japanese threat. Gulick's unique perspective allowed him to see the other side of the coin. White men were less numerous in East Asia than were Asian immigrants to the United States, but they came for far different purposes: Asians left home as long- or short-term immigrants, while most Westerners, aside from missionaries, came as temporary exploiters, even as would-be conquerors. Gulick observed daily the behavior of whites in Asia, and what he saw disturbed him.

The outbreak of the Russo-Japanese War in 1904 provided Gulick the impetus to put his thoughts about Japan on paper. Before he left Matsuyama he wrote friends about the war, complaining that it was difficult to obtain accurate news. But he could observe first-hand the Japanese treatment of hospitalized Russian prisoners, and it impressed him. "In truth, Japan is more truly a Christian nation than is Russia, if one looks at the principles that control her government and her civil and military administration," he wrote. Americans called Japan heathen, but he noted that in some respects the Americans were more so, for they still lynched Negroes and burned them alive.[13] The real issue, Gulick felt, was whether whites would attempt to continue exploiting the colored races, for that was unjust and might well be impossible in the future as the balance of power changed.[14] The yellow peril might prove a future threat, but the white peril was a reality.

Gulick's anti-Russian sentiments were shared by his fellow missionaries. One of them wrote that Japan was "morally superior to Russia in the war" because there was religious freedom in the former and a state-controlled church in the latter.[15] The noted popular historian of Japan, William E. Griffis, chimed in with the same tune,[16] and soon a majority of Americans shared their sentiments, cheering on the underdog and hissing at the bumptious and incompetent autocrat. As Theodore Roosevelt noted, albeit for quite different reasons, "Japan is playing our game."[17]

As Gulick traveled in the United States he was often called upon to lecture on the causes and implications of the war, and he began to consider the possibility of writing a short book on Japan's real war aims. He asked his siblings for their reactions to the idea on December 8, and a week later corresponded to Cara that he had already written about two hundred note pages.[18]

The White Peril in the Far East, finished before the war's end, was published in New York in late 1905, in time to capitalize on the interest the conflict sparked. The book clarified the author's position on the protagonists. He termed himself an admirer of Japan but not an uncritical patron who believed it free of faults. Briefly recounting the story of Japan's modernization, he praised the great progress made there by Christianity. He traced Japanese-American relations, noting proudly if somewhat simplistically that the United States had been the "single white nation always free from aggressive schemes and always regardful of Japanese rights and interests." His treatment of the xenophobic 1890s was balanced; he perceived the tenor of those years as a reaction to "the unreasoning rush after foreign things." Many reasons accounted for the decline of Christianity during that decade, including the spread of such competing ideas from the West as the higher criticism of the Bible and evolution. The repeated failure of treaty revision had hurt relations because the Western powers appeared to place demands on Japan "which would have been an insult if made of each other." Gulick also emphasized the disillusionment the Japanese felt with the West when the Triple Intervention powers, Germany, France, and Great Britain, deprived Japan of the Liaotung peninsula and then greedily claimed it themselves.[19]

Gulick remained optimistic, however, in his belief that Japan had transcended its antiforeign phase and now was able to borrow discriminately, keeping ideas that worked and opposing only those countries that sought to harm its interests. Christianity, Gulick felt, was enjoying a resurgence; the war had made Japanese society aware of its need for some kind of ethical values, and people realized that the theory of evolution had not destroyed the Christian faith.[20]

Gulick then turned to a discussion of the war, and his Japano-phile bias triumphed. Japan, he felt, aimed solely to protect its national existence and to achieve peace and security in the Far East. Russia epitomized the white peril—barbaric on the battle-field, deceitful in diplomacy, and sinister in its aims of controlling Manchuria and Korea. "The White Peril," he wrote, has "assumed its worst form [in Russia], for it adds hypocrisy to aggressive greed, and cloaks its crimes with the very religion which con-demns them." Japan, on the other hand, had learned humanitarian practices from its contacts with the West, to the point where it was almost more occidental than oriental. He depicted Japan as the international meeting place between East and West, interpreting each tradition to the other and fusing the best elements of each. Fortunately Japan did not perceive the war as a conflict of East against West; the solidarity of the West had been broken when Britain and the United States proffered Japan their support. "Ja-pan feels she is fighting in the interests of modern civilization. The real peril today in Japan is from Russia, backed by Germany and France. War is strengthening the moral fiber of Japan," he wrote.[21]

Gulick's assertions betrayed a boundless optimism and naïve faith in Japan, in contrast to criticisms expressed in *Evolution of the Japanese*. *The White Peril* also proclaimed his disillusionment with Western diplomatic conduct as he had observed it in the convoluted decade between 1894 and 1904. A Japanese victory in the war would bring great benefits, he felt—greater individual rights, freedom of travel, the stimulation of universal education and representative government, and an acceptance of the modern scientific world view. It would also be a victory for the Open Door concept, which he took at face value to mean equal trade opportunities and respect for the territorial integrity of China. China, too, would benefit, for Western interference would be thwarted and religious work stimulated. A Russian victory, on the other hand, would spell disaster for Asia.[22]

He concluded with a disquisition on the title theme, the white peril. "The white man's presence [in Asia] is the scourge of to-day," he wrote. "The Oriental has been debauched by the white man. The most serious hindrance to Christian work is the immoral life and selfish spirit so universally exhibited by white men in these lands." A fierce reaction was brewing, he warned, out of which a real yellow peril would emerge. The white race had to be taught to treat yellow men with the courtesy and dignity to which they were entitled as fellow human beings.[23]

This book, Gulick's first attempt to analyze East Asian international relations, is significant on several levels. It demonstrated simultaneously his perceptiveness as well as his naïveté. Tremendously optimistic about and supportive of Japan, he overlooked the sneak attack on Port Arthur and portrayed the Japanese as if they were Christians holding off the heathen hordes. Age and reflection moderated his subsequent books, which showed more ability to distinguish good from base in Japanese actions. But *The White Peril* does reflect his tremendous initial enthusiasm for Japan which appeared during the war years in America and declined only as a clearer apprehension of Japan's war aims emerged during the negotiation of the Treaty of Portsmouth.[24]

Despite these touches of innocence, Gulick accurately assessed the war's impact on Asian thinking about their position in the world relative to whites. The Japanese did view the outcome of the war as a "victory of the forces of progress and civilization over those of reaction and backwardness," as historian Akira Iriye has written. Some Japanese writers, notably Abe Isoo, asserted that a victory demonstrating Japan's advancement would make intolerable the discriminatory treatment of its emigrants abroad.[25] The Chinese also perceived Japan's apparent achievement as a welcome setback to the Western imperialists in Asia and a dramatic portent of future changes in the relationship of the white and yellow races. Gulick, drawing on over fifteen years of residence in Japan, correctly evaluated the consequences of the war. He saw the changing status of the white man in East Asia, the beginning of the decline of white power. He did not yet grasp the implications of America's shabby treatment of Japanese immigrants, who were as much a part of Japan's ideas of expansionism as was overt conquest. However, a later opportunity for observation would speedily repair that gap in his knowledge.

Gulick's perceptions of Japan's proto-Christian behavior were based on truth. The Japanese government did not want the war portrayed as a conflict between a Christian and a non-Christian nation, so it took pains to encourage the evangelists. Most Japanese believers demonstrated both their loyalty to the state and to their faith, although Christian socialists protested the war. Some missionaries were allowed to work among soldiers at the front. For a few years after the conflict the Japanese Christians were virtual allies of the government. The missionaries assisted in the management of education and medical work and redoubled their efforts at evangelism because their services as English teachers were no longer in demand. At the same time the Kumiai churches severed their financial ties to the American Board; the missionaries worked independently of them, but in cooperation, as they did in other denominations.[26] As John Howes noted, this was the "effective end of the period of apprenticeship in Japanese Christianity."[27]

Finally, neither Gulick nor the rest of the missionary community saw a contradiction between the notion of a "just" war, however defined, and the tenets of Christianity. Japan, struggling for its sovereignty and not, or so he believed, for empire, was fighting a "just" war, a legitimate conflict. No purist doctrines defining such a war as one fought only in self-defense troubled him; in fact, he seemed unaware that Japan had fired the first shot. His anti-Russian bias may have clouded his observations. The American peace movement, in which Gulick would later play a significant role, had always been to some degree intertwined with the historic peace churches, but Gulick's beliefs at this time displayed no pacifist tendencies. However, the Russo-Japanese War was easy to view in the abstract, unlike World War I, which, as will become apparent later, caused him much grief. Gulick was personally and emotionally involved in the latter, and the experience profoundly affected his thinking about the justification of violence.

The Russo-Japanese War came to a conclusion after the mediation of President Theodore Roosevelt. Although the Japanese had virtually exhausted themselves in the conflict, the Russians, beset by revolution, appeared the more obvious losers. Tokyo, seeking to maximize its temporary advantage, sought a huge indemnity, which the Russians rejected. Desiring to restore a balance of power in Asia, Roosevelt pressured the Japanese to concede the point. The resulting Treaty of Portsmouth ended the war, but

Japanese-American friendship was severely damaged by demonstrations in Tokyo over the terms of the treaty; young chauvinists
were especially quick to blame Roosevelt for Japan's concessions.
In 1906, after the San Francisco earthquake occurred, relations
between the two nations plummeted in the wake of even more
anti-Japanese actions in the devastated city. Added to that were ill
feelings over the war's outcome, resentment of Roosevelt's diplomacy, and mounting concern in Japan over American treatment of Japanese aliens.[28] Gulick, however, was in Europe during
the treaty negotiations and ratification, and he did not comment
on the outbreak of anti-American sentiment which accompanied
the announcement of the treaty's terms in Tokyo.

GULICK AS THEOLOGIAN AND PEACE ADVOCATE:

The Gulicks returned to Japan in December 1906, and settled in
Kyoto in time for Sidney to begin teaching at the Dōshisha in January 1907. He soon received the unusual offer of a part-time position at the newly opened Imperial University in Kyoto. With the
promulgation of the Imperial Rescript on Education the Japanese
had replaced most American teachers in government-sponsored
schools, if not with Japanese then with the more authoritarian
Germans. In fact, the total number of foreign "experts" employed
in Japan diminished during these years. Missionaries were
squeezed out of secondary schools desiring governmental accred-
itation, and few Americans were hired in state universities. Between 1902 and 1912 there were thirty-two foreigners at the presti-
gious Tokyo University, only four of whom were American. Kyoto's Imperial University, opened in 1897, utilized only two Americans part-time: Gulick to teach Christian religion, and Frank Lom-
bard to instruct in Shakespeare.[29] Although this employment put
him in the pay of the Japanese government, Gulick thought little of
the possible implications. The four hundred yen he earned in 1910
in that service enabled him to significantly supplement his teacher's allowance, and it supported his writing. (The sum was the
equivalent of the annual income of a lower-middle class Japanese
worker.) In fact he downplayed the significance of the position.
He wrote the American Board secretary in 1908 that he had only

one regular student and six or eight others who attended irregularly, but he hoped for a greater "payoff" in the future.[30]

Gulick enjoyed the new post of missionary theologian. He still gave occasional sermons and lectures and promoted the welfare of the Kumiai church, but now he had more time for scholarship. Bouncing ideas off Uncle John, he continued working on the unfinished book on the theory of evolution. His family also benefitted from the change. Leeds joined the two oldest children in the United States for schooling, and Sue rejoined her parents for a year's hiatus from Oberlin College, where she had gone after a year at Kobe College. Cara still worked too hard, Gulick thought, but then she chided him for his penchant for overwork, too.

An unexpected opportunity to return to Europe came Sidney's way in 1910, when he was appointed to attend an international missionary conference to be held in Edinburgh. Although the board did not provide travel funds, he received the necessary money through a gift from a fellow missionary in China, Arthur Smith, who was going on furlough anyway and had saved extra funds for the conference. Gulick traveled via the Trans-Siberian railroad and enjoyed the conference, especially the opportunity for a trip with his eldest son. He visited two relatives and then met Luther, whose way to the conference had also been paid by Smith. They traveled through the Lake District and the cathedral towns of England, and then traversed the Low Countries to Switzerland where they hiked to the base of the Jungfrau. The holiday also provided the opportunity for some parental guidance, for rambunctious Luther had been asked not to return to the Hotchkiss School in Connecticut and was transferring to Oberlin.[31] Gulick returned to Japan in time to resume teaching at the end of September.

His years in Kyoto brought Gulick into contact with a broader spectrum of the Japanese elite, as his own interests grew to include the nascent Japanese peace movement. Rethinking the utility of war in the aftermath of the Russo-Japanese conflict, he helped found the Oriental Peace Society in Kyoto in 1907, an outgrowth of the Japan Peace Society founded in Tokyo in 1906. He was also one of the vice presidents of the American Peace Society in Japan, founded in Yokohama in 1911. These organizations, although small, brought together American businessmen, Japanese officials, and missionaries who were dedicated to the cause of world peace. The Japan Peace Society promoted peace and goodwill, while the American Peace Society worked to improve Japanese-American relations.[32] In 1911 he met Hamilton Holt, the well-known writer and publisher of the journal *The Independent*. Holt, a member of the America-Japan Society (founded in 1907 as the Friends of America Association by Japanese who had spent time in America), was on a trip to the Far East. A long-time admirer of the Japanese, Holt met the emperor; this honor intensified his advocacy of better relations between the United States and Japan. Together Holt and Gulick drew up a proposal for a peace scholarship, which Holt promised to broach to the Carnegie Endowment for International Peace on his return. Gulick continued to correspond with Holt on the idea, which included a proposal for an exchange of Japanese students and professors of English to go to America, and American students to go to Japan. A version of the plan was adopted, and Nitobe Inazō was the first exchange professor in 1911.[33]

This interest in the peace movement stemmed in part from growing concerns the missionaries had over increased tension between Japan and the United States. During the period of harmony in U.S.-Japanese relations, up to 1906, most missionaries remained unaware of the trouble brewing over California's treatment of Japanese immigrants or its antecedents. Overt American hostility to Asians dated from the mid-nineteenth century, when Chinese who came to work on the transcontinental railroads were brutally treated and ultimately denied further entry by the Chinese Exclusion Act of 1882. The anti-Asian prejudice aroused by the Chinese was transferred to the Japanese, the next group of Asians who immigrated to America. The Japanese began to enter California from Hawaii in large numbers after 1900, and quickly encountered discrimination. Japan viewed the emigrants as a potential source of income, for they transmitted funds to their families at home, but it also considered them as continuing citizens who would maintain social and trade ties to their native homeland. Although most of the Issei were not well educated, they seem to have shared this concept of their role. For America to deny them the right to immigrate was resented by the Japanese government, and, from the earliest years of Japanese immigration, some Japanese officials dreaded a "Japanese exclusion act." Although the controversy was just one aspect of Japan's struggle for power, the missionaries did not see the ramifications.[34] They were probably also unaware that Japan envisaged a program of greatly expanded trade and peaceful migration to many areas of the world and believed its victory in the Russo-Japanese War had entitled its people to equal treatment.

The growing hostility against Japanese on the West Coast (where almost all of them resided) culminated with an incident in San Francisco. That city's school board, anxious about the increasing number of Japanese in the public schools, decided to segregate all Asian students in the primary grades. The incident brought a sharp protest from the Japanese ambassador, who objected to the principle of discriminatory treatment. Although President Roosevelt was sympathetic to Japan's complaint, he was disturbed to find that the Californians did not want to back down, for their prejudice ran deep. Roosevelt had some short-term success, but the prejudice continued. San Francisco became the home of the first anti-Japanese organization, the Asiatic Exclusion League, founded in 1905.

The Japanese press gave extensive coverage to the California situation. Denial of equal access to education and the right to acquire American citizenship made abundantly clear to the Japanese and the missionaries that Americans did not consider the former their equals. This posed a special dilemma for the missionaries, for how could a religion that preached the brotherhood of all mankind explain, much less rationalize, the fear, hatred, and hostility of their compatriots on the Pacific Coast toward their Japanese brethren?

The missionaries probably underestimated the extent and depth of the prejudicial feelings on the West Coast, much as did the Japanese government itself. They were no doubt relieved when a temporary solution to the immigration crisis was found in the Gentlemen's Agreement of 1907-08. A series of notes exchanged by the two governments delineating specific methods of restricting Japanese laborers from emigrating to America, the agreement effectively terminated the entry of male Japanese. While this defused the immediate war scare, the Californians were still unsatisfied and demanded total exclusion. The *San Francisco Examiner,* mouthpiece of William Randolph Hearst, led the attack.[35]

The missionaries reacted to this crisis by denying the fact that a war scare had existed in Japan as well. In 1909 the American Board passed a resolution about the San Francisco school situation, noting that the Japanese press and populace had not, on the whole, reacted with alarm to the immigration dispute. An article in *The Outlook* in 1910 also refuted rumors of war hysteria in Japan. The anonymous author, who wrote suspiciously like Gulick, urged Americans to discount stories that portrayed the Japanese as warlike. The missionaries were in a better position to judge people's feelings than sensation-seeking journalists, according to the writer, and they saw no sentiment for war.[36]

The next year at the Thirty-fourth Annual Mission Meeting, Gulick joined with two other distinguished American Board missionaries, Daniel Crosby Greene and James H. Pettee, in drafting a peace resolution. Expressing concern over rumors of trouble between the United States and Japan, they rejoiced in "the growing peace movement in Japan and in the growth of a calm spirit among its leaders." A suggested arbitration treaty between the United States and Japan won their approval.[37] The memorial was widely endorsed and circulated in America.

Gulick also tried the personal touch. When a friend sent him an article from the *Denver Post* that claimed Japan wanted to fight America, he responded with a lengthy letter. His experience had proven quite the opposite. He noted that the author of the *Post's* article, while a twenty-five year resident of Japan, was an art historian who did not know the language. He added that in 1908, when relations were poor, Japan had extended a cordial welcome to the Great White Fleet; Gulick had been appointed to the welcoming committee by the Kyoto Chamber of Commerce. Although the warmth that once existed between the United States and Japan had abated due to the immigration controversy, it certainly had not given way to antipathy. He enclosed a copy of the American Board's Peace Resolution and noted that seventy-five missionaries had endorsed it.[38] The passage of the Root-Takahira Agreement of that year had in fact defused many issues.

Gulick recognized, however, that the problem could not be glossed over by words alone, and he tried to devise some practical means of alleviating it. Japanese immigrants to America were disliked and suffered discrimination for what he considered basically economic causes—they outworked and out-produced their white competitors. The belief that they were unassimilable he attributed to their life-style. Rejected by the white community, they stayed together, thus seeming clannish. Their ignorance of the English language, Gulick felt, made it virtually impossible for them to acquire American culture. Gulick proposed to the eminent Christian writer and statesman Nitobe Inazō a plan whereby Japan would send secondary school graduates to the United States, either as students or workers. Because they could learn English and would have higher cultural standards than the poorly educated laborers, they might reverse this unfortunate stereotype. Gulick blamed sensationalist publishers and journalists like Hearst and Valentine S. McClatchy for unfairly portraying Japan in the press, and thus exacerbating relations between the two countries. He proposed to James Brown Scott of the Carnegie Endowment for International Peace that the endowment fund a new journal, to be called "Higher Internationalism," that would "educate Asians and Americans about one another in a beneficial way and undo some of the harm."[39] Although nothing came of either idea, they demonstrated Gulick's awareness of the complexities of the problem and his attempts to find a solution.

However, the response of the Californians to Japanese immigration was drastically different from Gulick's idealistic solution. They sought not only to exclude more Asians, but also to drive away those already there by socially excluding them and making their sojourn unprofitable.

THE MISSIONARIES AND JAPANESE-AMERICAN
RELATIONS:

Gulick's efforts had little impact on American public opinion. Although the signers of the missionary peace resolution ranked

among the most influential at that time in Japan, their names were
not well-enough known at home to attract attention. As Charles
Neu has noted, after the Russo-Japanese War the missionaries' influence on policymakers and the public was extremely limited,
despite the many articles they published and the talks they gave
while at home on furlough.[40] Although they reached a large religious audience, they were usually unknown to government officials or policymakers. In some ways they even abetted prejudice
through their criticism of Japanese mores, pursuant to the triumph of Protestant Christianity. While in Japan, missionaries
were often very isolated, and many lacked a deep interest in their
surroundings or in the political forces around them.[41] Gulick recognized this after he returned to America and sampled some of
their journal articles, so he printed and distributed a small brochure, labeled "Personal and Confidential," for the missionary
community. In it he cautioned his former colleagues that the articles they wrote to promote mission work in Japan tended to produce feelings of disdain or condemnation for the country, rather
than respect or goodwill. Writers needed to contrast the negative
with positive achievements to balance their accounts, he insisted.[42]

Gulick had made a significant point. The missionaries had
created a picture of an immoral society, and this no doubt caused
Americans to underestimate Japan's potential, particularly its
ability to take effective action against those who discriminated
against its emigrants overseas. Like American diplomats in obscure posts and naval commanders at sea, the missionaries were
also somewhat out of touch with events in America; their reaction
time was slowed by distance and poor communications. They
might have responded to the immigrants' plight as early as 1906,
instead of four years later.

An important question must be confronted at this point: why
did the missionary community in Japan have, relatively speaking,
so much less influence than its counterpart in China? China missionaries and their offspring exerted a significant impact on
American-East Asian relations throughout the twentieth century.
Their names are well known and include Henry Luce, Walter
Judd, and Pearl Buck. But the Japan mission produced only such

advocates as Gulick, Doremus Scudder, and Roger Greene, none of whom generated the amount of support for Japan as Pearl Buck did for China. Although no one single factor may be adduced to account for the differential, several explanations come to mind. First, the China mission was many times larger than that in Japan. Its leader, Bishop James W. Bashford, was an outstanding spokesman, but he was no more visible than Sidney Gulick would become. In neither land had the missionaries won vast numbers of converts. In fact, in Japan the small number of converts had had an impact far wider than their numbers alone would indicate. In addition, missionaries there had made great improvements in social conditions, education, the treatment of orphans, medical care, and attitudes toward women. The same was true of China, but in addition, the Japan missionaries had contributed toward the creation of a new generation of leadership because their converts came primarily from the upper class, in marked contrast to the situation in China.

However, the Japan missionaries faced several liabilities. Their message had not made Japan a peaceful member of the world community. They worked in a land where rising nationalism provided a motive force for expansion; this was a factor with which nineteenth century China missionaries did not have to contend. The China missionaries promoted a vision of a land almost innocent, at least peace-loving with respect to its neighbors. China was backward and needed help. Japan was hard-working and rapidly modernizing. In addition, the Japanese government was particularly sensitive to matters of "face," of equal treatment in the community of nations. Because of this, Japan was insistent that its emigrants to America be treated fairly and not made the objects of discriminatory legislation. This, as we will see, caused considerable friction for nearly two decades. The Chinese government was much more passive; its need for help was so manifest that it would tolerate much more in the way of discriminatory treatment, and it largely ignored the treatment meted out to the emigrants abroad.[43]

The missionaries themselves constituted a potent lobby in American foreign policy, as John Reed has noted. The American Board had considerable prestige, and its officials claimed to speak for five hundred thousand Congregationalists. The board's secretary, James L. Barton, actively promoted missions from 1894 to 1929, and the supporters of the mission movement constituted a "missionary mind," a way of looking at the world, that the State Department was forced to heed. But the impact of the message varied depending on the country or issue promoted. They had considerable influence, for example, in achieving the rapid recognition of the new republican government of China.[44]

Missionaries in Japan, however, did not have the clout that their China counterparts had. Before 1900 they had worked to achieve revision of the unequal treaties, and the peace resolution demonstrated their concern during the war scare of 1906. Only gradually did they become aware of the dangers the immigration controversy posed to the mission's success. The Congregationalists then sent Gulick to the Federal Council of Churches with a resolution on that issue. But they found it hard to generate sympathy for Japan. Had the country been a poor, backward, and passive land eagerly seeking Christ, it would have been a more attractive object of interest in America, but it was difficult to portray things that way. Attempting to depict it as peace-loving was an uphill battle, as Gulick had already discovered.

This difficulty prefigured the second factor. Japan's actions forced its friends to react, to explain, to take the defensive. Gulick tried his best to meet the challenge, explaining Tokyo's actions in a most sympathetic light. The problem, which was to become more acute as the century progressed, was how to accomplish that without appearing an apologist for aggression. No missionary successfully met that challenge, and in fact few tried. Until Gulick began writing, no missionary from Japan, with the sole exception of William E. Griffis,[45] who was primarily a teacher, had attempted to interpret Japan's actions for Americans. The China missionaries sought actively to influence the State Department regarding foreign policy; the Japan missionaries, by and large, did not.

GULICK THE SCHOLAR-THEOLOGIAN:

Along with his growing interest in foreign affairs and international peace, Gulick devoted himself to scholarship. His teaching at the Dōshisha necessitated writing just to produce materials his students needed. He and his Japanese assistant worked together translating two English-language theological studies into Japanese, B. P. Bowne's *Personalism* and William Adams Brown's *Christian Theology in Outline.* In addition, he wrote a book on systematic theology in that language, *A Sketch of the History of German Theology.* By this time he could use ten thousand characters, and his assistant, Tomita, a former journalist, knew twenty thousand, so they made an effective team. They completed a book entitled (in English) *Evolution: Cosmic, Terrestrial, Biological* which was published in Tokyo in 1910; a second edition, entitled *Evolution of the Human Race* came out in 1913. Gulick also authored a scientific work, *General Discussions in Science,* written in Japanese. He sent many letters to American pastors requesting recently published material that defended Christianity against scientific materialism, for his students were in great need of more sources.[46]

Gulick also began working on another book for his American audience, *Working Women of Japan.* Published in 1915, the book summarized the many occupations that employed Japanese women and the conditions under which they labored. The work clearly betrayed its author's social gospel leanings. He emphasized the immoral working conditions of factory girls and women entertainers, and discussed the efforts Christian missionaries were making to improve their lives. Designed to capture a general audience, the book nonetheless had a serious message: "No more urgent problem faces New Japan than the moral development of her workers."[47] They were capable of it; Christianity could provide it. This book showed how far Gulick had moved from the earlier concept of the missionary dedicated solely to individual salvation. As Akira Iriye pointed out, the emphasis of the missionary movement had shifted "from individual salvation to national redemption and regeneration,"[48] and Gulick's life exemplified that transition. Not that salvation had ceased to be important; it was now viewed in a larger context.

Meanwhile, and in a very dramatic way, Gulick's health became a major concern. In November of 1912, his doctor discovered a tumor in the groin, and the next month Gulick went to Tokyo for an operation for cancer. The operation itself was nearly fatal. Reacting adversely to the anesthetics used, chloroform and ether, he stopped breathing and was revived only with difficulty. The surgery was then continued without anesthetic. Although the cancer was successfully removed, Gulick nearly died of shock. He was soon on the road to recovery but on doctor's orders spent the rest of the winter and spring at his summer cottage at Karuizawa. In April he returned to Kyoto to begin the new semester's work, but in June he noticed sensitivity in the same area. Since his doctor had left the country, the family made a hasty decision to leave immediately for the United States.[49]

The Gulicks were already at sea before Sidney discovered the reason for his problem, and it was so simple as to be amusing. He had changed from heavy winter to lighter summer underwear in June, and the different weight of clothing caused a sensitivity in the area of the scar.[50] But the trip itself was no laughing matter. The more he considered events, the more Gulick became convinced that this error was in reality God's way of communicating to him that he had a new task, a new "calling." Believing in a personal God who communicated His wishes to each of His followers, Sidney felt this episode was as significant a statement as his original selection for missionary work had been. He had believed earlier that if God wanted him, He would tell him by providing him with a wife, and the results had been clearly affirmative. Gulick felt himself once more in God's hands.

While Gulick had not anticipated ever leaving the missionary field, he had very strong concerns about discrimination against Japanese on the West Coast of the United States, an issue which related indirectly to that work. Reports of pending alien land legislation had reached him in Karuizawa, and he foresaw the whole issue of American treatment of Japanese immigrants flaring anew. During his recuperation that spring, he wrote a series of letters on the subject to friends in both countries. Although he was concerned, he tried to calm his Japanese friends. He assured the editor of *Taiyo* that the legislation framed by the Californians would surely be found in contradiction to the U.S.-Japan treaty of 1911. Even if an alien law were passed, he believed it would be temporary and that ultimately no injustice would be done the immigrants. The true racists were few, he believed, and the heart of the problem was economic. But Japan insisted that the immi-

Karuizawa, 1913: The family gathered where Gulick recovered from the cancer operation. The servants are at left, Gulick's tutor at right.

grants retain their Japanese citizenship; this exacerbated the problem by encouraging the idea that they were unassimilable. Gulick urged the matter be treated with restraint.[51]

In a letter to a friend in Oakland, Gulick's deep concern was apparent. Pointing out how such legislation hindered the progress of the Gospel in Japan, he wrote: "The greatest obstacle to the growth of the Kingdom of God in Japan is the apparent failure of Christianity in so-called Christian lands to secure righteousness and justice toward other lands and aliens resident in Christian lands." Although he had no specific suggestions, he felt that Christians had to speak out against such injustice.[52]

Casting a wider net, Gulick next communicated with Secretary Barton of the American Board about the trouble the legislation would cause the missionaries; he knew its blatantly discriminatory intent would incense the Japanese government. He urged Barton to ask the board to issue a special bulletin on the subject.[53] Gulick had made two addresses in Japan during one week, he

noted, and both times dismayed Japanese called upon him to explain California's intent. The proposed legislation was rapidly
destroying the goodwill Americans had regained in Japan.[54] He
informed Barton that the mission board in Japan had passed a
resolution deploring the action and asking the American Board in
Boston to appoint a commission to study its effects. Gulick noted
that many Japanese believed only the American Christians could
remedy the situation.[55] It was time, he told Barton, for Christians
to take a stand.

The Gulicks stopped in Hawaii for ten days, then reached California in July. The ABCFM had already approved a furlough for
the family before the onset of Sidney's illness, for Cara needed to
take Sidney, Jr., and Ethel to Oberlin so that they, now eleven and
fourteen, could enter school. Gulick had postponed their scheduled departure so that he could be at Oberlin when Luther graduated in 1914. Because all the formalities for furlough had been
completed, however, there was no need to return immediately to
Japan, and Gulick took the opportunity for further medical diag-
nosis. He was relieved when the doctors pronounced him fit.
However, he decided to remain in California for a few months
studying the problem of the Japanese aliens. His subsequent plans
were indefinite, he wrote the board. Cara also needed some
surgery, and she planned to take the children to Oberlin in
November.[56]

In fact, Gulick's career in the mission field had come to an end.
He had evolved, to use a favorite concept of his, from a missionary whose preoccupations were the usual ones of evangelism and
education, to a scientist-theologian, and finally to an expert on
Japan whose interest in better Japanese-American relations transcended his missionary work. He recognized that prejudice and
discrimination at home would impede the spread of Christianity
in Japan, but his concerns were more catholic. At heart he was an
advocate of the social gospel, and this underlay his concerns
about the plight of the immigrants. Christian believers, he felt,
had a duty to mankind greater than just providing the key to salvation for the unconverted; indeed, they had to promote brotherhood and international goodwill and help to Christianize the conduct of life and the interaction between peoples. This was as

much a part of the reforming zeal of the social gospel movement as settlement houses or temperance reforms, and to the Reverend Mr. Gulick it was all-important.

In order to represent faithfully the Japanese point of view to the Americans, any missionary spokesman would have needed credibility with the Japanese and the ability to speak for both opinion leaders and the common citizenry. Gulick possessed that, and in addition had visibility in Japanese society and intellectual credibility because of his work on evolution and his positions at the Dōshisha and Kyoto Imperial University. Furthermore, events during his last year in Japan had improved his credentials as one who was influential with Japanese leaders in education and religion. In 1912 he participated in a meeting called "The Conference of the Three Religions" which was, as he described it, an official reception given by the Japanese government for the heads of the twelve Shinto, fifty-four Buddhist, and seven Christian bodies in the nation. Following that, he helped organize the Association Concordia, a group of Japanese leaders in education, business, and government, which sought to promote "better mutual knowledge by the East and the West of each others' moral and spiritual life." He was proud that through it he increased the number of his acquaintances in positions of leadership.[57] Clearly, if any one individual could explain Japan to the Americans and preach a message of Christian tolerance and goodwill, Sidney Gulick could. He stood ready to become a new type of evangelist. As he wrote later, "I am as truly a missionary working for Japan as if I were in Japan."[58] He became Japan's missionary to the Americans.

5

IN TRANSITION

The Gulicks arrived in California in late July of 1913 with future plans uncertain. While they received needed medical care Sidney reflected at length on his choices. Teaching was one possibility; Yale offered him a short-term appointment, which he briefly considered. But his chief concern was with the Japanese problem in California, and he wanted a position from which he could devote himself to that issue.[1]

In his customary fashion Gulick took advantage of his California location to investigate the situation thoroughly. For several weeks he traveled around the state; he gave a half dozen lectures in Northern California and seventeen more in the Los Angeles area, stressing the implications of the problem both for missionary work and for American-Japanese relations. Gradually he devised a solution which he termed "The New Oriental Policy." He tested it on audiences, then quickly set pen to paper, addressed it briefly in a pamphlet, and began writing a book.

CALIFORNIA AND THE "JAPANESE PROBLEM":

Gulick found that the tension over Japanese immigrants on the Pacific Coast was high, and in fact it was entering a new phase. The earliest immigrants had worked at menial employments in West Coast cities and farms, but, by 1908, many had established themselves as agricultural entrepreneuers. Their numbers were

78

small in comparison to immigration of other groups, never more than 2.1 percent of the population of California and one tenth of one percent of the population of the continental United States. However, they were a very visible minority. In 1908 the Japanese in America numbered some sixty thousand, two-thirds of whom lived in California.[2] Their willingness to work extremely hard for a pittance quickly aroused the ire of their neighbors, and anti-Japanese sentiment spread throughout the rural areas of California. The crusade to "keep California white" soon manifested itself in partisan politics. Although the anti-Japanese line was almost universally popular in the state, it was not a nationwide phenomenon, and national leaders of both parties restrained their local followers from pressing the issue in the state legislature. A few thousand Japanese women still entered the country annually, many of them as "picture brides" wed by proxy to laborers already in the country. While this was perfectly legal under the family reunification provisions of the Gentlemen's Agreement, it caught the Californians by surprise and led them to conclude that either they had been misled by the agreement or that they were being deceived by Japan.[3]

By the time the next session of the Republican-dominated California legislature met in 1913, Democrat Woodrow Wilson had been elected the nation's president, and the fiercely partisan Hiram W. Johnson, Republican governor of California, actually planned the strategy that led to the passage of the 1913 California Alien Land Act which barred the purchase of agricultural land by "aliens ineligible to citizenship," i.e., Asians. Wilson and Secretary of State William Jennings Bryan, dismayed by Japan's hostile reaction to the bill, made a showy but insubstantial and ineffective protest just before the gleeful Governor Johnson signed it into law.[4]

This was the situation that met Gulick when he arrived in California. He called it "California's Japanese question," but in fact with passage of the Alien Land Law and the resulting minor war scare with Japan, it had become a national issue. However, in 1913 most Americans were only vaguely aware of a Japanese issue in California.

Gulick attempted to see the situation from the Californians' perspective. He was a Christian, a believer in brotherhood, and a missionary who had lived abroad for over twenty years, and blatant discrimination was alien to his beliefs. However, on some issues he could agree with the Californians. His children had not been encouraged to play with Japanese youngsters, and he would have been distressed had any of them contracted an interracial marriage. He believed the two cultures had different values, but denied they were unequal in intelligence or civilization. The writer Carey McWilliams later called Gulick illogical, a fuzzy thinker who was out of touch with events in America, and termed his reaction to the problem part of a naïve "missionary habit" of seeing only good in the Japanese.[5] But Gulick did not deserve to be dismissed so lightly. Although his perspective was colored by his experience in Japan, his missionary years underlined for him the inimical impact of racial discrimination on international understanding and diplomacy. He had considerable experience with Japanese pride in which loss of face was no laughing matter. The repercussions of discrimination made the task of promoting Christianity more difficult, as he was well aware, but larger issues of peace, war, and equity were more significant than conversions. Most Californians did not know the consequences of their actions for the nation as a whole, and he believed that it was his duty to try to educate them. The task was immense and the consequences far greater than he dreamed, for a Pacific war might be the end product of failure. Although Gulick had no intuition of such a dread outcome, he was aware of the importance of his mission. Discrimination was not only unjust, it could be deadly dangerous.

Gulick began his task with a new book, *The American Japanese Problem: A Study of the Racial Relations of the East and the West* (1914), which analyzed from a liberal, nonracist perspective California's complaints and the Japanese response. Recognizing the Californians' fear of economic competition and their assertions that the Japanese were immoral, dirty, and unassimilable, he attempted to disprove their charges through illustrations showing very middle-class, well-dressed Japanese and their tidy, well-maintained homes. Californians, he asserted, had so set their minds against the Japanese as to prevent any possible assimilation. He agreed that unlimited immigration would cause economic disaster, but he denied that the Japanese government desired that anyway. Picking no quarrel with California's goal of restriction, he disagreed mainly with the methods they had adopted to achieve it. Anti-Japanese agitation was, he felt, "humiliating to Japan and disgraceful to America."[6] The Californians sought to drive the Japanese from the state by making it economically unprofitable and socially unpleasant for Asians to reside there; they had imposed a variety of irritating and unnecessary laws, the most significant of which prohibited the Japanese from owning agricultural land. Because the Gentlemen's Agreement was effective, these restrictions were needless, injurious, and contrary to the spirit of treaties with Japan, especially the 1911 Treaty of Commerce ratified by the Taft administration. He ignored the picture bride issue in his book, and concentrated on the fact that more Japanese were leaving the state to return to Japan than were entering.

The Japanese government, Gulick explained, recognized that the immigrants posed a problem to America, and had addressed it on several fronts. The Japanese Associations worked to mediate local difficulties and served as intermediaries for Issei who wished to travel to Japan,[7] while the Japanese government carefully monitored picture bride immigration to insure its legality. He claimed that the yellow press, particularly the Hearst and McClatchy papers, deliberately misrepresented Japan's well-intentioned actions, preferring instead to manipulate public opinion and exaggerate fears of war. Gulick did blame Buddhist priests in America for promoting a narrow patriotism and reinforcing Japanese customs. But the priests were the exceptions, he contended. By and large the Japanese in California were willing to "turn the other cheek" and accept their inferior status with regret but resignation.

Gulick then assured his readers that the Japanese were indeed assimilable. Through what he termed "social evolution," the manner in which a race changed through time, an immigrant population could easily be absorbed into a larger society; biological assimilation through intermarriage was unnecessary. The races were, after all, similar; he wrote that the Japanese are "fundamentally like us and wish to be regarded and treated so."[8] Although he deplored intermarriage in principle, its occasional successes intrigued him, and he later reversed his views on the subject.[9] Marriage between Japanese and whites disturbed him in part because the Japanese had a far different concept of the status of women and their place in a marriage, which would be unacceptable to Western women. He could at that time only explain the success of marriages between whites and Japanese that he observed in Hawaii on the shaky grounds that the latter race "already contains considerable white blood."[10]

The Californians should realize, Gulick stated, that they were dealing with a new Japan and that that nation, indeed all Asia, possessed race pride and rising ambitions. The new Orient offered tremendous potential for good or for evil, and much depended on the role the United States played. America could benefit from Asian trade and assist in its development, or the nation could prepare for war. If America tried to perpetuate the role of white peril in the East, it would force Japan to respond by becoming a true yellow peril, an economic and a military threat. Although to Gulick the notion of war between the United States and Japan was ludicrous, he recognized that many people in both countries believed it to be imminent. Even the notion of unrestrained economic warfare was based on fallacious thinking. The real yellow peril was the potential the anti-Asian policy currently in vogue had for producing ill will, injustice, brutality, and recurring outbreaks of lawlessness.[11]

Gulick's book proposed a multifaceted solution. First, total immigration should be restricted, but open to people from all lands. Their numbers should be based on a percentage of those from a particular nation who are already naturalized citizens in America, including their American-born children. (He at this point was ignoring the fact that people of Japanese origin were denied the right of naturalization.) Education in American history, civics, and English should be provided, and naturalization made available to all qualified foreign-born. The federal government should sponsor a positive program of citizenship training for aliens and should be responsible for all legal and legislative matters regarding aliens. He concluded with a strong statement endorsing the concept of acculturation. The Japanese, he felt, were intelligent, industrious, and had strong family ties; they were in many ways superior to immigrants from other lands. They would assimilate if they were accorded the opportunity by white society, and since they were more isolated from their mother country than European immigrants, they should be even more successful.[12]

The novelty of Gulick's approach to the problem of restricting immigration lay in his advocacy of a quota system. Like most Americans of his day, he shared the racist assumption that northeastern Europeans were the more desirable citizens. Although the quota concept was not unique with him, he was widely credited with its origin. In fact, it had been proposed in 1911 by the U.S. Immigration Commission, a joint body with members from both houses of Congress, but the commision dropped the idea without considering it, in favor of a literacy test.[13] Having arrived at the quota concept independently, Gulick amplified and popularized it and was identified with it in the public mind. As Roger Daniels noted, Gulick's positive approach and constructive proposals were unique even among the pro-Japanese, anti-exclusionist writers.[14]

America was anxious for a reasonable solution to the immigration dilemma, as the generally favorable response to Gulick's book attested. The work was termed "moderate and suggestive in its conclusions," a "fair-minded, closely reasoned survey," and "an eminently judicious handling of a perplexing question."[15] An articulate, well-organized counterforce to the exclusionists had begun to emerge. It was based on three groups, all Eastern: ministers, businessmen, and educators. Protestant missionaries and ministers worked through their denominations and the Federal Council of Churches. Businessmen anxious to avoid alienating Japan to the point of war spoke through commercial associations and the Japan Society of America, while educators and peace advocates often worked through the American Peace Society. The counterattack began in the spring of 1914.[16] Gulick's book articulated the opinion of no one of these groups, but he soon became the spokesman for the missionary-religious faction and a publicist for the hopes of all three. He was the key figure in the anti-exclusionist movement.

After Gulick completed his California study period, the family traveled to Kansas City in October 1913, for the meetings of the American Board, and then to Oberlin. Sidney, Jr., and Ethel entered school and Cara rented a house. Sidney went on to New York in late November, where he met with officials of the Carnegie Endowment for International Peace, with Hamilton Holt, and with the Reverend Charles Macfarland of the Federal Council of Churches of Christ in America (FCCCA). He also arranged for the publication of his *The American Japanese Problem*, and made arrangements to travel to Baltimore on December 3 to meet with the executive committee of the FCCCA on the Japanese question.[17]

Gulick's involvement with the Federal Council began in a minimal way. In the fall of 1913 he was appointed a member of its Commission on Missions, and Macfarland, its executive secretary, advised him that not only was he entitled to attend the executive committee meeting but that he ought to do so. Gulick had sent the council a resolution from the members of the American Board's Japan Mission. The resolution which he and Daniel Crosby Greene had authored discussed the deleterious effects of America's discriminatory treatment of Japanese immigrants on mission work, and called upon the Federal Council to appoint a commission to study the question and engage the Christian community in finding a solution. Macfarland advised Gulick that he should be prepared to discuss the problem with the Federal Council members. Gulick attended the meeting, and his views elicited a favorable response; he then traveled to Washington to discuss immigration and the new oriental policy with leading politicians.[18]

THE FEDERAL COUNCIL OF CHURCHES:

When Gulick met with the executive committee of the Federal Council of Churches he encountered a small group of men who represented a moderate-sized but growing constituency of Protestants interested in church unity and issues in international relations that impacted on world peace, justice, and goodwill. The executive secretary, Macfarland, was an eminent Congregationalist divine, and the council's president, Dr. Shailer Mathews, was a noted Baptist theologian from the University of Chicago. First proposed in 1905, the idea of such a council germinated over the next three years and the organization was officially founded in 1908. The FCCCA was a theologically liberal group representing thirty denominations whose social creed was critical of the laissez-faire individualism of the older Protestant evangelism. The leadership, even more liberal than the membership, was much in sympathy with the social gospel philosophy that Gulick himself espoused. The council's purpose, the promotion of church unity, was distantly related to two earlier but ongoing causes, the peace movement and foreign missions. The liberal agenda of the council had considerable attraction for Gulick, although at this point its concerns were basically domestic.[19] The general goals of the unified Protestant churches, as stated by the Federal Council in 1908 and 1912, did not specifically mention world peace or arbitration, although these aims were endorsed in various publications. Gulick was one of the few leading clergymen to support both the peace movement and the social gospel.[20]

The Federal Council of Churches appeared moderate and rather hesitant in its early years. It was not a "grass roots" organization, but was financed by a few wealthy organizations and individuals, and its leaders had to pick their issues carefully to avoid outdistancing their followers. As C. Roland Marchand has written, the FCCCA "almost instinctively seized upon those issues that would keep the churches abreast of popular current movements and give the Council something to do without alarming its constituent bodies. A mild form of social action and the peace movement conveniently met these specifications."[21]

In 1911 the FCCCA had acquired new and dynamic leadership. Macfarland sought out attractive causes that would draw outside financing. Through his friend the Reverend Frederick Lynch, Macfarland learned of Andrew Carnegie's desire to involve the churches in the peace movement. Lynch persuaded Carnegie to fund a program through the FCCCA to support the Taft arbitration treaties, and in 1911 Macfarland and Lynch established the Federal Council's Commission on Peace and Arbitration.[22]

It was at this point that Sidney Gulick entered the picture. Gulick convinced the executive committee of the FCCCA that the Japanese immigration question merited attention. The committee followed the suggestion proposed in the resolution of the Japan missionaries that Gulick had presented, and turned the issue over to the Commission on Peace and Arbitration.[23] Gulick's services quickly became essential to the cause. At first the FCCCA decided to support the furloughed missionary in undertaking a speaking tour of the country on behalf of improved Japanese-American relations, a journey funded by Carnegie through the Presbyterian Foreign Missions Board. The council members recognized that Gulick made a profound impression wherever he spoke, and soon they decided to involve him more directly in their work. He was appointed to the Commission on Peace and Arbitration in late February of 1914, and the FCCCA began negotiating with the American Board to extend his leave. Gulick himself was unsure about remaining away from the mission field. He wanted to evaluate the results of the current congressional action on immigration, particularly to see if a proposed literacy requirement would pass, before he committed himself to further work for the FCCCA, but he was clearly drawn to the idea. "This is as important missionary work as I can do," he wrote Barton, "I think . . . the Heavenly Father seems to have given me special opportunities along [this] line." The board was in agreement and Barton concurred. Gulick was doing "unique work that no one else could do," and his furlough was extended indefinitely.[24]

Even before embarking on the speaking tour, Gulick went to Washington to promote the three-point plan outlined in his book, *The American Japanese Problem.* In mid-December he met Senator William P. Dillingham, the chairman of the Senate Committee on Immigration, and he spoke with the head of the House committee. Although the book had not yet been published, he distributed copies of the first and last chapters, which contained his new oriental policy. Immediately after Christmas he began an extensive campaign, speaking across the country from Boston to San Francisco, visiting Buffalo, Cleveland, Toledo, Syracuse, then the midwest, and finally the Pacific Coast. He returned to Washington in late January to testify before the Senate committee and to meet with President Wilson and Secretary Bryan.[25] He was rapidly becoming, as Roger Daniels termed him, a "mass movement all by himself."[26] Energetic and inspired, he was the conscience of a nation.

JAPAN'S MISSIONARY TO THE AMERICANS:

Gulick entered his new work at the age of fifty-four with enthusiasm and a boundless energy. He had no intention of abandoning Japan or his work there; he viewed his assignment in the United States as an extension of it, and he renewed his furlough annually for the next five years. In 1917 he reluctantly resigned his position at the Dōshisha, recognizing that his continued absence was hampering their instructional program, but until 1923 he held out hope of eventually returning to the missionary field. When he wrote Barton for another extension of his leave in 1917, he asked that his name be retained on the board's rolls as a missionary to Japan, for as he said, "I am as truly a missionary working for Japan as if I were in Japan."[27]

The work he was soon engaged in concerned both Japan and the Japanese in America. His immediate task was to convince Americans that discriminatory treatment of Japanese immigrants and an immigration policy that unfairly singled out Orientals as lesser beings unfit for equal access to American residence or citizenship was un-Christian, unfair, and ultimately harmful to America's own best interests. These concerns were interrelated— discriminatory treatment of Japanese aliens irritated the Japanese government and jeopardized good relations between the two countries, and hence threatened the peace. But as Gulick elaborated on this theme he recognized the continuing need to interpret Japan to Americans, for not only did the white majority not understand people of Japanese origin, it misunderstood the actions of the Japanese government in relation to its neighbors, China and Korea. Japan was becoming hated and feared unjustly, and this in itself could lead to war. He may have underestimated the depths of American concern, for he had not shared the nation's slow identification of Japan as an economic and political competitor in the Pacific. Akira Iriye has noted that Americans concerned about Japanese competition were disturbed at the thought that "Japa-

nese, self-confident and cocky as a result of their victory over
Russia, [1905] would settle en masse in the United States . . . "28
But Americans were also concerned about Japan's foreign policy
aspirations. Over the next ten years a series of crises—the Twenty-
one Demands, the Shantung issue, the proposed racial equality
clause of the League of Nations Covenant—exacerbated ill will
between the two nations and intensified fears of an eventual conflict over Japanese expansionism. Gulick dedicated himself to
mitigating tensions by defusing the immigration issue and attempting to make Japan's actions comprehensible and acceptable
to a hostile American public. It was a task to which he would
devote the rest of his life.

The first issue to be tackled was domestic. Gulick advocated a
revision of America's immigration laws and a modification of the
procedures regarding naturalization of aliens. He promoted his
solution to the Japanese question through his position at the Federal Council of Churches and also in parallel, semi-independent
efforts, for he was aware that the FCCCA could not be overtly
politicized or it would risk losing its constituency and thereby its
effectiveness. Another dimension of his work was linked to the
Federal Council's espousal of Christian internationalism and
world peace. Gulick had been home from Japan less than a year
when the First World War broke out; he was in fact in Constance,
Germany, at a church conference on world peace when war en-
gulfed the continent. Suddenly his position on the FCCCA's
Commission on Peace and Arbitration took on a new dimension as
he and the churches had to contend with the demands of patriotism, the morality of war, and the need to construct a postwar
world free from the specter of war. Although the peace issue occasionally was sidetracked by the immigration issue, it never left
Gulick's thought. He was a convert to the cause and a dedicated
one.

Gulick's work for immigration reform and peace was interrelated and usually concurrent with his attempts to promote an understanding of Japan. They formed the basis of his association
with the Federal Council in the career that he pursued for the next
twenty years. In the course of this new work he was associated
with a myriad of committees and commissions whose often-

changing names and overlapping memberships were confusing to the public and later to historians, but whose goals were linked to his objectives—accomodation between a minority group and the larger society, and peace between the United States and Japan.

Gulick achieved considerable public exposure through his new assignments. He traveled incessantly for the next decade, sometimes giving two or three talks a day, often in different cities. A steady flow of publications streamed from his pen; he rarely let an idle moment pass without jotting something down. He was quickly identified as the FCCCA's "Japan expert," and his advice was sought from many corners. His reputation was such that scholars, politicians, and diplomats turned to him for advice. He corresponded with Stanley Hornbeck, then a professor of political science at the University of Wisconsin, and Kenneth Scott Latourette.[29] But he also antagonized certain segments of the public. One agitated listener wrote Secretary of State Charles Evans Hughes that Gulick was deceiving the people and was a "menace to the community."[30] Many politicians, journalists, and opinion leaders who gained considerable mileage from being professional Japanophobes identified him as the leader of the opposition and attacked him unmercifully. Eventually his outspoken views brought him to the attention of the Office of Naval Intelligence and then the Bureau of Investigation, predecessor to the Federal Bureau of Investigation.[31]

Yet this all lay in the future. As Gulick changed careers in 1913 he seemed the right man for the time, a leader for immigration reform who could provide the nation with an equitable, just solution to a difficult problem. He was the nation's conscience, reminding it of the promise of the Declaration of Independence— "all men are created equal." While "all men" could not reside in the United States, Gulick sought to promote a plan that would provide equitable access. It was a crusade in a time of crusading, and the opportunity for success looked promising.

6

THE FEDERAL COUNCIL OF CHURCHES, THE PEACE ORGANIZATIONS, AND THE WORLD WAR

THE FEDERAL COUNCIL OF CHURCHES AND THE CHURCH PEACE UNION:

Sidney Gulick entered the employ of the Federal Council of Churches at a time when that body was becoming more deeply involved in international relations and world peace. Although the FCCCA had established a Commission on Peace and Arbitration in 1911, its previous concerns had been primarily with church unity and domestic social issues. This new focus could not have come at a more propitious time; within a year after Gulick's appointment Europe was at war, and the united church group soon had an important role to play as the United States struggled to remain neutral. The FCCCA utilized Gulick's talents to respond to both the European and Japanese crises, and in so doing the organization itself moved from a domestic focus to a broader international outlook. From this wider perspective both the FCCCA and Gulick had to reassess their views on war itself and the role of the churches in promoting international peace.

Gulick was originally retained by the FCCCA to serve as secretary of its Commission on Relations with Japan, established in the spring of 1914 to investigate and try to ameliorate the deteriorating relationship between the two countries. Fellow Japanophile Hamilton Holt chaired the commission, the work of which was also closely tied to the immigration controversy. As the

90

Commission's focus was broadened, it was later renamed the Commission on Relations with the Orient.

In the same year, 1914, Gulick also became involved in a new organization funded by Andrew Carnegie, the steel baron and philanthropist. Although he was not a member of an organized religion, Carnegie had become convinced that religious groups ought to be associated with the movement to abolish war. The industrialist had already bestowed ten million dollars upon his primary peace effort, the Carnegie Endowment for International Peace, but that organization was primarily a cautious group composed of scholars, not peace activists. Two men, Congregational minister Frederick Lynch, and Charles Macfarland of the FCCCA, persuaded Carnegie to endow another organization to promote peace more widely among Protestants, Catholics, and Jews. Founded in the spring of 1914, the new group was named the Church Peace Union and endowed with two million dollars. The CPU became the "peace seeking bankroller of the country's major religions," working through their organizations to achieve its ends.[1]

The CPU and the Federal Council soon formed a symbiotic relationship that was facilitated by the work of three men, Lynch, Macfarland, and Gulick. Lynch resigned from the FCCCA's rather ineffectual Commission on Peace and Arbitration to serve as secretary of the CPU. Lynch, Macfarland, and Holt were trustees of the CPU. The CPU granted the FCCCA ten thousand dollars to establish the Commission on Relations with Japan and followed this with a grant of twenty thousand dollars to secure Gulick's services on a long-term basis. The other leading figure in the CPU at this time was the Reverend Charles Jefferson of New York's Broadway Tabernacle. After 1918 the executive secretary and chairman of the CPU were the Reverends Henry A. Atkinson and William P. Merrill.[2]

THE OUTBREAK OF THE WORLD WAR:

The first important function sponsored by the CPU was a world conference of Protestant church leaders to consider steps toward abolishing war and promoting international goodwill. Set ironically for early August 1914, the conference was called by CPU secretary Lynch to meet in the city of Constance, Germany; a Catholic conference was scheduled later at Liège. The leaders hoped that holding the conference in Germay would draw more support from that nation than was usually accorded peace meetings. Fifty delegates from the United States were selected on the basis of their leadership in the peace movement as well as their various denominations. Gulick and Macfarland, representing the FCCCA's Commission on Peace and Arbitration, were invited by Lynch to become part of the sixty-man delegation, whose costs were covered by the CPU. Gulick sailed for Europe in mid-July; the conference was to take place from August 2 to 5.

The travails of the delegation, which arrived in Europe amidst the growing tensions preceding the outbreak of war, were later described by Frederick Lynch in *Through Europe on the Eve of War* (1914). He narrated the reactions of the religious peace advocates to the turmoil and their impressions as to the causes of the conflict. When the fifty delegates left New York on July 21 there was, Lynch wrote, "no slightest sign or rumor of war."[3] Their train was rerouted and the trip delayed by the mobilization of Germany. But despite the mounting crisis, which had in fact begun in June with the assassination of Austrian Archduke Franz Ferdinand, they proceeded to Constance out of a sense of obligation and duty; they had, after all, organized the conference. Delegates came from Great Britain, France, Sweden, Norway, Switzerland, and Germany. When they arrived in Constance, they first passed a resolution appealing to all nations to avert war. The delegates then decided to begin the meetings despite the imminence of conflict. They would have persisted but for news that the German government was turning all the railroads over to the military. Deciding to adjourn to London, they pooled their gold and were able to purchase tickets on a special train through Germany. Although as neutrals they were entitled to safe passage, Lynch was grateful that their safety was personally guaranteed by Kaiser Wilhelm II. Safe in London, the delegates passed resolutions endorsing President Wilson's offer of mediation, his disapproval of loans by belligerents, and Secretary of State Bryan's "cooling-off treaties." They voiced support for American neutrality, and urged Wilson to set aside a special day of prayer for peace. Their contacts with one another proved so fruitful that they determined to form councils in each country to promote international friendship and a swift end to war.[4]

Lynch's book, full of poignant anecdotes about the travails of ordinary people caught up in the outbreak of conflict, was outspoken in its condemnation of the German government as responsible for war. He denounced the brutality with which its soldiers treated all foreigners, and pronounced the violation of Belgian neutrality a sign that Germany had become irrational. Although Lynch had been a pacifist, his anti-German sentiments became so strong that they overrode any prior experience, and they were doubtless shared by his colleagues, most notably Gulick. The trip from Constance filled them not only with a hatred of war but also with great animosity toward the German government, and most delegates carried home memories of the deep anxiety they had shared. Gulick was certain that he had come close to being trapped in Germany. He nearly missed the final train when he went back to check on his luggage the day before the border was closed.[5]

Like many churchmen in America, Lynch could only conclude that Christianity had somehow failed because war had come. It had not taught people sufficiently well a gospel of love that would prevent such horrors. The cause of conflict appeared self-evident. He blamed armaments for war, believing that the arms buildup had somehow made conflict inevitable. Patriotism, he felt, had to be "Christianized" so that it did not become blind jingoism. Lynch concluded that nations should be amenable to the same ethics that governed conduct between individuals; this rather unrealistic notion of the behavior of governments became entrenched in the postwar peace movement.

Gulick concurred in many of these sentiments. Before the conference meetings had adjourned to London, Gulick and a few others gave addresses on the most significant topics they would consider later. Gulick's, entitled "Constructive Methods for Promoting International Peace," received such favorable response that Lynch printed it as an appendix to his book. In this address he discussed factors which must be taken into account by those who would promote peace. The world lived in a "new era" of history in which nations were linked more closely by transportation and communication, he said. Greater contact between the races, many of whom sought a recognition the older powers had denied them, was the result. According to Gulick, the armaments race was the "most potent cause of this awful situation."[6] He praised the peace movement, but felt it was flawed because it dealt only with symptoms, with situations that were already dangerous, instead of seeking to prevent them from occurring in the first place. He castigated the churches for their indifference to the causes of war, particularly to the arms race, and for their apathy toward the peace movement. The concern with individual salvation, the focus on an otherworldly kingdom of God, and neglect of basic Christian precepts—the brotherhood of man and the need to love one's enemies—were to blame.

Gulick concluded his address with a positive program to promote peace. First, the churches as the most moral sector of society should assume leadership of the international peace movement, and not leave the task to jurists, statesmen, and economists. Christians should learn to respect the rights of every race, especially in Asia and Africa, returning to the gospel message of loving one's enemies and doing good to those who hated them. Only then could true peace come.[7] Gulick refined these arguments after the war and devised more detailed programs for their enactment.

Although Lynch and Gulick were naïve and somewhat simplistic in their analysis of the causes of conflict and their hopes for world peace, theirs were the feelings of their generation, possessing certain strengths and some basic limitations. Their loathing of war was passionate and sincere, but so also was their hatred of the German government, and this made them susceptible to war fever. Lynch also believed in the ability of strong leadership to set a wise course between good and evil; both he and Gulick believed Wilson would keep the country out of war. Neutrality was the best course for it provided a basis from which they could work to end the conflict.[8]

THE CHURCHES AND THE FIRST WORLD WAR:

American Protestants were shocked by the outbreak of war, which put a temporary damper on their hopes of avoiding conflict. The FCCCA's Commission on Peace and Arbitration (CPA) had been organized in 1911 to "promote through public opinion alternatives to war." The executive committee, in erecting the CPA, voiced the churches' traditional moral opposition when it declared that "war . . . is anti-Christian in its very nature." The commission had worked in a quiet way to promote the treaties of arbitration negotiated but not ratified during the Taft administration. Although its visibility was low, its secretary, Frederick Lynch, felt that the CPA's work had awakened "thousands of ministers to the importance of the peace movement,"[9] but in fact the commission had become virtually dormant in 1913 and was only revived when Macfarland took it over the next year. Gulick joined the staff in 1915. (The group underwent a name change in 1916, becoming the Commission on International Justice and Goodwill [CIJG]; in its later apotheosis it was the Federal Council's most effective voice in international peace work as well as the oldest surviving Protestant peace group.[10])

The FCCCA immediately reacted to the outbreak of war. The CPA/CIJG announced that the war "did not show the foolishness of Christian idealism, but rather the foolishness of brute force." It was the "reductio ad absurdum" of un-Christian civilization and proof of the need to "Christianize the spirit of patriotism."[11] Although the commission decried the use of force, the FCCCA did not condemn the war. The vivid scenes of suffering the conference members witnessed as they fled the continent of Europe for the relative safety of London reinforced the hostility most of them felt toward "barbaric" Germany, and all the Americans had the conditioned Anglophile tendencies of their generation of east coast leaders. They shared the sentiments of Lynch—indeed of society generally—that war represented a personal failure of Christian leadership, and that only Christian internationalism could prevent it in the future. Although the churches accepted blame for the outbreak of the war, as if they could have prevented it, many pastors reacted strongly to the charge, either denying it by claiming Christianity had never really been tried, or bemoaning their failure.[12] Yet at the same time many justified the use of force as necessary to achieve the "restraint of violence, the preservation of order, and protection of lives and legitimate interests of citizens."[13] This ambivalence over the nature and purposes of the war would haunt them at its conclusion.

The churches were caught on the horns of a dilemma as they sought to justify resisting a specific evil while opposing violence in general. Charles Jefferson and Lynch both felt the churches should oppose wrongdoing; Jefferson accused that the arms race was a misuse of a nation's resources, but he naïvely justified war as "occasionally a necessary means of developing character and disciplining nations." As Darrell E. Bigham has noted, many liberal Christian leaders fell into the trap of seeing the war as a crusade of good versus evil, and even as an opportunity for Christian work. This superficial understanding of the nature and causes of the conflict made them ready recruits to Wilson's crusade when he took the United States into the conflagration.[14] They decried war, yet became converts to the goals of a just and liberal peace. Some, like Wilson himself, used that end to justify the means—ultimate American involvement in the conflict.

Gulick's first reaction to the war was shaped by his personal experience of it. On the way home from London he wrote his sons from the liner *Laconia,* reflecting on the causes of the conflict. He had read the official British correspondence on shipboard and became convinced that although Austria bore the primary guilt, "Germany is the chief aggressor, and really responsible party for the terrible disaster." He recalled seeing carloads of German soldiers being rushed to the front, and he pondered how many of them were now dead or wounded. "War is hell, and it is all due to ambitions and race passions and injustice. Is it not worthwhile for strong and great men to make war on war?"[15] Yet he never denounced the European conflict, however much he deplored it, and when it spread to Asia through Japan's alliance with Britain he reaffirmed his anti-German sentiments.

In September 1914, Gulick gave an interview to the *New York Times* in which he supported Japan's war aims against Germany. He condoned Japan's seizure of the German concession at Kiaochow Bay on China's Shantung peninsula, and he maintained that after the war it would be returned. It was in "Japan's interests to preserve the integrity of China." He warned that the Germans were disseminating anti-American propaganda in Tokyo, building on the feelings of outrage over America's discriminatory treatment of Japanese immigrants.[16] Germany was clearly our enemy as well as Japan's, and he hoped this new bond would improve relations. He seemed to ignore Japan's use of the war as an excuse to take advantage of China's weakness.

Before they left Europe Gulick and the American delegates to Constance made plans for responding to the war. They especially favored the announcement of a policy of strict neutrality for the United States and the setting aside of a day of prayer for peace. The delegates also established a war relief fund for victims and refugees. Other suggestions were less realistic and deliberately vague. They called upon European churchmen to exhort the soldiers to somehow "reduce the horrors of war," and they asked for a treaty to proclaim that an interval of time must elapse before a provocation could be followed by a declaration of war. During this interlude the causes of a dispute could be investigated by some impartial body.[17] The FCCCA petitioned the president on these matters. As its involvement in international causes grew, it became a more effective lobby with the federal government, one that could not be ignored because of the size of its constituency.

CREATION OF THE WORLD ALLIANCE:

While at Constance, Gulick and his colleagues also decided to organize the World Alliance for International Friendship Through the Churches (WAIFTC), a voluntary body of individuals, including Protestants, Catholics, and Jews. Lynch was to be its secretary and William P. Merrill, chairman of the CPU, its president.[18] Gulick helped organize an American branch of this organization the following year, becoming associate secretary with Lynch. The WAIFTC and the CIJG formed a joint executive committee in 1916 to maintain liaison with the FCCCA while preserving the distinctiveness of the two organizations. They cooperated well for the next three years until certain points of friction began to drive them apart.[19]

The WAIFTC immediately planned a campaign for peace education through the churches. As part of this effort, and after a brief trip to Japan, Gulick wrote another book, *The Fight for Peace: An Aggressive Campaign for American Churches* (1915). The work, prepared at the request of the CPU, was intended as a handbook for pastors, discussion leaders, and Sunday school teachers. Four thousand copies were distributed for use in adult peace and international relations classes, most of which Gulick organized through the WAIFTC.[20]

The Fight for Peace opened with a discussion of the war, pointing out how paradoxical and tragic it was for Christians to be fighting Christians. Gulick attributed this to the failure of Christianity to deal adequately with large issues of war and peace because of the churches' preoccupation with individual salvation and with structure and ritual, and because of their lack of concern about the nation's foreign relations. Not only had Christians ignored the ideal of the brotherhood of man, but they had also neglected their duty to promote a foreign policy based on these Christian concepts. The churches would have to work for world peace through united action to regenerate society and nations.[21]

Gulick next explored a plan to abolish war. Calling for the universal application of the golden rule, he advocated more effective church organization to promote world peace. The Federal Council, which presumably represented twenty-four million American Protestants, should be strengthened, for its Commission on Peace and Arbitration was already a nucleus for an effective church peace organization. Also, the CPU could become the highest coordinating center of the peace movement, the apex of a pyramid whose base lay in community church peace leagues, and it could in turn link with international peace organizations.[22] This was a rather utopian scheme, as it turned out, but it was a beginning.

Gulick then castigated Americans for their treatment of both China and Japan, and he again decried the discriminatory immigration policy, which singled out their nationals as aliens ineligible for citizenship. He condemned the yellow press for its magnification of the war scare between America and Japan, and chastised the nation's Protestants for believing journalists rather than believing the better-informed missionaries. Newsmen, he felt, needed "training in honesty." Again betraying a utopian streak, he urged that the nation fund peace and goodwill efforts as handsomely as it supported the army and navy.[23]

Gulick ended the work promoting his quota plan. He faulted

the churches for not countering with reminders of Christian brotherhood the prejudice that underlay the demand for oriental exclusion. Christians did not realize the link between America's discriminatory practices and the hostility or indifference with which most Asians viewed Christianity. "This un-Christian treatment leads to anti-American feelings and thus to the creation of a barrier—Asians refuse to listen to the Christian message." Christianity also had failed to make the West moral and unselfish. "The wickedness of Christendom discredits Christianity everywhere," he wrote.[24]

The book met with a mixed reception. Critics praised Gulick for having written a "constructive study," and for having the "courage to break away from the usual generalities of the pacifist school and to formulate a definite program." But the *New York Times* doubted that the book would receive wide acceptance, and *The Outlook* disputed his notion that "the next great forward step for the Christian world is the crusade for peace." To that reviewer, justice was a more worthy goal.[25]

Gulick, however, was undaunted by the criticism, for he had written the book for a specific purpose. The WAIFTC was considering a plan to establish Peace Makers committees in thousands of churches around the country. These groups would educate Christians in the ideal of international justice and goodwill, in the application of the golden rule in international relations, and in the use of arbitration and conciliation to replace war. The committees were also potential advocates for an international league of peace, a world supreme court, boards of reconciliation and arbitration to which disputes could be referred prior to the outbreak of war, and lastly, for a reform of the nation's immigration laws and legislation to protect aliens in America. *The Fight for Peace* and other literature, much of it authored by Gulick, would be their textbooks. After his trip to Japan, Gulick promoted the establishment of these committees throughout the summer and fall of 1915, traveling primarily on the Pacific Coast. At the same time he spoke for his immigration plan. He persuaded the WAIFTC to adopt the peacemakers' program at its 1916 meeting.[26]

Gulick was appointed associate secretary of the American Council of the WAIFTC in early 1916 and given the tasks of in-

creasing the membership and holding a conference on world
peace. This organizational meeting took place at Garden City,
Long Island, from April 25 to 27, 1916, and attracted about two
hundred influential church leaders from all major faiths. Gulick
played a leading role in the conference, winning Macfarland's
praise as "the inspiration and administrative genius of the meeting." In succeeding months, the American Council of the
WAIFTC grew to four hundred members representing forty-one
denominations, and it operated through a joint executive committee, headed by Lynch, Gulick, and Macfarland.[27] The membership was very similar to that of the FCCCA. Gulick wrote one
supporter that "from the standpoint of the Federal Council this
World Alliance is identical with the Commission on Peace and
Arbitration." However, the WAIFTC did have a somewhat
broader base.[28]

Gulick continued to work for the establishment of the Peace
Makers committees. He drafted a petition to the president and
Congress urging their support for the idea, and he also prepared a
course on "the new internationalism" for use in the churches.[29]
Planning for future peace enabled the WAIFTC to avoid many of
the disagreements that the present war engendered among peace-
loving liberals. Military preparedness, conscription, and pacifism
were all hotly controversial topics in the years preceding America's actual entry into the war.

Gulick seemed to become even more hostile toward the German government during those years. He was never a pacifist, but
he supported Wilson's avowed determination to keep the country
out of war. While he did not record his views on the events of the
day, the outrage felt by most Americans at the sinking of the *Lusi-
tania* could not have escaped him. In December of 1915 he wrote
Macfarland from the West Coast, responding to Henry Ford's
plan to send an American peace delegation abroad. While the
Ford Peace Expedition was a good idea, he wrote, "I'm inclined
to think that the Allies have got to have more time to wear down
the Germans before they will think of peace. If peace is concluded now the importance of large preparedness will be more
convincing than ever and Germany's war plan will be completely
vindicated." He concluded by stating his fears that a peace based

on the status quo would only touch off a vast arms race that would involve even the United States.[30]

On the issue of the war Gulick was more bellicose than the FCCCA. The council, deeply concerned with preserving peace in America, never openly opposed the war, but it did promote efforts to keep America out. The pacifists urged an antipreparedness campaign in 1915 and 1916; the council gave it only lukewarm support and eventually backed out altogether. The church leaders feared that preparedness might be a first step to entering the conflict, but they trusted Wilson's rhetoric of peace. They suspected an arms buildup might have the same outcome that it had had in Europe and they were hesitant about measures taken in supposed self-defense.

Gulick had his own reasons for avoiding the preparedness issue. The controversial question could deflect support from his cherished new oriental policy, yet he could not oppose it. In June of 1917 he joined the American Defense Society, a very pro-preparedness group in favor of American participation in the war. His ultimate objective was to prevent future wars, but he did not believe in being unprepared if the United States should join in a cause he defined as just.[31] Invited to attend a meeting of the American Union against Militarism, he left when the meeting's tone, one of extreme condemnation of America, offended him. Although he was opposed to a militaristic spirit, he was not ashamed, as he put it, to be an American citizen, and he rejected the group's avowed opposition to conscription.[32]

It was far wiser politically to concentrate efforts on issues around which all religious leaders could agree. Macfarland as general secretary of the CPA/CIJG visited Europe in 1916, meeting with church leaders in The Hague, Berlin, Bern, Paris, and London to discuss the postwar world. The CPA/CIJG also began a War Sufferers' Relief campaign, which included participants from many member churches, and it cooperated with various other relief committees, including the WAIFTC. Gulick was one of the nine secretaries of the campaign, which raised money for war relief and special funds for the Huguenot churches in France.[33] Gulick's appeal to the WAIFTC churches called the program a most "important movement . . . for promoting international friendship."[34] Relief was noncontroversial and certainly a Christian duty.

The WAIFTC also appealed to President Wilson to arbitrate current differences with Mexico, whose ongoing civil war had created tensions along the border. In March 1916, Wilson dispatched General John J. Pershing to pursue the rebel Francisco (Pancho) Villa in Mexico. Gulick and Lynch reminded the president that war with Mexico would hinder efforts to help Europe make peace and might even prohibit the United States from taking the lead in forming a league of peace or a world court.[35] It was certainly no time for a Western hemisphere conflict.

Gulick was frenetically busy during 1916 and 1917. Heavily involved in the work of both the WAIFTC and the CIJG, he also served as secretary to the Commission on Relations with the Orient and continued to work on the problem of oriental immigration. He could not at that point contemplate leaving for the mission field, and asked ABCFM Secretary Barton for a two or three year extension of his furlough. His furniture and books remained in Japan, however, and he still hoped for an eventual return. But the entry of the United States into the war gave him a new reason to work for international peace. "The war is making our people serious, as never before, and . . . [causing them to] realize the vital importance of international justice and goodwill," he wrote Barton. Peace work and the immigration issue necessitated his staying in the United States where, at least for the present, he could do the most effective Christian work.[36]

His family life also took second place to his organizational activities. Gulick visited frequently with his eldest son Luther, who was in New York, and corresponded with the other family members. Luther completed his Ph.D. at the School of Public Services at Columbia in 1917; Sidney, Jr., was at Oberlin High School and briefly at a prep school in the East. Gulick managed a very occasional visit as he passed through Oberlin on his travels. In 1915 he spent Christmas with his family but missed the holiday the next year because work was too pressing. When Leeds decided to enlist in the Signal Corps his father had nothing but praise for him, for as Gulick wrote his family, German behavior showed the "outrageous, inhuman and absolutely untrustworthy character of the Prussian government. We can't make peace until the whole Hohenzollern brood is out and Germany has a government for which the people are responsible."[37]

The entry of the United States into the worldwide conflict prompted the Federal Council to call a special session in Washington in early May. The meeting was held jointly with thirty-five representatives of other religious groups, the YMCA, the American Bible Society, and the WAIFTC.[38] The mood was clearly one of cooperating with the government in promoting the war.

Gulick wrote a special message for the occasion, "The Duty of the Church in this Hour of National Need." In it he articulated the Federal Council's response to the conflict, its understanding of the reasons for America's entry, and its hopes for the future. The message opened with a statement about how the long-patient United States had been "forced to recognize that a state of war exists" between it and Germany. Although the council deplored war, the members were grateful that it was fought for such noble ends: to "vindicate the principles of righteousness" between nations, to safeguard the right of all peoples to live in freedom and peace, and to resist the forces which would prevent "the union of the nations in a commonwealth of free peoples conscious of unity in the pursuit of ideal ends." Although some of the members were pacifists while others believed in fighting for a just cause, all were loyal to the country, according to Gulick. All agreed that they had special duties, to purge their own hearts of selfishness and vengeance, to inspire the nation, to keep the noble aims of the war in mind, and to hold the nation true to ideals of justice, liberty, and brotherhood. They were also obligated to work for relief of war victims, to comfort and care for the soldiers and those they left behind, and to guard the rights of enemy aliens. Everyone needed to "keep the open mind and the forward look that the lessons learned in war may not be forgotten . . . [in] peace" and to help rebuild in the postwar world "the commonwealth of mankind."[39]

Gulick's statement judiciously avoided mentioning the agony the churches had gone through in determining a proper response to the war. Although Ray Abrams in *Preachers Present Arms* (1933) indicts the Protestant clergy for giving in to jingoism, the religious leaders had been divided over the issue from the beginning. While the historic peace churches such as the Quakers, Amish, and the United Brethren were pacifist, a majority of the other clergy believed in a "just" war. Preparedness was another controversial issue, for while many shared the notion that arms buildups caused nations to go to war, few wanted to be unprepared to fight in case war did come to America. By 1917 most church leaders, together with the rest of the nation, had moved from Wilson's "strict neutrality" to a position favoring a preparedness which was basically pro-Ally. Submarines and British propaganda had co-opted them. Lynch, Macfarland, Jefferson, and Merrill had deep pacifist sympathies but even they were wavering. Gulick was with the majority that favored arming for defense and fighting if necessary. Even the CPU had dropped its opposition to militarism in the spring of 1916. Most of the church leaders accepted Wilson's depiction of the conflict as a just war, and they pledged their support to the government. Certainly Sidney Gulick did.

THE NATIONAL COMMITTEE ON THE MORAL AIMS
OF THE WAR:

In 1918 the Protestant churches decided to create an autonomous body to promote their version of the war's goals and plans for a liberal peace. This new offspring, the National Committee on the Moral Aims of the War (hereafter referred to as the Moral Aims Committee), had many sponsors: the CIJG, the WAIFTC, the World Peace Foundation of Boston, and the League to Enforce Peace, which Gulick and Macfarland had helped organize. Chaired by Hamilton Holt, the committee was heavily influenced by Macfarland, who represented the FCCCA, and Gulick, of the WAIFTC; both were on its executive committee. The purpose of the Moral Aims Committee was to promote peace work vigorously, to prepare public opinion for a peace treaty that would be "fair and productive of enduring world peace," based on Wilson's Fourteen Points.[40] It hoped to rally support for that approach in order to influence Wilson to work for a just peace.

In April of 1918 the WAIFTC invited its members to a meeting that was to inaugurate a nationwide campaign proposed by the

Moral Aims Committee. This was in fact the first national assembling of the WAIFTC, because an earlier meeting had been postponed due to the outbreak of the war. Gulick addressed the membership, presenting a short history of the organization's accomplishments to date. The leaders, he explained, had promoted the goals of the committee in a variety of ways: writing and speaking, establishing CIJGs in various denominations and in individual churches, influencing pastors to study international relations, and helping churchmen remind their congregations of the high moral aims of the war and its ultimate goal of establishing a new Christian order in international relations. The Moral Aims campaign would focus on that purpose, he told the group, by seeking to influence Congress to establish a League of Nations and to readjust the nation's policies for dealing with oriental immigrants. Both goals were, as Gulick put it, "essentials of a peaceful civilization," along with a league and a world court.[41]

The Moral Aims Committee exemplified the idealistic vision of a majority of church leaders about the war. They believed it was, as Wilson said, a crusade to make the world safe for democracy, and they promoted the cause. The CPU, which funded the Moral Aims Committee, even had a representative on the Advisory Committee of George Creel's Committee on Public Information, and all these groups supported the federal propaganda campaign. If they erred, they erred together; only a tiny fraction of Protestant and Catholic church leaders in the country actually opposed the war once the United States had joined, and only the small, traditional peace churches held out against it. Not until the conflict ended, and the negotiation of the Treaty of Versailles brought out the seamier side of the Allies' real war aims, did some church leaders, in company with fellow liberals, begin to reject the notion of just, "noble" wars, and to truly embrace the cause of peace.[42] Gulick's own thinking paralleled this trend.

The Moral Aims Committee promoted the war cause in various ways. It supported the Liberty Loan drive and encouraged enlistment. Although the members found it difficult to promote the war effort without stirring up hatred against the German people and glorifying war generally, they tried. To some later writers this was complicity; this seems too harsh a judgement. A less stringent verdict is that the committee was "accepting what the government did and interpreting it in religious terms."[43] The churches generally aided the war effort, but they were more interested in promoting the ultimate goals for which this huge sacrifice was demanded. The Moral Aims Committee sought to keep its focus on these lofty aims and to avoid contributing to a war hysteria. Gulick tried to explain the purpose on tours he took on behalf of the committee: "The primary objective was to prepare for the peace—stressing a league of nations, trying to allay the passions of war, to develop a rational interpretation of it all, in order that the peace might be real and permanent."[44] Certainly to Gulick those were noble goals and not mere rationalizations to promote or sell a war.

The committee set about its task methodically. It divided the nation into eight districts and sought to reach all church people in each one, acquainting them with the war's purposes as defined in the Wilsonian program and promoting a postwar league of nations. The committee estimated its spokesmen addressed 1,259 meetings with approximately 771,000 listeners.[45] It believed it was "educating the people of the United States in these moral aims and . . . lifting their minds to their high level. No higher service could have been rendered."[46]

Gulick was very active with the Moral Aims Committee, which sent out teams of speakers all over the country in the spring of 1918. Gulick traveled with George Nasmyth, a fellow internationalist who opposed entering the war but supported the league. They addressed meetings throughout the South and West, and Gulick found an especially warm reception on the Pacific Coast. This was somewhat surprising since he took the opportunity to promote his favorite cause, better treatment of Japanese Americans, while discussing the war. In talks stressing the idea of a Christian world order Gulick cited examples from the relations of the western nations with East Asia to show how discriminatory treatment of minorities hurt the cause of peace. He was gratified to find Caucasians and Japanese getting along somewhat better on the West Coast. This improvement he attributed in part to the loyal response of the Asian community to the Liberty Bond drives, and Red Cross and YMCA appeals.[47]

Gulick believed strongly in moral internationalism as a deterrent to future wars. In early December of 1918 he wrote his wife, who still resided in Oberlin, that at the annual meeting of the FCCCA's executive committee he had secured a "strong declaration on the League of Nations and also a resolution appointing a commission to present it officially to [President Wilson at] the Peace Conference in Paris." He also nominated the members of the commission: President Henry Churchill King of Oberlin College, Hamilton Holt, Frank Mason North, later president of the FCCCA, and Frederick Lynch. Within a few weeks council leaders determined that Gulick should attend the conference as well, representing the Commission on Relations with the Orient and the CPU.[48]

THE VERSAILLES PEACE CONFERENCE:

Gulick left for Europe on January 25, 1919, traveling first to London to attend meetings of the British Council of the WAIFTC. Upon his arrival in Paris he met with a number of people about Asian affairs, including Stanley Hornbeck, Japanese delegate Viscount Chinda Sutemi, and China's C. T. Wang. Although his primary objective was to advance the cause of the League of Nations, he discussed the immigration issue with members of the Japanese delegation. He reported to the press later that the Japanese did not desire access to America equal to that given Caucasians but rather desired fair treatment plus support for the clause in the covenant on racial equality.[49] Gulick approved of both goals, although he did not lobby for the latter, and his concern for Japanese rights led him to overlook the demands Japan had made on China's sovereignty. Instead, he was preoccupied with other issues at Versailles.

The religious leaders' commission had been deputized to deliver a resolution supporting the League of Nations to Woodrow Wilson, and they met with him for an hour. The high point of the conference for Gulick came when he attended the second plenary session of the conference and heard Wilson read the Covenant of the League of Nations to the world leaders.[50] It was enough to make a Wilsonian of him for life.

Several other experiences also stuck in his memory. He lunched with Hornbeck and was pleased to find their opinions on Asia coincided, giving him, as he put it, "a friend at Court." He attempted to persuade the influential Colonel Edward M. House, Wilson's closest advisor, to include a guarantee of religious and educational freedom in the covenant. His nephew Edward Leeds Gulick, Jr., arranged his first airplane flight, over the city of Paris, and other friends took him by car to see the battlefield devastation at Chateau-Thierry and Verdun. Sidney was abroad for nearly two months.[51]

The churchmen were very supportive of the Treaty of Versailles. Although ten to fifteen years later they would be fashionably critical, only a small minority found it deficient in 1919, and Gulick was not among them. The Federal Council hailed the league as the "political expression of the Kingdom of God on Earth," and advocated its adoption without hesitation. The church leaders set aside a day of prayer on its behalf, and sent speakers to tour the country urging support. A monster petition endorsing the league without amendments or reservations requiring renegotiation was signed by 14,450 clergy, and even the Senate's rejection of membership did not immediately diminish their enthusiasm. The FCCCA promoted League membership throughout the 1920s.[52]

ORGANIZATIONS IN HARMONY AND DISHARMONY:

The alliances and interlocking memberships of the various commissions and committees with which Gulick was associated worked effectively for a few years. The war gave a tremendous impetus to organizing and doing public relations work for the peace cause, and both Protestantism and the Federal Council benefitted from this. The FCCCA's loyalty to the government and support for the war served it well; it was now viewed as a reliable and "mainstream" organization, not in any way fringe or radical. Its promotion and loyal advocacy of the cause of a liberal peace made it even more acceptable to the administration. As several authorities have noted, Protestantism reached the "apogee of its influence in modern America" at this time.[53] The Federal Council had been transformed "from a small, obscure organization to perhaps the most influential organization in American Protestantism."[54]

Such gains were not achieved without some minor dislocations on the interpersonal level. Gulick reflected later that the cooperation between the CPU, the FCCCA, and the WAIFTC, despite their similar goals, was not entirely harmonious nor to the equal benefit of all. Lynch was apparently a poor administrator, and in 1919 as the Moral Aims Committee came to an end, the CPU trustees voted to make Henry A. Atkinson the executive secretary of both the CPU and the WAIFTC. When a personality conflict developed between Atkinson and Macfarland, Gulick attempted to avoid being caught in the middle by resigning from both groups and the CIJG, and devoting himself entirely to the Commission on Relations with the Orient and the promotion of his immigration policy. However, under Atkinson's leadership the CPU and the WAIFTC soon surpassed the FCCCA in influence, and the CIJG receded into the background. Unhappy at this turn of events, the leadership of the FCCCA revamped the CIJG at its annual meeting in Boston in December of 1920, electing Gulick secretary and George W. Wickersham chairman. From that point on a clear rivalry existed between the CIJG and the WAIFTC. The members attempted to resolve this by appointing a "nexus committee" to serve as liaison between the two groups. Gulick was a member of this group, but he soon realized that Atkinson still intended to bypass the FCCCA by refusing or "forgetting" to hold meetings. Although the nexus committee remained on the books for years, it was moribund from the start. Gulick believed that the problem stemmed in part from the funding structure of the FCCCA; its cumbersome nature made it extremely difficult to provide financial support for a joint project. Atkinson's links to the CPU gave the WAIFTC readier access to Carnegie money. Under Lynch's leadership the CIJG had been funded by the CPU at the rate of twelve thousand dollars annually, but Atkinson diminished the amount and eventually discontinued it altogether. Gulick was displeased that the Atkinson-Merrill duo, which virtually ran the WAIFTC and the CPU, had succeeded in freezing out the CIJG. But not only personality conflicts and differences over money divided the groups; they had differing priorities as well. The WAIFTC was heavily Europe-centered, while the CIJG was more concerned about East Asia. The FCCCA and CIJG survived the freeze, however, and Gulick served the latter as secretary until his retirement in 1934.[55]

Gulick's work in the peace movement between 1914 and 1920 was an important part of his new career. Although he was not interested in partisan politics generally, he became an enthusiastic backer of Woodrow Wilson's crusade for democracy and an exponent of collective security. Like most Protestant leaders he advocated patriotism, not pacifism, and believed the war had to be brought to a successful conclusion. He wrote Macfarland, "Dreadful tho [sic] the continuance of the war is, will not the future peace of the world be promoted by delaying peace til [sic] Germany is pretty completely worsted and the failure of her methods proven?"[56] But a vengeful peace would be wrong; he found in the Fourteen Points a blueprint for a new world order. The work of the National Committee on the Moral Aims of War won his enthusiastic endorsement. Charles DeBenedetti has charged that "it served to polish the American war machine with a Christian sheen."[57] This may be so, but Gulick, like many others, did his part with good intent if a naïve heart.

Gulick never verbalized the disillusionment that came to so many others as their hopes for a liberal peace were dashed at Versailles. He had a psychologically beneficial ability to shift his priorities from doomed causes to more productive ones while still holding out hope that the original effort would some day be realized. Thus, like so many others, he gradually lost faith in the league while continuing to espouse *some* kind of world organization, and he championed instead disarmament, the world court, the abolition of war, and other Christian internationalist causes during the 1920s. Neither he nor the Protestant churches retreated to isolationism.

Not only did Gulick find other ways to work for peace, he had a major mission which had always been of transcendent importance for him, the cause for which he had given up his Japan missionary career. Although the war temporarily sidelined the immigration controversy, it flared up again and Japanese-American relations hit a new low once the war came to an end. There was still much work to be done.

7

CRUSADING FOR IMMIGRATION REFORM

THE IMMIGRATION CONTROVERSY:

Reforming the nation's immigration laws was the most pressing domestic need facing the country in the period from 1914 to 1924, Gulick believed. Prior to America's entry into the war this occupied most of his time; he feared that without an equitable solution to the problem, Japanese-American relations would quite likely deteriorate to the point of conflict. After April 1917, war sidetracked the issue, leaving it unresolved, though dormant rather than dead. Almost everyone agreed that unrestricted immigration must be abandoned; the beacon of liberty beckoning the world's poor and homeless had to be shuttered lest the social fabric of the nation be rent asunder. The question was one of means and also methods. Should restrictions be placed equally on all aliens desiring entry, or should some prospective entrants be singled out for special exclusion? The particular target of this selective exclusion, if there were one, was the Japanese.

The fight to limit immigration went through many phases. Although there had been much opposition to Irish and German immigrants before the Civil War, the first ethnic group to be collectively excluded was the Chinese, who were barred by the Exclusion Act of 1882. Prostitutes, contract laborers, polygamists, persons with certain diseases, and anarchists were also barred. Starting in the 1890s, strong opposition to the so-called "new immigrants" from southern and eastern Europe—Italians, Poles, Greeks, and Eastern Jews—developed, and, by the early years of the century many restrictionists, particularly those on the West Coast, began to focus on the Japanese. The 1890s also saw much agitation for a literacy test as a means of excluding presumed undesirables, and Congress four times passed such a measure. Presidents Grover Cleveland, William Howard Taft, and Woodrow Wilson all vetoed it, largely on the grounds that literacy reflected opportunity, not ability, but Wilson's second veto was overridden by a xenophobic Congress. This was only a stopgap solution, however. Congress sought answers to two issues: how to limit access generally, and what, if anything, to do about the Japanese.

Upon his return to the U.S. from Japan in 1913, Gulick threw himself with incredible vigor into the cause of a just immigration reform. He roughed out the outlines of a new oriental policy based on a quota system, elaborated on it in a book, *The American Japanese Problem*, and quickly began to publicize his ideas and seek support from those who could implement them. The first public statement of his proposed solution, the quota plan, was made in a speech in Los Angeles and later published in *The California Outlook*. His views so impressed his audience that supporters urged him to present his ideas in Washington.[1] William Dillingham, Republican senator from Vermont and chairman of the Committee on Immigration and Naturalization, was one of the first officials Gulick contacted; his interest prompted Gulick to send the plan to Wilson. He was invited to explain it in person and received a cordial if noncommittal response.[2]

Gulick's new oriental policy was presented to Congress January 31, 1914. Like a preacher seeking converts, Gulick outlined his ideas on a universal five percent quota to the Senate Committee on Immigration and Naturalization. Although he received some encouragement from his audience, he found the opposition stiffer than he expected. The highly influential Senator Henry Cabot Lodge challenged him at once, telling him he was wasting his breath and their time, that the American people had made up their minds on what to do with the "Asiatics," and there was no use his trying to budge them. Even Gulick's supporters had their lapses. Dillingham presented the policy but omitted one of Gulick's finer points, that the quota should be based on the degree of Americanization of each group of immigrants already in this country, not their sheer numbers.[3] Gulick was undaunted when he encountered opposition, and he determined to get the plan wider publicity across the nation. If only people understood his ideas and the rationale behind them, he was sure they would support him.

Gulick's views on immigration did receive wide publicity during 1914. The Federal Council *Bulletin* promoted the proposed policy, and Gulick toured the country, explaining it to church groups, civic organizations, and political meetings. Speaking with the ardor of a true believer, he aroused great popular enthusiasm wherever he went. The publication of *The American Japanese Problem* made his name more widely known. Funding for his speaking and writing was provided by the Commission on Relations with Japan, which had undertaken a study of immigration as its major issue for the year. The Federal Council published several of his addresses, including the January speech before the Senate Committee,[4] but although the leaders supported his ideas, they hesitated to endorse specific legislation. The campaign began to pick up steam.

TRAVELS TO FURTHER THE CAUSE:

In the middle of all this activity Gulick traveled to Europe for the Constance conference and the world erupted in war. The conflict caused a shift in priorities. Gulick had planned to promote the plan in California in the fall, after which he would visit Japan, but the war forced a six-month postponement of foreign travel.

The executive committee of the Federal Council and the leadership of the Commission on Relations with Japan agreed with Gulick that Japan's participation in the war as an ally of Great Britain made improving relations with that country a matter of utmost urgency. The Californians had to be dissuaded from passing any more anti-Japanese legislation, and clearly the Wilson administration could not be counted on to deter them, as the passage of the Alien Land bill had shown. Once in California Gulick did his best to rally the anti-exclusionist forces. He garnered support for the quota approach among educators and religious leaders, but the Hearst and McClatchy newspapers were implacably hostile. Throughout the state Gulick made contacts that he maintained by mail when he returned to the East Coast. The California situation alarmed him, and he wrote Wilson again, advising him that if the exclusionists were not restrained, their actions could precipitate war between the United States and Japan.[5] Gulick was nonetheless aware that the president was unlikely to pressure local politicians on that issue, however much he feared war.

Like the preacher he was, Gulick sought to convert the opposition as well as to rally the faithful. The American Federation of Labor president Samuel Gompers was a hard case; Gulick tried repeatedly to persuade him to drop his opposition to Japanese laborers, assuring him that American workingmen's rights could be protected "without racist legislation and treatment of the Japanese."[6] But organized labor, a key element in the anti-Japanese lobby, believed firmly in the economic component of the yellow peril hysteria, and nothing Gulick said could lessen its opposition. The stereotypical idea of those yellow workers undercutting the wages of honest union men by working for a bowl of rice a day was deep-seated and unshakable.

After California, Japan was next on the docket. The Federal Council decided to make a production of Gulick's trip and appointed him and the Reverend Shailer Mathews as a two-man goodwill embassy representing Protestant America and promoting friendship between the two countries. Seeking to ease the tensions their government's policies had created, they arrived in Yokohama January 27, 1915, and began a month of activities, addressing church groups, educational bodies, missionaries, businessmen, and government officials. Mathews gave a number of public addresses, while Gulick, who still remembered his Japanese, did more on a personal level, contacting old associates and giving interviews. The two sought to reassure Japan's small Christian community (less than two hundred thousand in total in a nation of fifty-four million) that they were not alone, that American Christians were at last working to improve American-Japanese relations. Despite a distinct and noticeable growth in anti-American sentiment, they were well received wherever they went, and they distributed a pamphlet, *The Friendship of America for Japan*, which contained supportive statements from Wilson, Bryan, and other distinguished Americans.[7]

Gulick had high hopes for the trip. He wrote to Chester Rowell, an influential Progressive California editor he hoped to win
away from an exclusionist stance, that they went "to do what we
may to convince the Japanese that the vast majority of our people
are truly friendly at heart, that there is not a particle of reason for
the belligerent stories that circulate on one side of the Pacific and
then on the other."[8] Their reception by prominent Japanese leaders was very heartening to them both. They were entertained by
Foreign Minister Baron Katō Komei and former Premier Ōkuma
Shigenobu as well as prominent business leaders and members of
the Association Concordia. Gulick's many contacts opened doors
for them, and they were quickly convinced of the trip's success.
But in the long run the goodwill they garnered netted them little.
They were shocked to learn later that Japan had presented China
with the Twenty-one Demands during their stay—an event which
further damaged America's image of Japan, as these demands
made Japan appear opportunistic and expansionist.

The Christian embassy to Japan received favorable publicity
in both countries. The Japanese were eager for any encouraging
words on the difficult subject of immigration, and Gulick promised to keep the journalists he met advised on immigration policy
and anti-Japanese legislation. In America the publicity testified to
the growing prestige of the organized churches. The *New York
Times* gave the trip favorable coverage, and a *Literary Digest*
article noted that Gulick's restriction plan appeared to be acceptable to the Japanese, but the author wondered if they assumed the
plan represented government policy since Wilson and Bryan had
signed the innocuous friendship document.[9] Of course it did not.
Although many Japanese opposed any restrictions on immigration, Gulick and Mathews concluded that many preferred a quota
system to the Gentlemen's Agreement because the latter was such
a source of misunderstanding.

When the two religious leaders returned to the United States
they drafted a report to the Commission on Relations with Japan.
The commission intended the goodwill mission to be one part of a
three-pronged program; in addition, it engaged Professor Harry
A. Millis of the University of Kansas to write a book on American-
Japanese relations, and it also sent a memorial to the president and

Congress urging a new oriental policy to meet the needs of both
Japan and the United States. The Gulick-Mathews report, published by the commission, emphasized the differing perceptions
the two countries had of each other, and called for the exchange
of delegations of workers—a suggestion the two had received
from the secretary of the California State Federation of Labor,
Paul Scharrenburg, one of the exclusionists. (Perhaps Scharrenburg thought a trip to the United States might convince Japanese
labor leaders that their countrymen were truly unwanted here. At
any rate, the Japanese did follow up on this.) Gulick and Mathews
also urged the churches to conduct an educational campaign on
the ramifications of discriminatory treatment. Congress was exhorted to protect aliens and to adopt an oriental policy based on
equality of the races and just and equitable treatment for all; other
groups were encouraged to endorse their appeal.[10] If it accomplished little else, the trip did demonstrate the churches' concern
about the Japanese question.

On his return from Japan Gulick spent a few days with family
and friends in Hawaii before resuming his travels. During the re-
mainder of 1915 he visited churches, business groups, clubs, and
labor leaders in major west coast cities speaking on the new oriental
policy and distributing pamphlets he had written, such as *Asia's
Appeal to America*, along with his book, *The American Japanese
Problem*. Wherever he could he gathered testimonials in support
of his proposal. Religious leaders could usually be persuaded, but
labor and the unions would be satisfied with nothing less than
oriental exclusion.[11] He feared that Senator Lodge was right—
most Californians' minds were already made up, and the exclusionists had a strong lead in winning the uncommitted.

OPPOSITION ARISES:

Although the war temporarily distracted people from the Japanese problem, Gulick's outspokenness had attracted public attention before the conflict began. The old Asiatic Exclusion League
had fallen apart in 1911, but a new coalition was forming, and it
singled out Gulick as a prime target. The appearance of *The
American Japanese Problem* had alerted the opposition to Gu-

lick's views. Montaville Flowers, a Virginian who had recently moved to California and had been giving anti-Japanese lectures on the Chautauqua circuit in the East, warned fellow exclusionist Rowell that the book was the latest in a concerted attack by Japan against their state: "It is ultra in its arguments against us, justifying the mixture of the races, etc." He feared that if it were widely promoted, it would have a "wide and powerful influence."[12] Rowell advised Flowers in the spring of 1915 that he had read Gulick's book and intended to present the author with substantial criticisms, as he had been requested to do. But the exclusionists agreed that Gulick was dangerous and had to be countered. "We will have to do some systematic organization in California against this sort of thing," Rowell cautioned. Although the anti-Japanese forces had tried to organize before, they had only collected "crooks and criminals." Now they must be much more selective to be really effective.[13] Flowers took a leading part in the new effort; he immediately began writing a book designed to vilify Gulick and destroy his influence.[14]

The exclusionists were not the only opposition Gulick drew. He also caught the eye of the Bureau of Investigation, forerunner of the F.B.I. Agent E. M. Blanford of Los Angeles began to send the bureau clippings from the local papers about Gulick's activities in that area.[15] The bureau was alerted to Gulick because of his many Japanese contacts and the generally pro-Japanese tone of his pronouncements. This was the only episode of surveillance in 1915; four years later the Bureau of Investigation files on Gulick bulged, as his case became one of many surreptitious investigations the bureau ran on people suspected of disloyalty, ranging from probable German agents to Japan propagandists and the occasional sympathizer. The file on him covered the years from 1915 to 1926, but it was most extensive from 1919 to 1924.

The surveillance of Gulick grew out of the public's general suspicion of Japan. When the Anglo-Japanese alliance brought Tokyo into the war against Germany, Japan's potential contribution was appreciated. However, Japan's war effort did not end the Japanophobia of the West Coast. Indeed, when Japan used its entry into the war to take advantage of China by announcing the Twenty-one Demands in 1915, public opinion became even more

hostile. China, with a more effective missionary lobby, was perceived as America's friend, and Japan's demands made that nation appear a villain. Particularly outrageous was the fifth group
of demands, which called for the stationing of Japanese "advisors" throughout China; this seemed, to Americans, to smack of a
protectorate. President Wilson was concerned when he learned of
the demands, which Japan had insisted China keep secret. China
missionaries dispatched Bishop James W. Bashford to Washington to urge the administration to pressure Japan to back down. He
went first to New York, where Gulick contacted him. The bishop
thought no one knew of his presence in the city, and concluded
that Gulick must have learned he was there from the Japanese.
(Gulick admitted that might well have been the case.) Bashford
concluded from this that Gulick was in Japan's employ, and he
most probably shared his conclusions with others.[16] Gulick also
drew suspicion on himself by his support of Japan's takeover of
the Shantung peninsula, Chinese territory alienated by the Germans into a sphere of influence, because he believed the occupation would indeed be temporary and that it was a legitimate spoils
of war. Both actions contributed to growing mistrust of Japan in
America. Even when the Japanese were forced to back down on
the demands, a legacy of ill will remained. That championing an
unpopular cause should warrant investigation by the Bureau of
Investigation seems outrageous, but given the vague parameters
of the agency's jurisdiction at the time, it was hardly surprising.

Gulick also ran head-on into the vicissitudes of California politics, in part through his own naïveté. He was a man of goodwill
and Christian charity who never ceased to think that reason could
convert his opponents, so he sent his publications to the exclusionist leaders asking for their response and commentary. But this
only served to tip them off and enable them to organize a more
effective opposition. While Chester Rowell was a reasonable
journalist, a Progressive influential in California politics who
seems to have considered Gulick sincere if misguided, two later
opponents were not as restrained in their attacks. Publisher V. S.
McClatchy, co-owner of the leading Sacramento and Fresno
newspapers, and U.S. Democratic Senator James D. Phelan,
former mayor of San Francisco in 1900 before anti-Japanese sen-

timent centered in the city, believed firmly in the yellow peril
concept and in the idea that Japanese were unassimilable. To
them Gulick was more than naïve; they believed it likely that he
was an agent of the enemy, and they may well have pointed the
Bureau of Investigation in his direction. Both men maintained that
exclusion was the only solution to the Asian immigration problem.
Phelan, a stupid if successful politician who believed his own anti-
Japanese rhetoric, also saw the issue as a popular vote-getting de-
vice, particularly useful when he battled in vain for reelection in a
year that witnessed a Republican landslide. The apolitical Gulick
missed the political overtones to Phelan's maneuvers and sought
to convince him with logic and reason. He was even willing to
debate Montaville Flowers if the Japan Society would sponsor it,
but Holt, its president, declined to provide a forum for the kind of
scurrilous attacks he had come to expect from the exclusionists.
Gulick was far less realistic than was Holt.[17]

To his enemies there was something suspicious about Gulick
anyway. His lengthy career in Japan seemed to have skewed his
vision. A Baptist paper in Cincinnati charged that his "long residence and position in Japan have made him Japanese rather than
American," and it warned that the quota idea might even have
Japanese origins. The writer maintained that Gulick "couldn't
serve Japan better if he were a paid agent."[18] While Gulick was
certainly American in his cultural framework and outlook, his
sympathies for the Japanese appeared to many as incomprehensible. Even Professor Millis, hired by the Commission on Relations with Japan to write a book that was very sympathetic to
Japan, doubted Gulick's loyalties. The problem stemmed from
the fact that Gulick, still uncertain about his ultimate career, continued to publicly identify himself as an American Board missionary and professor at Dōshisha and Kyoto Imperial universities,
and the latter position implied that he was paid by the Japanese.
Although in actuality his small stipend ceased when he left Japan,
his continued use of that title had unfortunate and unanticipated
consequences. Gulick wrote the doubting Millis that "not one cent
of money" that he had received for his work on immigration,
Japanese-American relations, or for the Federal Council, had
come from any Japanese source. The idea that he was either an

agent of the Japanese government, or paid to work on their behalf, was erroneous, as the bureau itself finally concluded, but once implanted in the public mind the connection did not die.[19]

Throughout 1916 the unsuspecting Gulick continued his campaign. He wrote articles for *Asia* magazine and *The Immigration Journal* explaining his proposals, and he authored a new book, *America and the Orient: Outlines of a Constructive Policy* (1916).[20] In it he described the awakening of Asia and reiterated how discriminatory practice and the violations of treaty pledges harmed our relations with China and Japan. He postulated three alternatives in dealing with the new, modernizing Asia. First of all, America could opt for white supremacy and oriental exclusion, becoming again the white peril that Asia hated. While he denied that the Orient would ever make war on the West, he reminded his readers that the democracies would have to be militarily prepared to counter Asian hostility. To Gulick democracy and militarism were incompatible. A second choice, mutual exclusion based on the idea of irreconcilable differences between East and West, would harm both, he pointed out, because of the advantages of trade, cultural and political interaction, and a modest amount of immigration. Instead he advocated a third approach, a "new internationalism" based on "equality and Christian principles of love and self-sacrifice," which would do away with the dread yellow peril menace by eliminating the white peril. (Although Gulick did not, because of the restrictions of his role for the FCCCA and WAIFTC, become involved in Japan's fight at Versailles for a racial equality clause in the Covenant of the League of Nations, his writings were fully consistent with that demand.) The West, according to Gulick, should lead the way in uplifting Asia, for mutual profit and advantage.[21] Advocating a policy that allowed a select quota of immigrants to enter the country on the basis of their skills and American needs, one that would encourage their Americanization and naturalization, he explained once again his new oriental policy. The book concluded with general suggestions about foreign policy in Asia. Reviews were favorable in the journals already predisposed to Gulick's views, such as Holt's *Independent* which called his immigration scheme "original and apparently so workable and just that one would like to see it tried."[22] The opposition ignored the book.

In addition to speaking, Gulick maintained a voluminous correspondence with influential political leaders and congressmen. He attempted to persuade California Senator John Downey Works that Japan had indeed carried out the Gentlemen's Agreement faithfully and objected to being accused of having violated it. Charges that Japan had manipulated that agreement were frequent, and Gulick constantly tried to refute them by statistics showing the reverse flow of population since the agreement had been in effect.[23] Unfortunately he could not deny that additional Japanese women had entered the country as picture brides, and this was a prime source of the exclusionists' charges. (Family members were entitled to entry; however, the manner of marriages had not been anticipated by the authors of the agreement.) Although he could not convince Works, he did acquire another supporter in Democratic Congressman Benjamin F. Welty of Ohio.[24]

Gulick also worried about the manner in which Japanese in America reacated to discriminatory treatment. He favored their turning the other cheek instead of pursuing courses of action that would increase public hostility. One incident prompted him to write fellow missionary Doremus Scudder in Honolulu and K. Kanzaki of the Japan Association in San Francisco which represented the Issei community. In 1914 an Issei, Takao Ozawa, had been denied citizenship by a district court in Hawaii. Ozawa claimed the right to naturalization by virtue of his Americanization. He had lived most of his life in the United States and Hawaii, had graduated from Berkeley High School and attended the University of California, spoke English at home, and was a Christian. The case became a test for the provision declaring Japanese aliens ineligible for citizenship.[25] Ozawa had appealed the original ruling in Hawaii's district court. Gulick wrote Scudder that he hoped the man would drop the suit if the original decision were positive and then overturned. Although he sympathized with the cause, he felt that a favorable outcome for Ozawa would only lead the Californians to agitate for even more discriminatory legislation,

which would worsen the situation.[26] The Californians should be
deterred from any more mischief, as he advised Scudder and
Kanzaki. He cautioned the latter not to test the Alien Land Law in
the courts, as that too would only arouse further hostility. Let
white friends do it for you, he advised.[27]

The attack against Gulick gathered strength with the publication of Flowers's book. *The Japanese Conquest of American
Opinion* (1917) was a diatribe against Japanese in America and
their American supporters. Flowers claimed that religious leaders
like Gulick had unfairly portrayed Californians as brutal and anti-
Christian. He charged that the Federal Council was committed to
a campaign to give the Japanese Americans citizenship and even
the right of intermarriage. The exclusionist trotted out the usual
arguments against the Japanese: they were clannish, unassimilable, and undercut the American standard of living through their
willingness to work for low wages. According to Flowers, Gulick
and the FCCCA were part of an interrelated group of Christian
advocates of Japanese equality who worked with the Church
Peace Union and the New York Peace Society. The idea that the
battle was one of Eastern interests pitted against the embattled,
misunderstood Californians was a recurring theme in the controversy. Gulick himself was depicted in vitriolic terms as a Japanophile so enamored of Japanese ideals that he spoke as "one
of them," and used the unsuspecting churchmen of the Federal
Council to promote a plan wholly political in its aims.[28] As Roger
Daniels noted, although Flowers's book exerted no appreciable
national influence, the volume opened a new phase of the anti-
Japanese movement and was indicative of things to come.[29]

The charge that he was unfairly stereotyping the Californians
upset Gulick, who corresponded with many supporters in the
state, among them Ray Lyman Wilbur, president of Stanford
University, and Benjamin Ide Wheeler, president of the University of California. One of his contacts, Harvey H. Guy of San
Francisco, urged him to widen the membership of the Commission on Relations with Japan to include some Californians, that
otherwise they would feel as if easterners were trying to "put one
over" on them. Gulick responded that the omission had been unin-

tentional. The original selection had been made on the basis of facilitating ease of meetings. He promptly invited Guy to join the commission. The San Franciscan advised him to ignore Flowers's book and let the venom published in the rabidly anti-Japanese Hearst papers run its course; further personal campaigns by Gulick would only encourage the opposition.[30] Gulick took his advice and concentrated his efforts on the East Coast.

Gulick made another nationwide appeal in yet another book, written in 1917 and published the following year. *American Democracy and Asiatic Citizenship* was basically a restatement of his 1914 proposals: a quota system to limit immigration, protection of aliens already in this country, and citizenship to all who could qualify. Once again he tied in domestic affairs with the international situation: "Americans should realize that modern Asia had rendered not only obsolete but dangerous any policy that ignores their [*sic*] problems, needs, and essential rights."[31] One of those "rights" was equitable treatment of their emigrants in the United States. The book was critically reviewed and widely acclaimed, but its message was ill-timed for the general public, whose interest in the immigration controversy waned when its attention was captured by the progress of the American Expeditionary Force in France.[32]

Congress in the meantime passed the first of a series of short-term immigration acts, the result of increasing demands for more effective restrictions. The law passed February 5, 1917, codified all previously enacted exclusion provisions and added new ones, including a literacy requirement which excluded illiterates of both sexes over sixteen but not illiterate wives of literate males.[33] Congress overrode Wilson's veto of the law. The law also created the so-called Barred Zone, which prohibited entry of any peoples from parts of China, South and Southeast Asia, and Asian Russia (but not the Philippines), part of Afghanistan, and most of Polynesia and the East Indies. (The prohibitions were phrased in terms of latitude and longitude, not peoples.) The Japanese were not included in the Barred Zone because their immigration was still controlled by the Gentlemen's Agreement.[34] This was but a temporary solution, and both sides girded for further battle.

THE NATIONAL COMMITTEE FOR CONSTRUCTIVE
IMMIGRATION LEGISLATION:

As the opposition coalesced, Gulick recognized that the forces
supportive of a quota system including Japanese would have to
organize to push their plan. The Federal Council of Churches and
its affiliated departments would not do, for if the council were to
maintain its credibility and its broad membership, it had to keep a
discreet distance from the fray. Besides, lobbying for specific legislation was a task better left to a group created specifically for
that purpose.

The needed impetus came from Gulick's success in recruiting
Ohio Congressman Welty to the cause. Welty told him that as a
newly elected member of the House, he wanted to build a broad
base of support for specific legislation along the lines of the Gulick plan. In response to this need, Gulick first formed a preliminary "Committee of One Hundred" which he described as "entirely outside the churches, a secular group to push the political
campaign."[35] Within a few months the new committee had
enough members to call a meeting and had expanded, hoping to
become in fact the "Committee of One Thousand." Soon it took
the name "The League for Constructive Immigration Legislation," a title later modified to the National Committee for Constructive Immigration Legislation (NCCIL). The new organization, which had enrolled 840 persons by mid-October, formed an
executive committee and proceeded to draft prospective legislation. Holt was elected chairman, and Gulick the executive secretary.[36] The group gathered considerable support for its restric-
tionist goals. As John Higham noted, the fact that its members
endorsed a plan which now recognized that some nationalities
were assimilated more easily than others was indicative of a real
change in public opinion, particularly liberal sentiment, from the
previous decade. It showed how far from the open door mentality
the nation had come. When fully constituted, the committee included such prominent liberals as Norman Hapgood, James Harvey Robinson, Vida D. Scudder, Oswald Garrison Villard, and
Lillian D. Wald. Gulick also enlisted George Kennan, John Col-
lier, Senator Dillingham, Harvey H. Guy, Frederick Lynch, William Howard Taft, and Benjamin I. Wheeler.[37]

Gulick's organizational skills were considerable. At each stage of the committee's evolution he informed those who had already enlisted of the names of the newly enrolled. He tried to obtain endorsements from the members to generate additional publicity, and he also sent out frequent appeals for money, hoping to raise fifty thousand dollars as a campaign chest. Proposed legislation was drafted with legal assistance, and whenever a word was changed, the membership was polled to ensure its continued support.[38]

Throughout 1919 the NCCIL was kept abreast of events through optimistically titled "Reports of Progress" chronicling the rise and decline of its fortunes. When Congress convened Gulick urged members to write their legislators, to promote his plan with local business and religious groups, and to persuade the local press to publicize the quota idea.[39] A second report informed members of the hearings conducted by the House Committee on Immigration on June 12 through 14 and 18 through 20, at which Gulick testified. V. S. McClatchy spoke for the exclusionists and delivered a personal attack on his opponent. Although Gulick did not advise his readers of his own personal discomfiture, the hearings, which had subsequent repercussions, provided the newspaperman with a golden opportunity to label him a Japanese propagandist. Gulick ignored the charge against him, and instead asked the membership to refute the publishers' wild and erroneous claims of a "Japanese Menace" and to promote in every way they could the quota plan. Because NCCIL funding proved inadequate to undertake that task, he had to rely on individual promotional efforts.[40]

McClatchy's charges touched off a barrage of personal attacks on Gulick that could no longer be ignored. Hearst's *San Francisco Examiner* blasted him, and his *New York American* called him a "liar and a hog for publicity." Gulick patiently tried to counter these distortions, and his friends came to his defense. But the publicity brought his plan widespread attention and that was desirable. The NCCIL held a general strategy meeting in Pittsburgh on November 12 through 14 that ran concurrently with the Third World Christian Citizenship Congress.[41] Gulick wrote Ray Lyman Wilbur that the introduction of the Treaty of Versailles into the Senate and demands for pressing domestic measures would make unlikely the introduction of new immigration legislation at this time. That was encouraging, for it would give the committee more time for its "educational campaign."[42] The strength of the opposition was becoming overwhelming.

In January of 1920 the NCCIL reported to its membership full of optimism for the next year, even as the opposition intensified. As hearings in the House Committee on Immigration continued, McClatchy and Senator Phelan elaborated on the idea of a Japanese menace and charges that Japan had violated the Gentlemen's Agreement. Gulick termed their allegations hysterical, full of misleading statistics and "the calm interweaving of fiction with fact." He patiently refuted the errors, pointing out that the net increase of Japanese in America was a mere ten thousand. Despite Gulick's predictions, a number of immigration bills were introduced in Congress, their provisions ranging from total exclusion of Asians to the complete suspension of all immigration for varying periods of time. A bill proposed by Senator Dillingham incorporated the quota features of the Gulick plan but subverted his intentions. His proposal stated that the legislation would not apply to countries with which immigration was already restricted in some manner— and hence the bill excluded Asians.

McClatchy also attacked the NCCIL itself before the House committee. He claimed that many members' names had been used without their permission, and he denied they endorsed Gulick's program. Gulick was shocked to have his carefully constructed lobbying effort discredited in this manner, and he jumped to rebut the accusations. He reported McClatchy's charges, and then explained to the members that in fact only twenty-eight had resigned; he urged the rest to hold fast. McClatchy's attacks were taking their toll, and the NCCIL was hard pressed to fight back. Gulick again pleaded for funds for the coming year's campaign.[43]

However, this time the appeal fell on deaf ears. The membership had been exhorted too much, and its loyalty waned in the face of the exclusionist fervor and the threat posed by the Red Scare then sweeping the country. Support for alien groups was not a popular posture to maintain in that climate of opinion. The many internationalists among them were also distracted by the opening of the fight over the Treaty of Versailles. Throughout the first six months of 1920 Gulick beseeched the members to renew their support for the committee, but by June 18, only six hundred had done so. On May 2, 1920, Congressman Welty finally introduced his bill, which most fully incorporated the new oriental policy. Gulick urged the members to support it or advise him of any specific objections they had,[44] but time was slipping away and his constituency was declining. The NCCIL continued to exist through 1922, but its effectiveness was so limited that it had, for all practical purposes, expired by the end of 1920. The tide seemed to be shifting in favor of the exclusionists, as Congress prepared to pass the most restrictive immigration bill yet.

8

THE EXCLUSIONISTS COUNTERATTACK

THE ENEMY ORGANIZES:

Despite occasional respites, California's hostility toward Japanese immigrants increased as the years passed, culminating in a drive to exclude them entirely. Arguments supportive of this movement were cast in many forms—social, economic, and political—but all were based on stereotypes originated at the turn of the century. Exclusionists added to their complaints against the Gentlemen's Agreement and the Alien Land Law. They recognized that this legislation had in fact only made it slightly more difficult for Japanese to purchase land; the Issei put their holdings in the names of their American-born children, and a few sympathetic lawyers retained by the Japanese Associations abetted them in this. But some Americans assumed all these strangers in their midst were future soldiers of our potential enemy, the Japanese emperor, and their dislike and hostility toward Japanese Americans focused upon the major spokesman of that group— Sidney Gulick.

Gulick attracted some very powerful opponents. Some were cynical politicians anxious to capitalize on popular opinion to win votes. Others were lecturers and journalists who pushed a cause in which they themselves believed. Aside from easily identifiable figures, Gulick had other enemies largely unknown to him at that time. The Office of Naval Intelligence, the Military Intelligence Division, and the Bureau of Investigation all had their eyes on him. Between 1919 and 1924 this opposition placed him on the defensive in the debate over immigration reform.[1]

THE FIRST SALVOS—FLOWERS AND PHELAN:

The campaign against Gulick's ideas began on the journalistic front. One of the earliest attacks came from Montaville Flowers, who claimed in a 1916 pamphlet that the former missionary was in the pay of the Japanese government. Although this charge soon became commonplace, Flowers was one of the first to publish it. Characteristically Gulick refused to join the battle, even in his own defense, but he did refute the allegation in a letter to Flowers's publisher.[2] However, Flowers was undeterred, and in his popular Chautauqua lectures he continued to spread the message of exclusionism throughout the eastern United States.

Flowers's next project, *The Japanese Conquest of American Opinion*, published in 1917, found no immediate audience because it dealt with a California obsession which the East Coast found rather incomprehensible, and even more because of the personal attacks and numerous inaccuracies it contained. The Bureau of Investigation agent reporting Japanese affairs in the Los Angeles area, Edward P. Morse, noted that the Japanese propagandist Kiyoshi Karl Kawakami claimed the book was offensive to the Japanese government, so he purchased and destroyed the plates for it.[3] Subsequently, Macfarland protested to the Federal Council that the book libeled Gulick, so the council forced its withdrawal from circulation. But truth was of little consequence in terms of the impact on Gulick's reputation, and the case against Gulick was building. Although Flowers soon dropped from sight, he was cited as an authority on Gulick by the Bureau of Investigation as late as 1921.[4]

If Flowers's polemics were irritating, Senator James D. Phelan proved even more visible. Phelan was one of the most prominent politicians in the anti-Japanese movement prior to 1920. Weaned on anti-Chinese activities in the 1880s, he saw the Japanese as the latest manifestation of the yellow plague to infect the Republic. He claimed no hatred for Japan per se, but he felt it could be a dangerous enemy, arguing that the Japanese immigrants were "an enemy within the gates," an unassimilable caste, a potential fifth column whose lifelong loyalties to their emperor made them forever untrustworthy.[5] Phelan needed a popular cause to overcome antipathy toward the Democratic party and his candidacy for reelection. Anti-Japanese rhetoric became a prominent feature of his campaign, even though it was not an issue on which he and his opponent differed.

Phelan accepted Flowers's charges against Gulick without checking his facts since they corroborated his own prejudices. He distributed copies of *The Japanese Conquest* to his friends and used the ideas as he opened a new campaign against the Japanese before a special session of the California state legislature on March 31, 1919—the opening salvo of his reelection effort. The slogan "Keep California White" expressed his fears of Japanese militarism and his suspicions that the immigrants were in fact colonists.

Phelan's own support was disorganized, but by fall of 1919, the California exclusionists had formed a number of groups that agreed on five basic principles: cancelling the Gentlemen's Agreement, excluding picture brides, prohibiting all Japanese immigration, forever barring Asians from becoming citizens, and amending the Constitution to bar children of aliens ineligible to naturalization from holding citizenship. The exclusionist campaign gathered momentum against the Japanese and against their friends. The sympathetic journal *Grizzly Bear*, the official organ of the Native Sons and Daughters of the Golden West, carried columns by Flowers denouncing Gulick, the Japan Society, the FCCCA, and the American Peace Society. Wide support developed among the American Legion and the labor unions and farmers of the Golden State.[6]

Despite Phelan's obvious political motivations Gulick did not give up on him. With the patience of Job and the diligence of a preacher, he continued to try to convert Phelan to his cause. When the senator introduced a constitutional amendment in early 1920 that would have denied citizenship to the American-born children of aliens ineligible for citizenship (e.g., Asians), Gulick gently took issue with him. He raised a multitude of quesions concerning just what groups would be affected, whether the proposed legislation would be retroactive, and suggested politely that it might have an adverse effect on international relations. Although one can read his despair through the lines, Gulick even attempted to pacify Phelan by assuring him he too was concerned about the problems raised by the presence of Asians on the West Coast, but he wrote Phelan, "I am trying to understand whether your proposed legislation would really solve it."[7]

THE HEARINGS OF THE HOUSE COMMITTEE ON IMMIGRATION:

The House Committee on Immigration conducted hearings in June of 1919 that added fuel to the debate. At that time Gulick encountered personal attacks from the men who had become his leading opponents. He gave a reasoned presentation of the quota plan, but when the questioning began the opposition drew its knives. Congressman John E. Raker, a Democrat from northeastern California who shared the common dislike of his state for Asians, was the first really hostile interrogator Gulick encountered.[8] Raker first centered his attack on Gulick's sources of income. Dissatisfied with Gulick's standard explanation of his current funding, Raker badgered him unmercifully. To Gulick the discussion was "quite irrelevant," designed to make him "look preposterous," and he believed it demonstrated Raker's disinterest in the real significance of the percentage plan.[9] In his "Reminiscences" Gulick recalled that this was a standard tactic of his opposition—discrediting him to make his ideas appear irrelevant.[10]

Raker touched the main issues subsequent opponents would belabor. A key topic was the connection between the Federal Council and the National Committee for Constructive Immigration Legislation. Raker, Phelan, and McClatchy were convinced, for example, that the latter was a front for the FCCCA, which stood behind a program that encompassed everything from repealing the Chinese exclusion laws to advocating intermarriage and encouraging picture brides. Charging that many members of the NCCIL did not really know Gulick's full intentions, opponents claimed that because the group as a whole had never met, Gulick simply used their names as a cover for his own activities.

Raker grew most vitriolic when he asked whether Gulick was, in fact, a paid Japanese agent. For several days the House committee examined details of his funding, which was indeed difficult to identify as it shifted from one agency to another, depending upon which one was using Gulick's services at the time. Finally Macfarland, who first hired Gulick to work for the FCCCA in 1914, explained the nature of his original appointment. Offering the FCCCA's financial records along with those of the Commission on Relations with Japan and of the Commission on Peace and Arbitration (the later CIJG), Macfarland testified that Gulick's three-thousand-dollar salary was paid in 1914 and 1915 by the latter group, then four thousand dollars were paid him from 1916 to 1918 by the WAIFTC, and in 1919 by the CPU. Macfarland denied that the FCCCA endorsed the details of Gulick's percentage plan, although he conceded that perhaps a majority of the members supported it. The Japan agent story he traced to an unsubstantiated charge in Flowers's book.[11] Macfarland, who respected Gulick highly, also made an impassioned defense of his friend in various books he wrote on the Federal Council and church unity, and his message probably did carry weight with persons who were open to persuasion.[12]

As the hearings continued Phelan picked up Raker's arguments and embellished them. Although he professed to believe MacFarland's testimony on the Japan agent issue, he did not drop his attack. Instead he presented two hours of testimony which Gulick later described as a diatribe "full of self-contradictory absurdities and fictions."[13] He continued his attacks on Gulick for the next year, and they became part of his campaign rhetoric as he fought for reelection to the Senate in November 1920.

However, his attacks against Gulick paled before those of V. S. McClatchy, who next entered his words into the testimony. McClatchy was a much more formidable opponent than Phelan. He was, as Roger Daniels has said, a "leader behind whom the whole movement could rally." He retired from his position as publisher of the *Sacramento Bee* in 1919 after a dispute with his brother, who succeeded him in that position. Instead of depriving him of access to the media, his retirement instead gave him even more time to devote to the cause of Asian exclusion. Because he had been director of the Associated Press he had extensive contacts among influential people and was, in addition, a close friend of Hiram W. Johnson.[14]

McClatchy testified before the House committee June 19 and 20, 1919, not only speaking but including an appendix to his words entitled "Japan's 'Peaceful Penetration' of the United States: How American Commercial and National Interests are Affected." In this he laid out his charges against Gulick, whom he claimed was nothing more than a shill for Japanese interests, "the promoter and manager of Japan's propaganda organization in the United States." He reiterated the claim that the sinister Gulick had duped the innocent members of the NCCIL into supporting his nefarious schemes. The organization was, he said, a "remarkable tribute to the cleverness of the Japanese in the work of propaganda in this country." To McClatchy the Japanese were undesirable and unassimilable, but more than that, they posed an economic threat to California labor and agriculture. Gulick's plan would let more in when in fact "we should let none in."[15] He later warned that the Japanese were the "Germans of Asia," and they would turn the United States into a Japanese province through their immigration unless it was absolutely prohibited.[16] Although Gulick refuted McClatchy's charges point by point, he had difficulty denying he was a propagandist, and many observers concluded that he was therefore an agent. Since no one ever claimed he was a spy or saboteur it is difficult to fathom what precisely his opponents thought an "agent" or a "propagandist" did that would be so harmful to the nation's interests. In a letter to McClatchy written a week later, Gulick identified the problem: "The way . . . in which you speak of me as a 'Japanese propagandist' implies that you regard my purposes and procedure as dishonorable because tainted with ulterior motives for benefitting Japan and for injuring America."[17] Animosity against Gulick can best be explained in the context of the times, against the background of the Red Scare, as a paranoia over affiliation with or sympathies toward a foreign nation with whom the United States might one day be at war.

GULICK, McCLATCHY, AND PHELAN:

Throughout the next three years Gulick battled with McClatchy, but it became an uphill fight once the publisher seized the offensive. Gulick polled his California friends for suggestions but received nothing very concrete; he contemplated traveling there again, but few friends encouraged him. Although McClatchy's sentiments seemed "radical" to Gulick, he learned that they did represent exclusionist opinion in the state. R. N. Lynch of the San Francisco Chamber of Commerce agreed with Gulick that Phelan, Raker, and McClatchy should not be allowed to appear as spokesmen for the entire state, but the chamber was unwilling to tackle the trio except through a discreet article in *Review of Reviews*. Lynch claimed the chamber could not openly support the percentage plan however much it desired to do so because public opinion was too hostile toward Japan. That nation's current suppression of a rebellion in Korea, its takeover of Shantung, its suspiciously large expedition to Siberia, which ran counter to American interests, and its exploitation of China, all evoked wide opposition in this country. Such advice persuaded Gulick to abandon the idea of a personal campaign on the West Coast, and instead he spent the summer of 1919 attempting to refute his enemies in print.[18]

McClatchy had greater access to the press than did Gulick, so that strategy also foundered. The publisher's testimony at the June House hearings was reprinted by the *Sacramento Bee*, together with other broadsides and editorials, and they were given wide circulation.[19] Gulick collected all these missives and attempted piecemeal to refute them in letters to McClatchy and his friends, but it was the public that needed convincing. In August the personal allegations against Gulick were picked up by Hearst's *San Francisco Examiner* in an editorial portraying Gulick in even harsher light than had McClatchy—as a deliberate liar who had attacked the Hearst press unjustly because it had exposed Japanese atrocities in Korea. The *Examiner* even used his own words against him, quoting from *Evolution of the Japanese* to show that Gulick had once decried Japanese inhumanity, lack of integrity, immorality and lying, yet now he saw the Japanese as saints. Clearly such contradictions in his position could be explained only if he were in Japan's pay.[20]

Gulick's counterattack was far more dispassionate. He exposed the illogic of McClatchy's argument and revealed the publisher's misuse of immigration statistics. The two dueled in the

New York Times but McClatchy published articles or made charges that ran as news items, while Gulick's rebuttals were often just letters to the editor. Macfarland even persuaded the Commission on Relations with the Orient to pass a resolution denying that Gulick had ever accepted Japanese money,[21] but again the statement missed the target. Gulick wrote a pamphlet published by the Federal Council that attempted to disprove charges by Phelan and McClatchy that Japan was violating the Gentlemen's Agreement. Citing their June 1919 testimony before the House committee, Gulick argued that McClatchy's statistical evidence was misleading, as his figures included women who came to Hawaii with those who arrived in California. He denied that picture brides reproduced like rabbits. The charge that the agreement was being violated by Japanese crossing the border illegally was also unwarranted by the evidence, he claimed; in fact, said Gulick, Japan had lived up to the terms of the agreement.[22] Phelan, defeated for reelection in 1920, countered with a book written after his retirement, *Travel and Comment*, in which he again charged Japan with building a colonial empire through the birthrate of its emigrants, and he reiterated his demands for total exclusion.[23]

Gulick made a second appearance before the House committee on May 22, 1920, when he presented a revised version of the quota plan. Responding to criticisms, he amended his original scheme to provide for a board of immigration that would set a yearly quota of immigrants based on America's needs and the assimilability and adaptability of the immigrants. Under Raker's intense questioning the harried Gulick admitted that on the basis of "assimilability" he himself would probably exclude Africans, East Asians, and Hindus entirely at the present time. Why then would his plan be any improvement over the Gentlemen's Agreement and Chinese exclusion? Gulick could only admit that Japan was dissatisfied with the agreement because of the discriminatory treatment and denial of naturalization. He admitted, too, that his new bill could allow entry to more Japanese than the highest number that came before the war.[24] To the exclusionists that damned his proposal.

Although Gulick held his tongue in public, privately he

writhed under McClatchy's attacks, which he considered slanderous and designed to undermine his influence and discredit his proposals. He knew the charge that he was a Japanese agent was widely believed, influenced by the Hearst papers, yet he was unable to shake it. "But for this campaign of misrepresentation and personal slander," he reflected later, "I am convinced my percentage plan would have been promptly accepted by Congress, with incalculable beneficial results to American-Japanese relations." But his tactics failed, even the occasional personal appeals to McClatchy. In fact, Gulick found himself charmed by the publisher's seeming sincerity, but Gulick recognized later that for all his efforts, his replies "never caught up with his [McClatchy's] lies." The former missionary despaired that California's church leaders would not confront McClatchy, but they felt he was so clever and devious and had such access to publicity that "to try to unhorse him would do more harm than good."[25] Gulick never ceased battling, although he was clearly on the defensive against the exclusionists' charges in California. He hoped a rallying of opinion in the rest of the country might save the percentage plan, for the nation as a whole did not share the western state's prejudices.

UNDER SURVEILLANCE:

The investigation of Gulick by Military Intelligence and the Bureau of Investigation bear out all the assertions made by Frank Donner in *Age of Surveillance*. Donner's words merit quoting:

Even the selection of a target embodies a judgment of deviance from the dominant political culture . . . the investigation [is not] embarrassed by seemingly barren results, for an innocent fact may turn out to be a clue to a sinister, yet-to-be revealed conspiracy. . . . Even though the target is an American national, engaged in lawful political activities in his own country, he is viewed in an adversary context. Life in a relatively open society makes the target enormously vulnerable when his politics come under hostile investigation by a secret police unit with an anti-subversive mission. The individual's vulnerability is intensified by the secrecy of the probe and the knowledge that even if no "derogatory" information is developed, he or she will become a permanent file subject.[26]

Gulick's name first came to the attention of the Bureau of Investigation in July 1918 when it was called upon to consider publications of the WAIFTC to determine if their material for use in the churches was in any way suspicious because of its obvious pacifist slant.[27] The surveillance proceeded from the assumption that a man who consorted with Japanese nationals and espoused the welfare of Japanese immigrants had to be dangerous to the welfare of the United States. Japan was an unpopular country whose goals and motives were mistrusted, a yellow peril all the more threatening as it became more powerful. Japanese immigrants were discriminated against, perceived as economically threatening and generally socially unacceptable. The investigations seemed clearly predicated on suspicion rather that fact, and the agents themselves contributed to the rumors surrounding the subject, Gulick, and shared the prejudices of his accusers. Although no hard data ever emerged to prove the allegations against Gulick, they were accepted as true and used to justify further surveillance. Gulick became the enemy because he associated with them. He learned of the investigation as it proceeded, but he could not confront his tormentors until it was too late.[28] Their allegations became a part of a permanent file, and were repeated whenever Gulick tried to influence public officials about later events.

Gulick was not the only victim of the official harrassment associated with the xenophobia that followed the war, but he stands out because his "crime" was his support of Japan. During the war German sympathizers were similarly suspect, and the inclusion of reports on Gulick among hundreds of German cases in the FBI files demonstrates the link. However, the surveillance of Gulick was most intense after the war, when the Bureau of Investigation was concerned about Japan as a possible threat because of its expansionist aims and the immigration controversy at home. For several years, from 1919 to 1923, agents reported on him, often weekly, even when he was traveling in Japan in 1922 and 1923. Clearly his ties to Japan singled him out for special treatment. Agents watched any activities of the Japanese government; in Boston, for example, they observed all Japanese in the vicinity and even infiltrated the local Japanese Society, a group promoting friendly relations. Japanese officials in this country were also accorded close scrutiny, but were watched closely only if they, like Gulick, were considered propagandists. J. Edgar Hoover, who ordered the surveillance, certainly believed Japan was a threat to American security and that Gulick was in its pay, the head of a vast propaganda operation that included such "dupes" of the Japanese cause as professors Payson J. Treat and Kenneth Scott Latourette.

The investigation of Gulick proceeded from two bits of hard information—his known association with Japanese officials and his specific dealings with Kawakami—and from a continuing concern over his source of funding. The first of these is easy to document and is innocuous in the context of Gulick's past career. He did know many minor bureaucrats when he left Japan, he renewed their acquaintance when he returned there, and he felt at ease writing them about his new career, sharing his plans and soliciting information. For example, in 1916 he wrote a friend in the Gaimushō, the foreign office in Tokyo, about his campaign for his new oriental policy on the West Coast and asking how Japan had reacted to recent modifications of the immigration bill presently in Congress.[29] The impact of America's treatment of Asians on Japan's foreign policy had concerned Gulick since his missionary days. He discussed the matter further with acquaintances in Tokyo on his visit in 1915, and he communicated with consular officials in New York as part of his regular activities there. Because he was well known to Japanese bureaucrats in this country, they no doubt regarded him as an advocate. Being in their pay was quite another matter, however.

Gulick's relationship with Kawakami was closer, but also of a business nature. Kawakami, an Issei, had an American-born wife and had been in the United States nearly twenty years. He was a prolific writer in both English and Japanese. His position with the Japanese press bureau was funded by Japan; he acquired a reputation as a propagandist for that government.[30] Whether Gulick knew this at the outset of their relationship is moot. Gulick later learned of allegations that Kawakami was a paid propagandist and apparently believed them; he tried to avoid too close contact with the man, but the two did correspond on a number of occasions about the Gentlemen's Agreement and immigration.[31]

Rumors about Kawakami led to his surveillance by Military Intelligence in 1919. An agent followed him for several months investigating his activities for Japan at the Paris Peace Conference. The agent noted that Kawakami's writing was propagandistic although not especially offensive to the United States. His reports indicated that he had read Kawakami's correspondence as well as his latest book, *Japan in the League*, in galley proof. The investigator's findings seemed to substantiate that the man was a paid propaganda agent, part of a network the Japanese government had in the country. Kawakami advocated Japan's territorial expansion and commercial domination of the Orient, but the agent found no proof that he was engaged in espionage.[32] However, like McClatchy, Military Intelligence seemed to regard propagandists as figures almost as sinister as spies.

Gulick and Kawakami corresponded regularly in the spring and summer of 1919 and all their letters were intercepted and read by Military Intelligence. Although the letters concerned mainly immigration statistics, one bore more significance. On July 7, 1919, Agent F. W. Wilson sent Military Intelligence a letter from Kawakami to Gulick written June 25, 1919, in which the former discussed the activities of Phelan, Hearst, and McClatchy against Gulick's immigration bill. Kawakami then mentioned a trip to the West Coast that Gulick was contemplating. He concluded, "If you still think that your trip to California will do much good, I think we can find the way to bring you here. I should be interested to have your opinion on the matter."[33] The agent also reported Gulick's answer: "I would be glad to take advantage of the trip to the Pacific Coast provided the same could be financed by American citizens interested in the matter." Gulick apparently advised Kawakami that he thought a visit would be worthwhile despite the severe criticism of the proposed immigration bill, but neither he nor the Federal Council could finance it.[34]

Military Intelligence concluded that both Gulick and Kawakami were suspect. A report entitled "Japanese Activities in the U.S." maintained that the Japanese had a "carefully laid plan" to utilize current antiradical public opinion in support of a new immigration plan. Allegations were frequently inaccurate; Gulick was often described as "the head of the Federal Council of Churches," and Agent Wilson claimed, "It is an established fact that he is a Japanese adherent."[35] Kawakami was ostensibly in charge of the Pacific Press Bureau, but according to the bureau, was "in fact a propagandist in the direct pay of the Japanese government."[36]

The Department of Justice files present a more complete picture of the intelligence agencies' investigation of Japanese activities in the United States. Throughout much of 1919, Edward P. Morse, now the special agent of the Department of Justice in San Francisco, reported weekly on the activities of known propagandists, pro- and anti-Japanese organizations, Japanese-owned property, and the movement of Japanese nationals back to the mother country. Other investigators watched Japanese known to be operatives or propagandists and any Americans suspected of working with them. Although they also observed Gulick's friend Frank Waterhouse and a fellow missionary Doremus Scudder, Gulick's activities were so extensive that he was a prime suspect. They had covered him sporadically prior to 1919, for example, noting the previous year that his correspondence about the war did not warrant prosecution since he had not advocated supporting Germany.[37] They read Gulick's private correspondence for at least a year prior to the appearance of the Kawakami letter. At the outset of the investigation the agencies were simply "fishing," hoping to come up with something positive; in the Kawakami letter they seemed to have found it—if one specifically ignored Gulick's reply to that communication, as the Department of Justice did.

The Gulick-Kawakami correspondence story blew up in the summer of 1920 when Phelan obtained the incriminating letter through dubious means and then made it public. The occasion was a San Francisco hearing conducted by a subcommittee of the House Committee on Immigration and Naturalization. Phelan presented testimony which included three letters from Kawakami, including one to Gulick. When asked how he acquired them, the senator, according to Colonel John P. Irish, who heard him, admitted they might have been lifted from the mail. Kawakami, outraged, wrote a pamphlet giving his side of the story. Suspecting that the letters had in fact been stolen from his office, he had planted two more letters in his wastebasket specifically as "bait," and found they too were made public by Phelan. While maintaining his own innocence, Kawakami claimed the decoy letters had in fact never been mailed. He was convinced that someone had been rifling his trash nightly and purloining the contents.[38]

There are at least two possible explanations for the leaked correspondence. One is Kawakami's version, endorsed by Colonel Irish, a California farmer, politician, and propagandist for Japanese Americans, who was the intended recipient of one of the fake letters. The other is that Military Intelligence might have lifted the letters from the trash and made them available to Phelan. Such an explanation is more likely, in fact, because the agents following Gulick and Kawakami were clearly supportive of the goals of the exclusionists. Morse reported weekly on Kawakami and other Japan-related matters in the fall of 1920, while B. C. Haworth, who apparently was a freelance operative, kept the Office of Naval Intelligence informed. The latter files wound up in the office of the counsellor of the State Department, while the former became part of the records of the Federal Bureau of Investigation, the successor agency to the Bureau of Investigation. Morse also monitored the contents of the Japanese language newspapers and activities he considered "propaganda and espionage," and translations of Japanese language articles were made for him by Haworth.[39] Editorial comments in Morse's reports revealed his own sentiments. He noted that although one of the newspapers was "more in harmony with American interests and ideals," although it shared "the common blindness of the Japanese . . . to the real issue in the California question, viz., American repugnance to a new race struggle on our shores."[40] Unable to understand how white men could champion their cause, he reported a "pro-Japan" advertisement in the San Francisco papers, noting that it included the signatures of Stanford professors Payson J. Treat and David Starr Jordan.[41]

By November 1920, the Bureau of Investigation had also become suspicious of the operations of the Federal Council of Churches, whose interest in social and economic problems seemed to smack of radicalism, a dangerous tendency during the height of the Red Scare. The council's decision to incorporate the Interchurch World Movement, and its condemnation of the

Palmer raids against suspected anarchists, raised doubts about its "loyalty." The bureau was particularly curious about Gulick's activities; he was then secretary of the Commission on the Orient and the Commission on International Justice and Goodwill.[42] A weekly intelligence report dated November 13 concerned itself entirely with the activities of the supposed "agent of Japanese propaganda," stating that he had been "for many years a salaried employee of the Japanese government." It covered the June 1919 House hearings in detail and alleged that Gulick had, on his 1915 trip to Japan, not only assumed the right to speak for California but had also promised the Japanese government an "open door" for Japanese subjects into California. Raker, the report claimed, was unable to get Gulick to admit who financed the trip or paid his salary. The agent who authored the report concluded that it was not purely coincidental that Gulick had returned to the United States just as the "first attempt of California to check the land-grabbing schemes of its Japanese subjects" had occurred; this new post was assigned him by the Japanese government. The investigator assumed he had duped the Federal Council into supporting his schemes.[43]

The next week the bureau obtained a file on the Federal Council from Military Intelligence. "This organization seems to be in sympathy with a movement to allow larger immigration of Japs [sic] to the U.S.," it reported, documenting this conclusion with Gulick's statements over the years opposing exclusionary legislation.[44] A week later a memo detailed contents of letters Military Intelligence had intercepted between Gulick and some London-based organizations, specifically the National Peace Council, the Peacemakers, and the National Union of Women Workers. These letters attacked the anti-Japanese propaganda in the Hearst press and reported Gulick's queries to the Japanese government regarding its attitudes on the Gentlemen's Agreement, immigration, naturalization, and various foreign policies.[45] Morse warned the bureau a few days later that "the hand of Sidney Gulick" was evident in a Federal Council report urging promotion of goodwill between the United States and Japan, and he reminded the bureau that Gulick was a "paid Japanese propagandist" and a Federal Council secretary.[46]

The bureau did not pinpoint the supposed source of Gulick's Japanese funds until 1921, when several reports stated that Baron Shibusawa had provided twenty thousand dollars for Gulick in November 1920, and that the money had been delivered by Dr. Harada Tasaku, a professor of Japanese history and literature at the University of Hawaii and former president of the Dōshisha. The source, name censored, was a female agent employed by the Department of Agriculture, who resigned her position April 21, 1919, giving as a forwarding address Tientsin, China. However, in 1926 a report of the bureau indicated that it had been unable to substantiate this charge.[47]

A General Intelligence Division, created in August 1920 and headed by young J. Edgar Hoover, began a probe of the Federal Council in early December. Hoover asked his New York office to check on the organization's principles and activities, its officers and prominent members—tasks he interpreted as part of his mandate to ferret out radicals. Hoover even reported placing an inside informer to discover who had condemned the Palmer raids. Nothing in the files of General Intelligence or the State Department linked the council to subversive organizations, however.[48]

Next the bureau turned its focus on the National Committee for Constructive Immigration Legislation, beginning an intensive investigation in January 1921. A lengthy report by Agent H. B. Pierce labeled the NCCIL "pro-Japanese propagandists" and termed it an outgrowth of the Commission on Relations with Japan of the Federal Council. The latter body had been organized "at the instigation of Sidney Gulick," ostensibly to promote goodwill but in fact to advocate unrestricted immigration of Japanese to the United States and their admission as American citizens. Gulick's life was reviewed fairly accurately in the report. Pierce noted that when Gulick left Japan the tension in American-Japanese relations had discredited the work of American missionaries, making the American Board uneasy. "While it is hardly possible to prove, your Agent has been reliably informed that prior to the coming to the U.S. of Dr. Gulick he spent more than three months' time in conference with the Military Intelligence and Naval Intelligence of the Japanese government." Whatever the truth of that allegation, Pierce charged that Gulick clearly had used the Commission on Relations with Japan to secure the endorsement of the entire Federal Council for his nefarious plans. It was part of "an elaborate scheme by Gulick and his pro-Japanese associates" to draft legislation to remove all restrictions on the immigration of Asians and their ultimately obtaining American citizenship. Between 1914 and 1918 all propaganda and legislative work had been handled through that commission, but when it became necessary to enlarge the constituency and the campaign, the FCCCA decided it was "inappropriate" to link that body directly to the legislative goals. Thus the National Committee was organized as a front to lend influence and respectability to Gulick's activities.[49]

Pierce's report then detailed the organization, structure, and finances of the committee. Gulick's brainchild was headed by Holt, who was, the agent claimed incorrectly, responsible for the initial employment of Gulick by the Federal Council. "Stripped of its camouflage, the National Committee for Constructive Immigration Legislation is merely a committee of the Federal Council," separate only because the council did not approve of Gulick's plans to bring in "unlimited numbers of unwanted and unassimilable Orientals." The agent then raised the issue of financial support of the committee. If not from the Federal Council, then from whom? Pierce doubted that the National Committee by itself had the funds to pay Gulick's salary and expenses. The resulting legislation, Pierce charged, represented the "friendship of Dr. Gulick and Hamilton Holt for the Japanese government—demonstrated regardless of their prostitution of American ideals and standards."[50]

The report closed with a discussion of a two-hour meeting Pierce held with Gulick on January 23, 1921. According to Pierce, Gulick admitted the close ties between the National Committee and the Federal Council. "As a result of leading questions during the conference" Pierce concluded that the committee was apparently receiving contributions for publicity purposes from foreign governments. Gulick also acknowledged being the originator of the Sterling immigration bill.[51] Pierce's unsubstantiated report was damning, and a similar report was filed in February, including a detailed breakdown of the committee's expenditures for 1920.[52] The bureau's agents filed occasional reports on Gulick thereafter, noting his activities on behalf of Japan and his work with the National Committee on American-Japanese relations. His mere presence in that organization was enough for the bureau to suspect the "true nature of the organization."[53] In 1924 he was listed in an alphabetical index of names of persons associated with pacifist and radical organizations.[54]

Military Intelligence conducted a simultaneous investigation. It too reported on contacts between Japanese officials and their supporters and occasionally used Haworth's services to translate the local Japanese language press, and it repeated the story of the twenty thousand dollar slush fund provided by Baron Shibusawa. Its agents also claimed Gulick received a monthly retainer from the Japanese government. Some of the reports were circulated between Military Intelligence and the Bureau of Investigation. Although Gulick ceased to be a subject of primary concern, his name appeared in files twice during the war years. A final reference to his status as a Japanese agent was made in a 1952 security check on his youngest son.[55]

What is one to conclude from all this? Clearly all U.S. intelligence agencies believed Gulick was a Japanese agent. They reported their findings to one another, and inaccuracies crept into the story in the process. The charges essentially were these: that Gulick had been recruited as an agent by the intelligence branch of the Japanese government before he returned to America, presumably while he was recovering from the cancer operation; that those ties were reaffirmed and strengthened during the 1915 trip to Japan; and that he received money, at least twenty thousand dollars, for his propaganda work in connection with Japanese immigration. While agents admitted they could not prove the first two allegations, they claimed to have evidence for the third. However, they did not obtain the documentation they requested from the Department of Agriculture and their case was weakened by their citing of Montaville Flowers as a source. Gulick would certainly not have told Flowers that the Japanese government had promised to pay his expenses as a propaganda agent. The twenty thousand dollar payoff and the monthly retainer appeared highly unlikely since the NCCIL's effectiveness had been hampered and its early demise ensured by the lack of funds, and Gulick had been unable to make the trip to California because he had insufficient money. (It is curious that the figure, twenty thousand dollars, was precisely the sum of money the CPU had originally allocated to pay Gulick. Perhaps this is the source of the figure in all the rumors.) In retrospect, and by the Department of Justice's own admission to the author, it is clear that Gulick was not a paid agent.[56] He became the prey of the neophyte intelligence operations of the American government, who responded to the Red Scare by attempting to root out un-American activities wherever they were suspected. Although the major focus of their efforts were communists and other radicals, they also followed pacifists and people connected to a country they believed intended war with the United States. Gulick was their innocent victim.

The Bureau of Investigation did not lose interest in Gulick in the 1920s. It watched his involvement in the disarmament movement and acted to impede his effectiveness. But its main work had already been done. Gulick was labeled a Japanese agent, and the charge stuck. If he was not, in Donner's words, a "permanent file subject," he had become one long enough for his reputation to be seriously damaged. In his "Reminiscences" Gulick called the investigation part of the "McClatchy poison germinating rapidly in the war and navy department." Someone told him his name was in a card file of dangerous persons, and he recalled that in 1917 or 1918 two military intelligence officers had tried to gain admittance to his office to search his letter files. When he told Macfarland, the churchman brought the matter to the War Department and was told there that Gulick's name was "on the list of persons who might be useful to the government in case of difficulty with Japan." In 1924 or 1925, Gulick recalled later, he was called a Japanese agent by a congressman on the Chautauqua circuit and refuted it to the man's face. From him he learned that the basis of the allegation was "current gossip in China and Washington."[57] The China aspect is interesting, especially in view of the connection between that country and the source for the story of the twenty thousand dollars. Gulick visited China in 1922 to 1923 and found many Chinese leaders regarded him as a secret agent and spy for Japan. He attributed that to Bishop Bashford who had believed him an agent ever since encountering him in New York at the time of the Twenty-one Demands controversy.[58]

Gulick did try to clear his name by confronting his accusers. In March 1921 he wrote Attorney General Harry M. Daugherty, telling him that he had learned from a number of sources that he was being investigated by the Department of Justice. He asked Daugherty to please send an official to his office, if indeed he were under investigation, so that "I may show and tell him everything he may desire to see or know. I have nothing whatever to conceal." Daugherty replied, merely acknowledging receipt of his letter.[59] Perhaps the visit of Agent Pierce was an outgrowth of the correspondence. At any rate, the Bureau of Investigation did not lose interest in Gulick for the next five years, but ceased its surveillance in 1926, compiling a dossier on Gulick that ran to over five hundred pages. In the end it concluded that he was not in fact an agent of Japan, but that information was never made public. The damage to Gulick's career was already done, and in retrospect it seems to have been substantial.

Gulick's opponents did not allow the Japan agent charges to die. In June 1924 former Senator Phelan repeated them to the *New York Times*. The executive committee of the Federal Council of Churches, understandably angered that he should reiterate such a canard, charged Phelan with "falsehood and malicious insinuations" and claimed his attack was "poor sportsmanship." Phelan then reiterated the allegation, claiming that if Gulick were not in Japan's pay, his actions were even worse, "helping Japan in its silent penetration of the United States." He remarked snidely, "I didn't know Japanese money was so dirty that it would be disavowed." He still believed Gulick was a professor on furlough from a Japanese university, whose sole assignment was to help the Japanese cause. "Gulick is an able adversary . . . but a poor loser," he concluded. Once again the faithful Macfarland came to the rescue, refuting Phelan point by point, but clearly to no avail.[60] Phelan's outrageous attack was one more blast in the exclusionists' successful campaign against Gulick.

In fact, some people perceived Gulick not only as an agent but a tiresome public nuisance as well. A woman in New York wrote Secretary of State Charles Evans Hughes in November 1924 when Gulick addressed a luncheon of the Upper Montclair Women's Club. He had, she noted, "exhausted the women's clubs of New York with his propaganda" and was now going further afield. "Is there anything to be done to stop the deception of the public by this man who is a menace to the community?" she wrote.[61]

In conclusion, one must tie Gulick's case to the slovenly way in which these intelligence agencies operated. They were, indeed, as Donner stated, secret police units with antisubversive missions, but the idea that Japan was a source of subversion was ludicrous. Pro-Japan sympathies should hardly have qualified as "radical," but the proponents of the Red Scare of 1919 and 1920 were notoriously unscrupulous in their choice of targets. Gulick's name also appeared on the voluminous list of suspected radicals compiled by the witch-hunting Lusk Committee, appointed by the New York State Legislature in 1919.[62] He had no radical sympathies whatsoever but merely championed an unpopular cause. Given such a climate of opinion, he was a likely target for surveillance, a victim of "guilt by association" with an unpopular country. To the intelligence operatives, Gulick's crime lay in fact that he appeared, as one report labeled him, "anti-American."[63]

9

THE EXCLUSIONISTS TRIUMPH

CALIFORNIA TAKES THE LEAD, THE NATION FOLLOWS:

California's drive for Japanese exclusion gathered momentum in the election year of 1920. The exclusionists introduced an initiative that would tighten the restrictions on alien land ownership and close the loopholes in the state's 1913 law. Carefully arranged House Immigration Committee hearings throughout the West Coast in the summer preceding the elections added to the anti-Japanese emotions.[1] Despite Phelan's defeat, the Alien Land Law passed, and anti-Japanese forces basked in success.

For a brief time both the pro- and anti-Japanese forces in the state were well organized. Colonel John P. Irish's American Committee of Justice, vocal if not large, worked for the Japanese cause, while the opposition reorganized in September of 1920 as the Japanese Exclusion League. Irish was motivated by principle and politics. A retired farmer from the Sacramento delta area, he liked his Japanese neighbors and went on speaking tours on their behalf. Although Irish did not know Gulick personally, he found his work inspiring.[2]

On the national scene, the drive to protect the nation permanently from masses of unwanted immigrants was also building strength. In December 1920, Congressman Albert Johnson of Washington, chairman of the House Immigration Committee, introduced a bill proposing total suspension of immigration for fourteen months to allow Congress to analyze the postwar situation before drafting new legislation.[3] Johnson's bill, itself a stop-

149

gap solution, attracted some support. Gulick's National Committee for Constructive Immigration Legislation, trying to fight off imminent demise, deemed the bill worthy of discussion and convened a conference at the Broadway Tabernacle in New York City. Hostile feelings quickly became aroused. While Gulick attempted patiently to explain the Johnson bill, one speaker demanded to know if this were a "pro-Japanese meeting in disguise." Gulick defused the attack, which he attributed to McClatchy's propaganda, by carefully explaining the origins, aims, and purposes of the NCCIL. Several other ministers spoke on the subject of immigration, and Gulick added only that he sought to "protect America from contaminating immigration" but at the same time wanted all peoples to be treated fairly.[4] The quota system that the committee advocated had become highly controversial, and Gulick sought to allay fears by emphasizing that he too sought to control the problem of excessive immigration.

Congress was determined to enact strong restrictions on immigration. Since the Johnson bill was temporary, the Senate Committee on Immigration, chaired by Senator William P. Dillingham, changed the method of restriction to the quota system, setting as a base figure five percent of any nationality resident in the United States in 1910. Dillingham's proposed legislation would not affect Japanese immigration, however, for it did not disavow the Gentlemen's Agreement. Although Congress passed the substitute legislation after the Senate reduced the quota to three percent, President Wilson, who favored impartial restriction, killed it with a pocket veto. However, the measure was reintroduced when Warren G. Harding took office, and within a few months the same act was passed with only a few minor changes. Harding signed the Dillingham bill into law in May 1921. A temporary measure, it was to expire on June 30, 1922.[5]

While Congress continued its search for a permanent solution to the immigration issue, Gulick conducted his public information campaign on the universal percentage plan, taking advantage of the media's interest in the controversial subject. The *Annals of the American Academy of Political and Social Science* ran a special issue on immigration, focusing on the Japanese question. Both sides were represented, the exclusionists by their big guns, Phelan, McClatchy, and labor leader Paul Scharrenburg. Those favoring a quota for Japan also had persuasive advocates: Colonel Irish, Kawakami, Doremus Scudder, Baron Gotō Shimpei, a leading Japanese bureaucrat, and Sidney Gulick.

Analyzing several documents, including a report of the California State Board of Control and the west coast hearings of the House Committee on Immigration in his article, Gulick reviewed the usual points of contention—the Gentlemen's Agreement and the unassimilability of the Japanese. Assessing the so-called economic threat they posed to California, he stated that the value of the crops they produced had increased by 479.5% (presumably since they first entered California agriculture). He argued for a moderate policy, but said he saw the handwriting on the wall: "The enactment by Congress of a drastic Japanese exclusion law is to be expected in the near future . . . . It will be obnoxious and humiliating."[6]

Gulick continued his efforts through the NCCIL, attempting to pump life into that moribund operation. Every few months he sent a form letter to members, detailing the progress of legislation and his frequent trips to Washington to confer with the sponsors of his quota system bill, Senator Thomas Sterling and Congressman Welty. He published another pamphlet, *A Permanent Immigration Policy,* which addressed the need for new legislation following Wilson's pocket veto. Clarifying what he felt were basic criteria for effective legislation, Gulick endorsed the Sterling bill, which not only established a quota for all groups but also made all qualified immigrants eligible for citizenship.[7] Such an enlightened measure, however, could not pass. The Dillingham bill was the best Congress would do.

Meanwhile, the fight between Gulick and McClatchy shifted to another forum, as the exclusionists sought to make immigration a foreign policy concern. The total California congressional delegation, Senators Hiram Johnson and Samuel M. Shortridge, together with members from each of the eleven House districts, submitted a brief from McClatchy, representing the Japanese Exclusion League, to Secretary of State Charles Evans Hughes, using as pretext Japan's unpalatable expansionist foreign policy.

The McClatchy brief was a classic exclusionist compendium that included the California legislature's resolutions on exclusion, the Alien Land Law of 1920, a digest of testimony presented to the House Immigration Committee, resolutions of the American Legion and the American Federation of Labor, statements from the *Sacramento Bee,* and McClatchy's own extensive remarks.

The publisher also reprinted the same anti-Japanese articles he had published in the *Bee* in June 1919, which had blasted Gulick. Part of his attack was somewhat novel. He cited Gulick against himself, quoting from a pamphlet the latter had written in 1915, *Hawaii's American-Japanese Problem,* in which Gulick examined the rapid growth of the Japanese population of the islands. Gulick noted in the pamphlet that within a score of years they would dominate the Hawaii electorate. McClatchy remarked that the leading Honolulu Japanese newspaper was concerned that teachers of Japanese students lacked sufficient skills to instruct their students in the English language and American history and civics. Depicting Hawaii as the dread example of Japan's true aims, a colony created by immigration, McClatchy claimed the Japanese-dominated islands were now in danger of "being lost to democracy." Japan had violated the Gentlemen's Agreement, he asserted, since the government alone could determine who was a "laborer" and thus ineligible to immigrate, and he concluded that Gulick's quota would be no solution. Only the five points of the exclusionists' program—cancellation of the Gentlemen's Agreement, exclusion of picture brides, ending of all Asian immigration, barring Asians from citizenship permanently, and denying citizenship to the children of Asian immigrants—would satisfactorily solve the problem.[8]

The American Committee of Justice, the group organized by Colonel Irish to counter the exclusionists, fought back, submitting a counterbrief in the form of a pamphlet, *Japanese Immigration and Colonization.* Charging that McClatchy's brief was "tiresomely repetitious, apparently in the belief that a fiction often enough repeated becomes a fact and proper foundation for national policy," the Justice Committee singled out as the only real questions of substance the Japanese birthrate in California, whether Japan had violated the Gentlemen's Agreement, and the situation regarding Japanese land tenure in the state. Its answers— that the actual Japanese population was a mere two percent of the state's total, and its birthrate not excessive—were meant to appease. Denying charges of violations of the Gentlemen's Agreement and charges that the Japanese were buying all the state's best agricultural land, the pamphlet closed by urging the Senate to recognize that in fact only a minority of Californians supported exclusion.[9] Gulick's assertion was incorrect, but the effect of this pamphlet was minimal anyway as opposition lines hardened.

THE NATIONAL COMMITTEE ON AMERICAN-JAPANESE RELATIONS:

Gulick, meanwhile, formed yet another committee to continue his quest for an equitable immigration law and also to consider the broader question of American-Japanese affairs. The old Commision on Relations with Japan, founded by the FCCCA in 1914, had been broadened two years later and renamed the Commission on Relations with the Orient; in 1921 that body was included in the jurisdiction of the successor to the Commission on Peace and Arbitration, the new Commission on International Justice and Goodwill.[10] As Japan seemed again a focal point of tension, Gulick thought it deserved its own study group, which would have much the same agenda as the old CRJ had had, but would take a more evenhanded approach that advocated urging concessions on both sides. His intentions were reasonable but the formation of the new committee triggered a sharp response from the intelligence agents following him. This new emphasis on Japan appeared to them as renewed evidence of his subversive tendencies.

On February 19, 1921, Gulick invited a dozen men to a dinner meeting where a temporary committee tentatively named the "Committee on Right Relations with Japan" was founded. The program adopted was Gulick's: to promote education and study of that country; to cooperate with groups in the United States and Japan that sought better relations; to publish short pamphlets; and to speak and travel on that behalf. The founders favored a "square deal" for Americans in Japan and Japanese in California, and immigration legislation based on justice and goodwill. This proposal, however, was coupled with a statement requesting Japan to eliminate dual citizenship and supporting China's territorial integrity.[11]

Within a month the committee had been renamed the Committee on American-Japanese Relations and permanent officers chosen: Jacob Gould Schurman as chairman (soon succeeded by George Wickersham), Hamilton Holt vice-chairman, and Gulick, Linley V. Gordon of the WAIFTC, and Charles Levermore of the New York Peace Society as secretaries. Gulick was also on the finance, research, and publicity committees. The platform included the new Asian policy, but went beyond it to broader concerns like the limitation of armaments.[12] Its primary task was to replace animosity with feelings of amity and goodwill between the two countries.[13] By the time the committee went public in June, the platform had been further revised to include a statement opposing "anti-Japanese jingoes." Honorary members were added to the letterhead for prestige, including the reformer Jane Addams, suffragist Carrie Chapman Catt, Reverend Shailer Mathews, and John Mott of the World's Student Christian Federation and the Student Volunteer Movement.[14]

The committee did public relations work to promote Japanese-American friendship and also lobbied politicians on Japan's behalf. In July 1921 the CIJG and the new American-Japanese committee held a joint dinner and reception for visiting members of the Japanese parliament.[15] That fall the group hosted Japanese political and business leaders and prepared replies to anti-Japanese articles in the *New York Herald*.[16] Gulick wrote President Harding to refute the perennial charges that Japan had violated the Gentlemen's Agreement, and he followed the progress of California's 1920 alien land legislation through the State Supreme Court. He also briefed the committee's members on the Washington Arms Conference, which he praised as a key to reducing tensions with Japan. His only concern was that liberals in Japan would have to work to ensure that the agreements were carried out.[17] For the time being the committee's activities remained rather low-key.

TO JAPAN AGAIN:

In September 1921 Gulick took time off from the immigration fight. The Dillingham bill was law, if temporary, and was to expire on June 30, 1922, with the Sterling bill proposed as a replacement. But Congress bypassed the nettlesome issue and extended the original legislation to June 13, 1924.[18] The exclusionists were also quiet due to recurring organizational difficulties. In the spring of 1922 the Japanese Exclusion League ceased to function, and Phelan and McClatchy began to subsidize the whole anti-Japanese movement themselves. Deciding to wait until Congress should take up the immigration matter again before opening a new campaign, they even ignored the Japanese issue in the fall 1922 elections. Since the Supreme Court had rejected Ozawa's petition for citizenship and thereby reaffirmed the "aliens ineligible for citizenship" formula, there was no specific reason to agitate. No general immigration bill was considered prior to the convening of the sixty-eighth Congress, which opened in December of 1923.[19] The Red Scare had abated; Gulick could afford to leave the country.

In mid-1922 the executive committee of the Federal Council decided to send Gulick and Dr. John Finley on a special mission to the churches of the Far East. The trip was broadly financed. Sponsors included Gulick's new American-Japanese Relations Committee, the CIJG, and the American Council of the WAIFTC, for whom Gulick was serving as secretary on Asian affairs. These domestic groups supported the broader issue of improved relations with Japan, even if they were unwilling to risk unpopularity by backing Gulick openly on the immigration issue, which they perceived as too political. Additional encouragement came from a committee of the Kumiai churches of Japan.

Gulick began the trip alone, traveling first to Japan. He used the opportunity to assess whether he wished ever to resume his missionary career. At sixty-two he was not too old to return, and retirement in Japan offered certain attractions. His son Leeds was now a missionary there, and his two youngest were considering making Japan the focus of their careers as well. Although he was surprised and gratified to discover that he had not lost the language, Gulick soon realized how out of touch he was with that world. His heart was in America with the immigration crusade; he could not leave that mission undone. He reluctantly settled his remaining personal affairs and admitted to himself that that chapter had ended.[20]

The trip also provided an opportunity to visit family and friends in Honolulu and Japan. He saw ninety-three-year-old Uncle Orramel and Aunt Julia, and met his sister Hattie in Miyazaki. She accompanied him from Japan to China for a little trip, but died there quite suddenly from pneumonia, a poignant reminder to Sidney of just how hard the missionary life could be.[21]

The venture turned into a solo effort for Gulick when Finley was unable to carry out plans to join him in China, so the itinerary changed accordingly. The planned agenda called for a quick week in Japan and then for travel throughout China with Finley. When the latter cancelled, Gulick spent almost two months in China, two weeks in Korea, and then returned to Japan where he remained until early June of 1923. The purposes of the trip also expanded to suit Gulick's own needs. The original intent was to assure the Asian Christians of American support, to enlist them in a new campaign, the "crusade for a warless world," and to establish a branch of the WAIFTC in China. After accomplishing those tasks, Gulick returned to Japan to work toward improving relations between Japan and America, a task that took longer than he had intended.[22]

Gulick's weeks in Japan became a personal crusade for better understanding between the United States and that nation. He met with the premier, the minister and vice-minister of foreign affairs, navy department officials, and a number of influential businessmen. The Japanese freely exchanged ideas with him, and Gulick relayed current American attitudes toward their country. When high officials enlisted his support, asking his assistance in identifying mistakes they had made in China so that they could correct them, he was even more sympathetic to their cause.[23] Since the passage of the Washington treaties had improved relations, the Japanese found it harder to understand the persistence of anti-Japanese agitation in America. Impressed by a meeting sponsored by the Japan Peace Council, which represented seven internationally minded organizations, Gulick wrote his family: "They say they have done everything that America has asked;

they have stopped the Picture Bride movement; they continue to administer the Gentlemen's Agreement most rigidly; they are not asking for any labor or other immigration to America; they ask only for justice and humanity for their fellow nationals in America."[24]

Gulick's trip to Asia merited attention from the Office of Naval Intelligence. That agency issued weekly reports between 1921 and 1923 on Japanese activities in California, and in these Gulick's name was frequently mentioned. The Honolulu office also reported on Gulick's trip to Japan. At a farewell banquet given for him in Tokyo sponsored by the American-Japanese Relations Committee an agent reported that Viscount Shibusawa Eiichi had proposed a joint high commission to settle the "question of equal treatment for all Japanese living on American soil with that of other nationalities." The agent, who said Gulick spoke at the banquet, gave as his source the *Japanese News*.[25] The naval attaché in Peking also reported on Gulick's activities in China. No particular significance was attached to his trip; he was simply a subject whose activities merited attention.[26]

On his way home Gulick stopped in Hawaii, where Military Intelligence continued its surveillance. Agent Major P. H. Bagby informed Washington of the arrival of the "prominent pro-Japanese propagandist," after a seven-month trip to the Orient. Gulick spoke to the Hawaiian Evangelical Society, urging it to pass a resolution calling for the naturalization of all eligible resident aliens. Bagby noted with some pride that his agents had managed to have the proposal tabled. It would have been most undesirable if Gulick had returned to the mainland with such a declaration as ammunition in his fight for equal treatment for the Japanese, he noted. Bagby was convinced that Gulick had come to Hawaii "to perform some mission in behalf of the Japanese," figuring that he could easily take advantage of the "ignorance of local organizations with the national aspects of the Japanese problem."[27] That Gulick had family in Hawaii and invariably stopped there on his trips to and from the Orient was irrelevant or unknown to the agent.

When Gulick returned to the United States his vivid impressions of his trip became the basis for a new book, *Winning the Far*

East (1923). In it he discussed the state of Christianity in each of the countries he had visited, and he concluded by calling on all nations to create institutions that would establish and maintain justice, honor, security and fair economic opportunities.[28] He again promoted the quota system of immigration. The trip had convinced him that it was essential to understand Japan's foreign policy, and that it was equally urgent to prevent the passage of any additional anti-Japanese legislation in the United States.

The American-Japanese Relations Committee circulated the book and some pamphlets Gulick wrote about the Japanese in Hawaii and the United States, and Chairman George Wickersham attempted to raise funds for the work ahead. The committee remained quiescent while its guiding spirit traveled abroad and the hostility toward the Japanese in America lay dormant.[29]

A FIGHT TO THE FINISH:

Gulick returned to America determined to secure justice for the Japanese. He settled into larger quarters in New York, and also into a pleasanter lifestyle, for Cara's task of providing a home for their offspring studying at Oberlin College was completed and she now joined him there. The Asian respite was a needed one for Sidney, as the battle for a permanent immigration law was about to commence.

The exclusionists' campaign opened on December 5, 1923, in the House of Representatives, just three months after Gulick returned to the United States. Albert Johnson of Washington and John E. Raker of California introduced a bill entitled the National Origins Act that established a 2 percent quota based on the "Nordic" census of 1890; it specifically excluded "aliens ineligible for citizenship." Although Secretary Hughes personally protested Japanese exclusion, Johnson modified the bill only slightly, resubmitting it March 24 with the Japanese exclusion provision intact. The measure passed by an overwhelming majority on April 3, 1924.[30] The Johnson bill abrogated the Gentlemen's Agreement.

The advocates of equal treatment had not been silent during this event, just unable to stem the tide. In early February 1924 Gulick alerted members of the National Committee on American-

Japanese Relations to the pending struggle. Chairman Wickersham issued a strongly worded statement to the press on February 26. Declaring the exclusion clause "discriminatory and humiliating legislation which will be resented by Japan as a gratuitous act of unfriendly character," Wickersham announced he was sending a letter to each congressman and senator urging that if a change in the Gentlemen's Agreement were needed, the proper method would be through negotiations at the executive level. He reminded them that immigration statistics showed that exclusion was not only unnecessary but also contravened the existing treaty with Japan and the Gentlemen's Agreement.[31] The House ignored his appeal, but the Senate was somewhat more open to such reasoning; it generally evinced more concern about the international implications of domestic legislation. The exclusionist leaders made a final pitch. McClatchy, Phelan, and California Attorney General Ulysses S. Webb gave long presentations before the Senate Committee on Immigration. They trotted out all the old racist shibboleths: Japan's alleged violations of the Gentlemen's Agreement; the immigrants' enormous birthrate; their lack of assimilability; and the speed with which they were acquiring California's choicest land. McClatchy charged that the brave state of California had for twenty years made "the fight of the nation" against the incoming of alien races whose "peaceful penetration must in time inevitably provoke international trouble across the Pacific."[32] And, once again, the exclusionists dragged Gulick's name through the mud. Phelan asserted that the man generally regarded as the author of the quota system was a paid Japanese propagandist. And once again the Federal Council of Churches sent a telegram of denial.[33]

Gulick appeared after McClatchy, once again on the defensive. Speaking on behalf of the groups he represented, he refuted McClatchy's allegations about Japanese land ownership and immigration, and again proposed his favorite solution, "a constructive program" based on an equitable quota for all nations, and naturalization to all who qualified—in short, no discrimination. Gulick pleaded with the committee to listen to the message of one who had lived among Asians for a quarter of a century: they were basically no different from Westerners, he contended. While he did not wish to see them overrun the United States, he saw no reason why the two peoples could not live harmoniously with one another.[34]

The Senate inclined more toward Gulick's view of the matter than McClatchy's. California's senior senator, Hiram Johnson, was absent from the debate, stumping the country for the Republican presidential nomination, and the junior senator, Samuel Shortridge, proved so ineffectual that when he rose to denounce the Japanese his audience departed. Senator LeBaron Colt of Rhode Island proposed a bill with a quota and the Gentlemen's Agreement intact, reserving the diplomatic issue to be settled by the State Department. As the debate continued it appeared that a majority preferred that approach, including Secretary Hughes.[35]

Then came the event that changed everything. Hughes, responding to allegations that the Gentlemen's Agreement was a secret document, decided to ask Japanese Ambassador Hanihara Masanao to write a letter detailing the arrangement. Hanihara responded on April 10, and Hughes presented the reply to the Senate. The ambassador first summarized the workings of the agreement and expressed Japan's willingness to renegotiate it if necessary. Then he turned to the pending legislation, noting that Japan was interested merely in preserving its right to respect and equality of treatment. Pointing out that the quota would allow only 146 Japanese a year to emigrate, Hanihara stated that the rejection of such a reasonable proposal would cast aspersions on the Japanese government's good faith. In a phrase that had enormous and unforeseen results, he concluded that enactment of exclusion would have "grave consequences" for relations between the two countries.[36]

Hughes did not establish that in fact he had solicited the letter, and to many observers, including Phelan, Hanihara's statements appeared reasonable enough. But one man, Henry Cabot Lodge, took exception and used the unfortunate phrase as a lever to wedge exclusion into the law. Lodge, senior senator from Massachusetts and chairman of the Senate Foreign Relations Committee, was a wily old exclusionist who looked to this issue as his final coup. Calling the "grave consequences" phrase a "veiled threat," he charged that the letter was improperly sent to begin with since an ambassador had no business discussing domestic legislation with Congress. Lodge "turned the discussion into a stampede" in an action Roger Daniels has correctly described as "wanton."[37]

Gulick's committee was frantic. It had already published a last-minute pamphlet, *Should Congress Enact the Japanese Exclusion Section?*, which spelled out reasons why the Senate should oppose the provision. When Hanihara's letter was published and Lodge's strategy became clear, Gulick and Wickersham urged the committee to write their congressmen and to request a provision be added to the bill asking the State Department and Japan to confer. They also sought to delay the date of effectiveness of the bill, and if all else failed, planned to urge President Coolidge to veto it.[38]

But the vote was overwhelming, seventy-six to two for exclusion. Lodge was too influential and Hughes's strategy too inept. The secretary's attempt to use the Japanese ambassador to influence the passage of domestic legislation was a perilous course at best, and his submission of the Hanihara letter to the Senate with no explanation as to its origin was needless. In fact, the ambassador's letter damaged the cause in several ways, for it reminded the senators how the Gentlemen's Agreement worked. The Japanese government had not violated it; the agreement contained a loophole quite unintended by its negotiator, Theodore Roosevelt. No one at the time foresaw the emigration, quite legal, of the picture brides, and it was they and their offspring who so outraged the Californians. Hughes and Hanihara, in fact, became "the unwitting accomplices of the exclusionists."[39]

The National Committee on American-Japanese Relations met again in late May to confer on last-ditch action. The group considered asking the president to veto the bill but decided against that course, which would have been futile anyway, considering Coolidge's lack of political courage and the upcoming elections. Instead, they decided to urge a revised policy: Japan should be admitted to the quota system in 1927; qualified Issei should be naturalized; Japan should be urged to end dual citizenship; and the two countries should be allowed to maintain the status quo regarding naval bases on the coasts and the Pacific islands.[40] But it was too late. The National Origins Act, signed by

Coolidge with ostensible "regret" about the exclusion clause, became law on July 1, 1924.

THE IMMEDIATE AFTERMATH:

Passage of Japanese exclusion brought some sharp responses.
Japanese ambassador Hanihara and American ambassador to Japan, Cyrus E. Woods, both resigned in protest. Woods called the
act an "international disaster of the first magnitude" for American
diplomacy, for business, and for "the effective work of our American churches in Japan."[41] The Japanese government lodged a
formal complaint against the law as discriminatory on the basis of
race and a violation of the treaty of amity and commerce.[42] Much
of the Japanese press went wild with outrage; one paper even
insisted that American missionaries go home. There were prayer
meetings, boycotts, demonstrations, and a suicide in front of the
American Embassy. The day the law went into effect, July 1,
1924, became a day of national humiliation in Japan.[43]

Reaction in the United States varied according to region.
While most of the West Coast was pleased and Phelan was jubi-
lant, the rest of the country was more concerned about the consequences and regarded the Senate's actions as rash. The *New York
Times* said the action showed "shocking disregard of the feelings
of the Japanese," and it feared the law would inflame Japanese
hatred of the United States.[44] Other newspapers echoed that sentiment. According to a survey by the *Christian Science Monitor*
forty out of forty-four newspapers east of Chicago criticized the
action.[45] The major Protestant denominations issued highly critical statements, and a host of religious and professional organizations joined them, including the American Board of Commissioners for Foreign Missions, the YWCA, the World Peace Foundation, and the National Chamber of Commerce. The Church Peace
Union and the WAIFTC added their voices to the cries of protest.[46] The Federal Council called it a "needless and wanton act"
and warned that the consequences would slowly appear in succeeding decades.[47] Cables crossed the Pacific expressing regret.
One was signed by a group of prominent New York business and
professional men, another by thirty heads or presidents emeriti of
leading American universities and colleges.[48]

Gulick took a hard line publicly against the bill, calling it a "wanton affront to Japan."[49] But in letters to his sons he downplayed its significance. To Sidney, Jr., who was in Japan teaching music, he pointed out that the tension over the bill's passage had been worsened by "Japanese misunderstanding and misinterpretation as well as similar blunders in the U.S." The Japanese had taken the whole matter much more "tragically" than was necessary or even logical. They had, he felt, "given way to emotionalism," while the Senate "gave way to bad temper and to politics." He hoped that Japan would not erupt again when Coolidge signed the bill, for "the more the Japanese rage, the more difficult it will be to straighten things out and the more will Americans think their exclusion was wise."[50] To his missionary son Leeds he reported that the bill on the whole was fairly satisfactory, Japanese exclusion notwithstanding. He blamed the Senate for the manner of its action rather than the substance, for on balance he favored a quota approach. The Gentlemen's Agreement should have been rescinded diplomatically rather than by means of domestic legislation.[51] A small quota for Japan would have allowed wives and children entry, while still excluding laborers.

Clearly Gulick did not consider the matter ended. He felt that Congress would come to its senses after a while and undo the mistake of excluding Japanese, and he urged his Japanese friends to remain calm. With regret and deliberation he prepared to work to turn things around, little dreaming that the quota system and Japanese exclusion would remain the law of the land until 1952.

PICKING UP THE PIECES:

In his initial attempts to put the best face possible on the situation, Gulick underestimated the devastating effects of the legislation upon subsequent Japanese-American relations. Probably the single act most damaging to goodwill between the countries, it stimulated the growth of Japanese militarism. As time passed Gulick perceived this, but in the immediate aftermath of the passage of the bill, he decided to let the dust settle and then to begin a slow and careful campaign to change the law.

One of the first actions the National Committee on American-Japanese Relations took was to circulate a pamphlet written by the missionary William Axling, *Japan Wonders Why*.[52] Axling pointed out the destructive effect exclusion had had on the liberal movement in Japan, and attempted to explain the shock felt there. How could a country that, on one hand, had been so generous with aid after the 1923 Kanto earthquake, be now so insensitive, he asked, not recognizing in fact how typically American such behavior was. Axling urged including Japan in the quota system and providing for naturalization of the Issei. But only those already converted to the cause read his words.

Although Gulick would have liked to reopen the question and press for different legislation, he took care not to act precipitously. He wrote Ray Lyman Wilbur asking his support for a new "Committee of One Thousand" whose purpose would be to express the outrage of America's leading citizens over the exclusion bill. Nothing could be done for the present, he admitted, but he felt that something should to done to "remove the sting" from America's actions; advocates of better relations with Japan had to be organized for that cause.[53] He got no response to that, but the Federal Council published a pamphlet, *Reestablishment of Right Relations Between America and Japan*, in which Gulick explained Japan's shocked reaction. The situation was dangerous, he warned, and goodwill had to be restored. However, Japan must accept America's need to restrict immigration. A quota for Japan must come some day, and the law should be changed to provide for naturalization for the Issei. He concluded that "discriminatory legislation is not in accord with American ideals."[54]

In these days of anticlimax the National Committee on American-Japanese Relations continued a tepid existence. Gulick used the group to sponsor a "quiet educational campaign" to improve relations between the two countries in the wake of the immigration debacle. A leaflet printed in 1926, *What Can I Do To Help Reestablish Right Relations with Japan?*, suggested that members try to urge civic, religious, and educational groups to study and discuss the Japanese question. The group promoted formation of a "Committee of Five Thousand" to carry on the program, but subscribing entailed neither contributions nor dues, only offering one's name. Gulick also suggested keeping interest alive through debates about exclusion or discussion of pertinent books. He recommended his own books, several of Kawakami's, and Raymond Leslie Buell's book on Japanese immigration.[55] The CIJG, of which Gulick was secretary, also studied relations between the United States and Japan, but it too was discreet about raising the sensitive immigration issue.

For two months in 1927 Gulick toured the West Coast, attending, some religious conferences and checking if the time was right for a renewed campaign against exclusion. Reporting to the Commission on Relations with the Orient that the situation appeared calm and anti-Japanese agitation had ceased, he stated, "It is generally assumed that the problems have been permanently settled by the Alien Land Laws and the Exclusion Law of 1924." Prejudice against Japanese was simply dormant, not dead; no real opposition would surface, however, unless the Japanese tried to better their status. Although he felt the country as a whole believed exclusion unnecessary, the sentiment that gave rise to it was still alive in California. That state's Japanese farmers suffered from the general economic situation, overproduction, and only secondarily from the easily evaded Alien Land Laws, but as few of them prospered, the white community ignored their existence.[56] During his trip along the coast, many people asked Gulick if the Federal Council and the American-Japanese Relations Committee advocated introduction of new legislation placing Japan on the quota system. He denied such intentions but admitted that both groups would continue their educational programs.[57]

Gulick himself was not optimistic as America's Japanese faced a "discouraging situation with dogged determination to make the best of it, but with little hope of seeing any change made in the present laws either by California or national legislators." The exclusion provision affected Japanese Americans only in matters of "race dignity and honor." Although humiliated, they did not discuss their plight and would certainly do nothing to change it. Gulick deplored their loss of faith in "what they had supposed to be the American sense of fair play and freedom from race prejudice," and he discounted the possibility that American-Japanese relations had been permanently damaged by the Alien Land Laws or the exclusion provision of the National Origins Act. America, he concluded, was hurt more than Japan, for its reputation for just, honest, and courteous treatment of all peoples had been undermined.[58] Gulick published a summary of his report in the journal *Trans-Pacific*.[59]

The National Committee had hoped that in 1927 new immigraton legislation might be introduced, placing Japan on the quota system. Gulick's study convinced the group, however, that the time was not yet ripe, and they ceased operations. Perhaps Gulick missed an opportunity to persuade America; he felt later that sentiment from 1924 to 1929 generally supported the idea that exclusion had been a mistake. He was most likely in error. However, Japan itself killed any hopes for repeal by its actions in 1931. The Manchurian crisis and the Sino-Japanese War put an effective end to attempts to revise immigration legislation until after World War II. Once again, Japanese Americans were held hostage to Japan's good behavior.

10

CHRISTIAN INTERNATIONALISM
IN THE TWENTIES

Throughout the fight against Japanese exclusion Gulick was also involved in the postwar peace movement. To him the two subjects were deeply intertwined. A satisfactory solution to the immigration question would improve relations with Japan and hence improve conditions for a lasting peace between the two nations. But he also sought peace through other approaches. He shared the concerns of many churchmen who, disillusioned by the experience of the First World War, hoped to find alternative methods of conflict resolution. There was no longer any excuse for war; methods of avoiding bloodshed had to be identified and promoted, for peace had become, in Charles DeBenedetti's words, the "necessary reform."[1] Gulick participated in all the endeavors the Christian internationalists upheld as means of promoting world peace: disarmament, international organization, a world court, and the outlawry of war. In addition, he even organized and promoted a cause of his own creation, the involvement of children in the movement for international peace. Working through his positions as executive secretary to the FCCCA's Commission on International Justice and Goodwill and the Commission on Relations with the Orient, Gulick sought to bring about a world of equity where all peoples could live together in harmony. In order to achieve that lofty goal, the first objective

167

was the reduction and eventual elimination of armaments, for the churchmen still believed that weapons systems were a fundamental cause of war.

THE CHURCHES AND THE DISARMAMENT MOVEMENT:

The Protestant churches of America thus became a powerful force pushing the indifferent administration of Warren G. Harding toward naval disarmament. As a first step, the Church Peace Union's Committee on Armaments, of which Gulick was a member, and the WAIFTC held a Congress on Reduction of Armaments. Meeting May 17 to 19, 1921, in Chicago, four hundred official delegates from twenty states, representing twenty denominations, discussed the topic. The Federal Council issued a formal statement calling for arms reduction; it was joined by the National Catholic Welfare, the Central Conference of Rabbis, and the United Synagogues.

This gathering inaugurated a nationwide drive similar to that launched on behalf of the League of Nations. The churches circulated pamphlets and petitions throughout the country as a means of galvanizing public opinion. This pro-disarmament sentiment was then directed toward the Senate and President Harding. The FCCCA proclaimed June 5, 1921, as Disarmament Sunday, and the churches and CIJG members sent resolutions to Washington calling for a conference of nations. Their efforts produced results. Twenty thousand clergy signed petitions presented to Harding. On July 10 the reluctant president took the first steps, inviting four nations to convene, and the other Pacific powers were soon included. Only Japan was an unenthusiastic participant in the endeavor.[2]

By fall the Federal Council effort had swung into high gear. The organization began an educational campaign as a means of stimulating and informing congregations on the topic. Constituent churches were asked to set aside November 6 as a special day of prayer, and articles on arms limitation were published in religious journals, as pro-disarmament sentiment quickly developed into a groundswell of public opinion. The Associated Press, prompted by Arthur Hungerford, who had been with the *Baltimore Sun* before joining the Federal Council, devoted many articles to the churches' interest in peace. Gulick's own efforts were tireless. He authored a new pamphlet, *The Church and a Warless World;* 120 thousand copies of it were circulated to church members, and copies sent to the secretary of state and the president. Gulick also began work on a book, *The Christian Crusade for a Warless World*, and the CPU gave considerable financial support to his publication efforts.

The Federal Council proclaimed Armistice Day, 1921, a day of "solemn dedication to the cause of peace." Gulick's commission, the CIJG, called not only for arms reduction, but for a Christian settlement of the Far Eastern problem, equal treatment of all peoples, and a "world combination of nations for world peace," international law, and a warless world. The churches also advocated nondiscriminatory immigration laws, an end to the building of naval bases in Hawaii and the Pacific, and even consideration of a plan to free France from payment of war debts.[3]

Gulick was especially anxious that the arms limitation conference, which met in Washington from November 12, 1921, to February 6, 1922, negotiate a settlement of the problems of the Far East. Great Britain was still bound to Japan by the alliance of 1902 which concerned not only the United States but also the British Commonwealth. The United States opposed what to it was unprincipled Japanese expansionism on the Asian mainland, but it was rigid on the subject of immigration, which remained a continuing irritant between the two nations. Gulick hoped the delegates would address all these issues. Prior to the opening of the conference he wrote a confidential memo to the FCCCA's executive committee on behalf of the CIJG, the American Council of the WAIFTC, and the National Committee on American-Japanese Relations. He pointed out that the meeting would provide an ideal opportunity to announce a new and equitable immigration policy. It would also be an appropriate occasion for the United States to grant China a restoration of rights denied by the unequal treaties as well as early withdrawal of all foreign troops. He also urged that Japan's special problems of overpopulation and inadequate resources be recognized and the country be helped to secure legitimate industrial and commercial expansion without military control.[4] The council chose not to urge these additional objectives, however.

As the conference drew to a close, its achievements were applauded by the Federal Council, which prided itself on having helped to originate the gathering. Another minor coup for the council was the opening of the sessions with prayer, a nice symbolic touch, the inspiration of Macfarland. The council's rallying of grass roots support had been spectacular. It claimed that the 12.5 million signatures received by the State Department had been the result of the council's efforts. Secretary Hughes received a telegram congratulating him on his part in the conference; the council reminded him that 24 million Protestants in 150 thousand member churches of the FCCCA endorsed the arms reduction program and desired speedy ratification of the treaties. To the CIJG the conclusion of the meetings was just the beginning of a movement for the eventual abolition of war; Gulick urged the membership to work for the ratification of the Washington treaties and to continue their study of international relations. As DeBenedetti has written, "The Federal Council had renewed its commitment to a formal liberal world order."[5]

Gulick was particularly interested in the impact of the Washington Conference on Japan. He noted that opening the sessions with prayer had impressed the Japanese, who were convinced that they were "in the presence of Christian America." After the conference Japan removed its troops from Shantung and Siberia, which pleased him since it confirmed his optimistic expectations. Although public opinion in both the United States and Japan was initially opposed to the Four Power Treaty, which replaced the Anglo-Japanese alliance with a far weaker agreement, Gulick urged its ratification because he saw it as a way to reduce tensions.[6] Elihu Root, former secretary of state and a delegate to the conference, expressed his appreciation of the churches' support for ratification of the disarmament treaties.[7]

The churches' campaign for ratification helped ensure support for the treaties in the Senate. All three passed, although the vote on the controversial Four Power Treaty was close. The results of the Washington Conference strengthened Japan's liberals although it displeased the navy; it did, however, cause a decline in tensions between Washington and Tokyo. The council, highly optimistic for the future of relations between the two countries, chose this time to send Gulick on his nearly year-long goodwill trip to Asia.

The churches saw the conference as a first step on the road to permanent peace. Gulick described their goal in *The Christian Crusade for a Warless World* (1923), which was published before he departed. Intended as a manual for church courses or discussions on the peace movement, it stressed the international aims of the Federal Council. These had earlier been formulated in a statement, "Declaration of Ideals and Policy Looking Toward a Warless World," passed by the FCCCA executive committee in December of 1921. The "Ideals" emphasized the need for justice, unselfishness, and goodwill in international politics. Although the document did not mention the League of Nations by name, it called for a permanent association of nations to promote world peace, and in a bold step away from the churches' prewar position, denounced war as un-Christian. Gulick wrote that Christians should seek to establish the Kingdom of God on Earth through methods of international righteousness and helpfulness. He spelled out how this could be done: through philanthropy, exchange of students, and fair and generous relations in politics and trade. Racial and economic factors remained potent threats to world peace, he wrote: "The danger of war today lies in the amazing economic and industrial expansion of modern nations. And inextricably intertwined in this economic competition is the clash of race prejudice and race pride."[8] He deplored both racial discrimination and the rise of militarism and advocated working for peace through the League of Nations, arbitration, and the World Court. The book, as John Hutchinson has noted, came to the same utopian conclusions about the imminence of peace as most prewar tracts had. A warless world would someday come about when people had studied the folly of war and the need for international understanding: "Over all [would be] the spirit of a kindly and loving religion, which together with education has been responsible in bringing this fair world into being."[9] Gulick's thought retained its idealistic flavor, even though the plans he promoted for achieving peace were tied to a realistic concern with ways to achieve that goal.

Gulick's involvement in the movement for naval disarmament

brought him once again to the attention of Military Intelligence, now concerned about a possible pacifist movement in the country. Agent Major W. H. Cowles submitted a sheaf of papers to the State Department, including a proposed Federal Council press release comparing army and navy expenditures for select years. The council generally considered such expenditures proof of militarism, a subject it opposed with vigor. However, a commotion quickly developed over the press release. The Federal Council planned to issue the statement—which listed American expenditures for armaments and gave a breakdown on what proportion of one's taxes paid for past wars and what proportion paid for preparation for future wars—just prior to Armistice Day. The State Department learned of the statement from Military Intelligence, whose agents immediately (and, as it turned out, incorrectly) assumed that Gulick was the source. Cowles referred to him as "the well-known Japanese propagandist."[10] The State Department copy of the press release was annotated with comments that Gulick was "suspected to be a paid Japanese agent." Cowles had attached to it a page of corrections of the figures and a copy of Gulick's pamphlet, *The Church and a Warless World.*[11]

When the State Department contacted the Navy Department, attempting to verify the totals the Federal Council had used, the former learned that Gulick had also tried to confirm the figures there. Although the statement seemed harmless, if somewhat erroneous, Edwin Denby, the secretary of the navy, was outraged by Gulick's action. He wrote Secretary of State Hughes that Gulick not only erred, but that he had neglected such information in the public record as past legislative acts or the congressional committee hearing data. His failure to use primary instead of secondary sources was "deplorable under any circumstances, . . . [especially] when material is prepared with a view to influencing public opinion in reference to a proposed action . . . regarding the national welfare." The official then excoriated Gulick's research methods.[12] These objections, blown out of proportion, quickly reached the Federal Council, which cancelled the offending release upon Hughes's request.

Macfarland once again came to Gulick's rescue. He wrote Hughes that the figures in the press release had been prepared by

Arthur Hungerford and only verified by Gulick, who found their source in other published material. The former missionary, he noted, had written fairly about Japan, and had in his recent writings even urged the overthrow of Japanese militarists and emphasized the necessity of protecting China from Japan. He enclosed Gulick's latest pamphlet, *Far Eastern Problems and the Conference on Limitation of Armaments*, which proposed a seven-point program to solve East Asian problems. One of the points advocated the replacement of Japanese militarism by liberalism.[13] With the offending press release killed, the incident ended. Gulick's name and the causes he championed had become linked to Japanese propaganda in the minds of the State Department and Military Intelligence. The episode also demonstrated how notorious Gulick had become, and how sensitive intelligence agencies were to anything connected with disarmament or pacifism.

The Office of Naval Intelligence reached a similar conclusion about Gulick. It reported to the State Department on the activities of a Japanese man in the United States who was considered part of the Japanese propaganda machine. Among the man's suspicious activities was a close association with Gulick, the "well-known Japanese propagandist in America."[14] Gulick could not escape the label.

THE WORLD COURT AND THE OUTLAWRY OF WAR:

During the decade following his return from China and Japan Gulick devoted most of his energies to working for peace. This occasionally involved foreign travel and in 1925, he journeyed to Stockholm as a delegate from the American churches to the Universal Christian Conference on Life and Work. There he addressed the conference, emphasizing that "if the churches don't destroy war, war will destroy the churches."[15] He condemned conflict and called for its outlawry; except in cases of self-defense, making war was a sin against God. After his address he traveled to Geneva to attend the Assembly of the League of Nations, a cause he still supported. Japanese delegates Nitobe Inazō and Viscount Ishii met him there, and he spoke to their delegation about the situation of Asians in the United States.[16]

But Gulick's work was primarily at home, where he became involved in the major battles of the so-called conservative wing of the peace movement in the 1920s, the first of which was the campaign for the World Court. The Federal Council saw the court as a major institution for the promotion of peace, and it sponsored a campaign similar to the one for the Washington Conference, hoping to gain America's entry. The leadership again circulated petitions and met with President Harding, Secretary Hughes, and Vice-President Coolidge. Every senator was personally contacted by a representative, and Bishop Charles H. Brent, vice-chairman of the CIJG, testified before the Senate Foreign Relations Committee.[17] The battle began in 1923 and went through several phases. The CIJG worked with the CPU and the WAIFTC, distributing pamphlets on the court and promoting a World Court Week. The groups sent the Senate and administration a memorial of support containing the signatures of several hundred religious leaders.[18] Both political parties endorsed the court in the elections of 1924, but the isolationists, convinced the court was just a first step into the hated League of Nations, blocked it, using the delaying tactics they had so perfected on the league fight.[19] The pro–World Court push was as surprising and humiliating a failure as the defeat of the league had been. When the effort came to naught, the Christian internationalists temporarily abandoned it.

In 1925 the churches tried again. Working with women's clubs and peace groups, they mounted a third major effort. Gulick was involved with both the WAIFTC as its secretary for oriental relations and as the CIJG's secretary. Again those organizations sent letters urging members to lobby. Gulick met with Coolidge and later addressed the House Committee on Foreign Affairs, advocating that the nation join the court while observing the restrictions supported by Presidents Harding and Coolidge. Like most court advocates, Gulick saw it as a universal panacea that would save the world from war. He overlooked structural limitations that would have prevented it from hearing any but minor affairs. He called its work "a step in the direction of establishing the Kingdom of God among men."[20] But again the churches proved unsuccessful. The court fight stirred the isolationists to even greater tides of denunciation, and they tacked new reservations onto the hapless measure. When the European members expressed doubts about accepting American restrictions precluding the possibility of any compromise, the Coolidge administration dropped the stalemated proposal.[21]

Christian internationalists next turned to an even broader scheme, the outlawry of war. This movement was the brainchild of Chicago attorney Salmon O. Levinson, who in 1918 discovered that war was not against international law. Astonished, he sought to remedy that defect. Although the notion of making war a crime was simple and popular among many groups, its advocates differed on whether the League of Nations could provide some enforcement machinery more effective than an aroused world opinion. The Federal Council of Churches was an early supporter. The idea was included in its 1921 list of ideals, "Looking Toward a Warless World." The council favored the particular plan for outlawing war endorsed by Senator William E. Borah, which lacked any provisions for enforcement; the lack of a resort to force, even in maintaining peace, appealed to the leadership. This idealistic version fit in well with the churches' objectives for a ten-year peace crusade.[22] In 1921, the statement of ideals had been transmitted to the State Department along with an endorsement of the Washington Conference and the World Court, but outlawry was sidelined while the court campaign was under way.[23] The council formally adopted the outlawry of war campaign in 1924, hoping to link it to a renewed World Court fight and support for eventual membership in the League of Nations.

Gulick was involved in the outlawry campaign from the outset. His 1923 book, *The Christian Crusade for a Warless World*, provided one rationale for the movement, and he continued to support it in speeches and letters to peace societies. When the Geneva Protocol outlawing war in Europe was proposed to the League of Nations, Gulick called the CIJG together to discuss it. The commission voted to send copies to all Federal Council pastors. Gulick and the leaders of the council called on the churches to observe Armistice Day, November 11, 1924, by discussing the horrors of war and mobilizing sentiment for a warless world. They issued a pamphlet to guide discussions planned for the holiday, and in it they encouraged church classes to study the Levinson-Borah plan.[24] Gulick wrote another pamphlet on peace education in the churches and helped determine the FCCCA's policy on disarmament. The council did not favor unilateral disarmament but yet, as Gulick wrote his son Leeds, its support for arms limitation caused it to be labeled both pacifist and militarist by its ideologically diverse opponents.[25]

Needing some outside impetus for success, the campaign to outlaw war limped along throughout 1926. The Nexus Committee held a meeting to increase support. It invited James T. Shotwell to speak on the issue for the Carnegie Endowment for International Peace. Shotwell was one of the chief advocates of the abolition of war as an instrument of national policy. His address was followed by one from Gulick, who presented a program calling for church support for the World Court, for arbitration treaties, and for world peace. The three constituent groups of the Nexus Committee, the CPU, the WAIFTC, and the Federal Council, endorsed his proposal. In an article in *Christian Century* Gulick elaborated on the plan. He explained that the churches advocated a three-part world peace program—outlawing war by promoting arbitration of disputes, gaining pledges from the nations to refrain from war, and defining an aggressor as one who refused to arbitrate. Those actions would make war illegal, he believed, and an international court of justice could somehow enforce it.[26]

Such vague principles were not enough to prompt legislative action, however, and the outlawry plan might well have drifted into oblivion. But in March 1927, Shotwell provided the necessary impetus. He helped French Foreign Minister Aristide Briand draft a message calling for a bilateral pact of perpetual friendship that would set a precedent for outlawing war. Although the Coolidge administration was extremely indifferent to the idea, the American public quickly became enthusiastic.[27] The Federal Council drafted a confidential memorandum calling the proposal a "rare opportunity" to examine the peaceful settlement of disputes, and a month later it adopted a statement supporting the plan as "a more immediate goal than disarmament." The confidential memorandum provided local churches with a form for petitioning Congress to adopt such a treaty, and the authors suggested Armistice Week as an appropriate time to collect signatures. The failure of the 1927 Geneva conference to achieve a limitation on cruisers provided further incentive to adopt the Briand proposal. The memo even spelled out a daily program of activities for the churches during Armistice Week, culminating on November 11 with a two-minute period of silence and a community mass meeting.[28] The churches were mobilizing for peace. The Federal Council passed a formal resolution of endorsement on May 22.

The plan had wide appeal, and the council believed that world opinion would be an effective lever to compel compliance. Although the FCCCA had lobbied diligently to secure American membership in the League of Nations, that particular brand of collective security had lost the support of many churchmen as the twenties progressed. Gulick remained a steadfast, if solitary, adherent. The council's resolution marked the beginning of a bandwagon for the Briand proposal; only the day before, Charles Lindbergh had successfully flown across the Atlantic, landing just outside Paris, and an outpouring of pro-French sentiment added to the growing lobby in favor of outlawing war. Briand himself proposed the wording for a suggested treaty and presented it to the American ambassador on June 20, 1927, touching off a huge publicity campaign. Organizing in early November, Shotwell, Wickersham, President Nicholas Murray Butler of Columbia University, and Gulick galvanized the peace activists to work for the project. On November 10 Senator Borah was scheduled to make a speech before the Federal Council proposing a multipower outlawry pact; although he was forced to cancel it, he publicized his intentions in a message to Gulick which was published in the *New York Times*.[29] The Federal Council leaders petitioned President Coolidge, and public opinion provided incontestible support for the French offer. Although some advocates were more interested in naval disarmament, others were enlisted to back Briand's proposal. Gulick solicited personal letters of support from influential people to national leaders. The Federal Council mailed a flyer urging the Senate and president to support the treaty; church members were asked to sign petitions and return them to the council by the end of April 1928.[30] It took almost that long for the administration even to answer Briand, and when it did, it advocated broadening the bilateral pact the French foreign minister had suggested.

Secretary of State Frank B. Kellogg was responsible for substituting a multilateral treaty in place of the bilateral Franco-American pact. Hoping that extending the outlawry idea to the whole world would kill the dangerous notion of a French defense treaty, Kellogg believed he had found a formula to neutralize that idea. The French tried desperately to recast the motion, but Kellogg's idealistic gesture proved irresistible to world opinion. Fifteen nations signed the pact August 27, 1928, and by December it had reached the Senate floor, complete with the inevitable reservations regarding the necessity of congressional approval before any action. The Federal Council worked throughout the year building public support for the treaty, and had increased pressure in the autumn of 1928. As the campaign reached high gear, the CIJG published a four-week study course to brief the populace on the pact's history, contents, and meaning.[31] The peace advocates formed a grand alliance for ratification. On December 17, 1928, the FCCCA presented the White House with petitions signed by 185,333 members of its constituent churches. One senator read into the *Congressional Record* a letter of December 17 from Gulick describing the effort in terms of the number of signatures per state.[32] These petitions took their place among the thousands of letters and appeals urging the pact's approval.

Gulick also published an article, "The Meaning of the Peace Pact," which stressed that the pact's significance would depend on how serious people and their governments were in desiring to end war. Their sincerity would become evident only after the treaty had been ratified, he wrote. If people truly wanted peace, they would have to strengthen agencies for peaceful settlement of disputes, such as the World Court, and proceed with the codification of international law. The rapidity of disarmament would also be "an acid test of a nation's earnestness," he added. There were other prerequisites for peace, such as the reduction of German reparations and the Allied war debts, the ending of monopolistic control of raw materials, and the achievement of freedom of the seas. However, everything would depend on the "goodwill and

brotherliness of people."[33] Nowhere did Gulick mention the need
for some mechanism of enforcement stronger than public opinion. If only the schools and churches truly promoted brotherhood,
the nations could live in peace. He further demonstrated his support for the pact by attending a WAIFTC-sponsored Armistice
Day rally in New York where Secretary Kellogg spoke for peace.

The Federal Council too was optimistic. "We rejoice in the
Pact of Paris. It ushers in . . . the dawn of a new day. It opens the
door to a new era in human history—an era free from the wrongs
of war, an era glorious with the happiness and prosperity of a
brotherly humanity."[34] The council was not alone in its enthusiasm, and the pact was opposed only by big navy advocates, some
Senate Irreconcilables, and a few critical realists. On January 15,
1929, the Senate ultimately passed it, after much debate, by a vote
of eighty-five to one. It was indeed the "supreme isolationist
achievement," but testimony to the more cynical mentality of the
times was the fact that it was followed by a bill appropriating $270
million to build fifteen cruisers. While most Americans believed
with Gulick that world opinion would keep the peace and if it
failed we were safe behind our ocean moats anyway, the world
was already arming for the next war.[35] Gulick had worked hard to
bring about a treaty outlawing war, but it was a dubious
achievement.

THE DOLL CAMPAIGN:

Gulick believed that internationalism, like prejudice, could be
taught, and that the best place to start was with children. If the
nation's youth could learn tolerance and understanding of other
countries, perhaps then they would be less likely to fight as adults.
A simple notion, yet the idea had a certain appeal. Gulick persuaded the CIJG to hire two additional secretaries, Mrs. Jeannette
Emrich and Walter W. Van Kirk, with whose services in 1926 he
organized the Committee on World Friendship among Children.
The new group was chaired by the well-known former ambassador to Great Britain Alanson B. Houghton, but its guiding genius
was Gulick.[36]

The commission's first project, testimony to Gulick's influence, was Japan. He planned to teach American children about Hina Matsuri, the Festival of the Dolls, and then to send dolls to Japan as "messengers of goodwill and friendship." Sunday schools, educational institutions, and families could purchase the dolls, enclose a message with them, and for a dollar obtain a "passport" and ticket to send them to Japan. The gifts were to be distributed to schools in Japan by the Ministry of Education.[37]

Gulick considered the doll project a great success; thirteen thousand "messengers of friendship" were sent, and Japanese children responded by returning dolls of their own to America. The next year friendship school bags were packed and sent to Mexican school children, and in the years 1929 and 1930 friendship treasure chests containing books, toys, and trinkets were sent to the Philippines.[38] These subsequent projects met with mixed success: thirty thousand bags were sent to Mexico, but many of the Philippine gifts were left over. Additional projects were planned for Puerto Rico, India, Germany, and China, but the Depression made severe inroads into the financial support for the endeavor, and by 1931 the commission's activities had dwindled to sponsoring essay contests and distributing peace literature.[39]

Gulick devoted long hours to the World Friendship Committee, and was particularly excited about the doll project. But not all of his colleagues shared his enthusiasm. Henry A. Atkinson chided him for his misplaced efforts. The CPU leader noted in 1926 that war between the two nations seemed imminent as Japan's resentment of America had reached the boiling point. In such a serious crisis, "asking funds to buy dolls is 'adding insult to injury,' " and belittling to the cause they both represented. Atkinson was offended that the project's fund appeal appeared on stationary of the National Committee on American-Japanese Relations, on which letterhead his name appeared.[40] Although he took pains to make his criticism privately in order to avoid embarrassing Gulick, whose motives he respected, Atkinson's strong feelings would not permit him to remain silent. In retrospect the effort does appear a bit naïve if well-intentioned. However, it made a deep impression on the Japanese, who were remorseful when the Second World War ended that they had destroyed the dolls during the war.[41] Gulick intended the enterprise to be a way of stimulating real and lasting friendship among children of different nations, and he wrote several pamphlets and a book, *Dolls of Friendship* (1929), which he felt the schools could use.[42] As his boundless energy declined and his hearing failed, the sixty-six-year old Gulick turned increasingly to educational activities to perpetuate the goals he held dear.

PUBLISHING FOR PEACE:

Most of Gulick's work for peace emanated from his position as executive secretary for the CIJG. That body, composed of thirty to forty members, one from each of the constituent denominations that formed the Federal Council of Churches, had labored for peace since its founding in 1911. Under its auspices Gulick authored a series of publications that sought to inform the members on significant issues of the day and to help them to reach intelligent decisions. Gulick also raised funds, organized meetings, personally solicited political leaders, and delivered addresses.

Gulick authored nearly a hundred short pamphlets and brochures for the CIJG between 1924 and 1934. He first edited a biweekly newsletter, *International Goodwill*, which became a forum for his own ideas. The brochures covered a variety of international topics but focused mainly on the Far East and Japanese-American relations. They also included statements on disarmament and universal military training, as well as news of the activities of the CIJG. Addressing his own priorities, Gulick used the pages to remind his readers of the ongoing humiliation experienced by Japan because of the exclusion provision of the 1924 immigration law. In March of 1927 *International Goodwill* merged with the Federal Council *Bulletin* to form a new, thirty-six-page monthly magazine, and Gulick continued to write an international section.

A few months later in 1927 Gulick launched another publishing venture. Using a single page brochure format, he began a series for the CIJG entitled *International Relations of the United States: Brief Summaries for Busy Men and Women.* Designed first as brief discourses, the format was simplified to permit quick scanning. Gulick hoped the brochures would be passed on, reaching a wider audience than would a weightier tome. The topics varied. Some brochures attempted to encapsulate the history of relations between the United States and another nation, such as Mexico or China.[43] But the majority of them discussed important items on the peace agenda. He reviewed the Kellogg-Briand Peace Pact, stressing how important it was for nations and statesmen to attempt seriously to accomplish its purposes.[44] In a discussion of disarmament he cited figures on the cost of past wars, as well as President Hoover's 1930 budget, singling out the huge sum, $692 million, which was proposed for national defense. He also analyzed the president's peace program and urged people to write Congress about it.[45] Another brochure informed church school teachers about ways to educate youth for peace.[46] The World Court was the subject of another issue that reviewed its history and advocated American membership,[47] and in fact, at its December 1930 meeting, the Federal Council's executive committee adopted a resolution to that effect which Gulick described in still another brochure, *Why the United States Should Join the World Court.*[48] The council continued to advocate the court throughout the decade as a politically safer if more innocuous topic than the League of Nations.

The ongoing arms race deeply concerned Gulick, who believed military buildups led inevitably to war. The Federal Council proclaimed the London Naval Conference a necessary corollary to the Pact of Paris, and set aside November 8, 1931, as a day of prayer for its success. The CIJG began an educational campaign to acquaint church members with the issues, and several brochures addressed this topic.[49] In one, Gulick and the council advocated a reduction in military expenditures. He described the resulting pact, which included a 10:10:6.5 ratio in cruiser strength for the United States, Great Britain, and Japan, and a 10:10:7 ratio on destroyers, as "one more step toward a warless world."[50] Arguing that building to the amount allowed was "permissive, not mandatory," he next opposed any suggestion of a billion-dollar naval building program.[51] The cost of armaments prompted frequent communications with the State Department throughout 1931; Gulick tried to persuade Secretary of State Henry Stimson to support fiscal restraint: "To the lay mind budgetary limitation would seem to be one of the very effective methods for restricting armaments," he wrote.[52] Routine acknowledgements greeted his efforts.

The London Naval Conference of 1930 was only a partial success. It did achieve a large-cruiser ratio of 10:10:6, but in fact the Japanese succeeded in gaining a 10:10:7 ratio. Robert Ferrell has concluded that it was "a failure so far as concerned anything really new, and a very pronounced failure in that it aggravated old issues."[53] However, Gulick was not disheartened, and he continued to work for arms limitation. He urged suppport for the World Disarmament Conference scheduled for February 2, 1932; if the conference failed to achieve its goals, it would mean "blacker war clouds" and possible war within "a decade or two or three." The nations must observe the pledges made in the Pact of Paris and drastically reduce their military budgets, he felt.[54] He wrote Stimson again, urging that the United States take the lead in proposing massive reductions as it had done so successfully at Washington in 1922. Dismayed when Stimson informed him he had "nothing to trade" the other nations, Gulick encouraged taking the initiative anyway.[55] He believed the ultimate triumph of the peace movement would come in battles over funds for armaments: "Steadily decreasing military budgets mean decreasing war preparations, increasing adoption of peace policies and organizations, growing confidence among the nations and a safer world to live in." Since he discounted the possibility of war, he asked people to write Congress and the president supporting disarmament, and advised church school teachers to promote it.[56]

Gulick's fervent advocacy of arms reduction and his letters to the administration did attract its attention, although not always in the manner he wished. President Hoover was apparently disturbed by one of Gulick's communications to the executive committee of the Federal Council, which the president interpreted as an attack on the peace policies of the administration. Samuel McCrea Cavert, general secretary of the council, hastened to assure Stimson and Hoover of Gulick's benign intentions,[57] but Gulick continued to be viewed with skepticism if not distrust—the legacy of his old image as a Japan agent.

In 1932 Gulick changed his brochure series to a question-and-answer format, using a hypothetical situation where an "informed citizen" advocated his, i.e., Gulick's, cause to a questioner. In these later issues he discussed the Hoover moratorium, militarism and disarmament, the World Court, war, patriotism, and sanctions. Even more facts and figures were crammed in, interspersed with bits of homey folk wisdom. A complicated issue like the relationship between war debts, reparations, and the tariff was explained in simple terms, and the reader was led to the conclusion that the debts and reparations question was for all intents and purposes, dead.[58] In a similar fashion Gulick proved that big navies only increased the likelihood of war. He also advocated multilateral disarmament based on mutual reduction, as was proposed at the 1932 Geneva World Disarmament Conference.[59] He maintained that support of arms reduction was not the disloyal, communist plot that opponents of the Federal Council had charged it with being.[60]

Gulick devoted several more brochures to the interrelated questions of international tension, the World Court as a way to prevent conflict, and patriotism. He was a member of the Federal Council's World Court Executive Committee, a group that continued lobbying efforts for the cause. That group refused to accept the Senate Foreign Relations Committee's decision to postpone consideration for a year. The members advocated a special session of Congress to consider the court and lobbied for that throughout 1931. Although they finally abandoned that notion, they continued to hope that Congress would act before the World Disarmament Conference met in 1932. Gulick believed Congress was shirking its role as a world leader by ignoring the court issue and disregarding the will of the people. But all his efforts came to naught.[61]

Gulick and the Federal Council represented what Gulick termed the "peace mind," the persuasion that international controversies should be solved legally through arbitration and conciliation procedures rather than by armaments. Although economic sanctions might deter conflict, Gulick did not endorse them because they could be construed as an act of war. Only the World

Court and arbitration seemed to offer a method of conflict resolution that did not risk bloodshed. To that end he opposed compulsory Reserve Officer Training Corps and universal military training and instead supported membership in the League of Nations. The "problem of abolishing war and of establishing grounds for permanent peace . . . is the most urgent issue ahead for the world," he wrote.[62]

As international relations became more turbulent and regional conflicts intensified, the Federal Council's leadership found it increasingly difficult to equate international justice with goodwill. World order and indiscriminate opposition to war appeared to be irreconcilable goals. Although the Federal Council held them in unstable equilibrium, it became harder to do so. Throughout the 1930s the Federal Council continued to oppose the increase in military budgets, and it was implacably hostile to suggestions of a draft. Although the council supported the Nye Committee's investigations of the munitions industry and the neutrality acts, Gulick was more ambivalent. He wrote President Franklin D. Roosevelt expressing his disappointment with the Johnson Act, which restricted the president's ability to differentiate between an aggressor and its victim. He still rejected a totally pacifist, isolationist approach to conflict resolution.[63]

As Gulick prepared to end his public career he summarized in writing his thoughts on world peace for a possible address. Certain things were essential to him: ending armed intervention anywhere for any purpose whatsoever, abandoning enforcement of neutrality, and the right to trade with belligerents. He advocated scrapping all types of aggressive weapons and supported a strengthened World Court and League of Nations. His political thinking was supportive of the New Deal; he had moved far from the moderate republicanism he had once espoused. The fundamental cause of war now seemed to him "a social system that puts vast wealth in the hands of small groups," resulting in excessive inequality of income, overproduction and inevitable underconsumption, great disparities between rich and poor, and conflict among nations. Peace organizations that effectively rallied world opinion against war could achieve nationwide cooperative action for peace through such actions as a general strike. The selling of arms and munitions and the loaning of money to belligerents should be outlawed, and ROTC and compulsory military training abolished. And once again he favored ending Japanese exclusion, abandoning America's naval bases in the Philippines, and reducing forces in Hawaii.[64]

Gulick's views, which had changed dramatically since 1917, were very similar to the program for world peace adopted by the Federal Council in April of 1934. It too called for arms embargoes on aggressors and "strict control of the international traffic in arms and munitions" rather than a prohibition. The council also favored abolishing aggressive arms and all military aviation. It supported the World Court and urged a defining of "the terms upon which it [the nation] would be willing to officially . . . relate itself to the League of Nations." The Federal Council, unlike Gulick, made no attempt to analyze the causes of war, but advocated international cooperation to remove the economic reasons for conflict.[65]

Was anything wrong with such thinking? Although Gulick and the Federal Council were idealists who believed almost nothing was worth a resort to arms, Gulick could see that "have-not" nations such as Japan had needs for raw materials that might justify their acting to remedy their deficiencies. The council and Gulick had unlimited faith in the power of public opinion and neither could conceive that such a positive force could be enlisted for war as well as peace. They were so firmly rooted in a democratic society that they could not envisage that a nation might freely choose an authoritarian system and follow its leader to war. In short, they did not see the darker side of circumstances, but then neither did most of those they represented, nor for that matter did the nation's leaders. The goals of Gulick and the council were very much this-worldly and in that respect they were the inheritors of a legacy of social gospel rhetoric and belief. Yet one cannot escape the notion that there was an ultimate escape clause in their reasoning: if the Kingdom of God did not come to fruition on Earth, there was still a heaven for believers, another world where indeed the Prince of Peace would reign eternally. For the Federal Council that was salvation enough; for Gulick it was not, and he continued to work to increase public understanding of Japan's problems until the outbreak of the Second World War.

Gulick's focus remained fixed on peace. Although his physical faculties began to fail in 1928 when his hearing diminished and he was forced to curtail his public activities, his mind remained sharp. In 1930 he and Cara finally took the vacation so long denied them by his heavy schedule. They made the grand tour for the last time, visiting England and Scotland, then Paris, Switzerland, and Germany.[66] As the Depression affected the American economy more deeply they too felt the pinch, for the Federal Council was funded by contributions from wealthy benefactors who no longer had as much money for benevolence. By 1932 salaries and work had been cut back drastically, and this too stimulated plans for retirement. They considered various missionary retirement homes as their own funds dwindled.[67]

Gulick's last work for the Federal Council was with China Famine Relief. For six years he had served as secretary for this special fund-raising group, and in its annual report for 1933 he noted with pride that it had raised over $215,000 for assistance after a flood of the Yangtze and Yellow rivers produced widespread food shortages. He noted that since the Chinese government had now accepted responsibility for disaster work, the group's assistance was no longer necessary. In any case, the Depression made it unlikely that the members could ever collect that much money again.[68]

In January of 1934 Gulick celebrated the anniversary of twenty years' service with the Federal Council and announced his pending retirement. Council president Samuel McCrea Cavert congratulated him on his efforts to rouse the churches to their international responsibility. Gulick's work had been "more important than that of any other member of [the] staff," and Cavert felt the present Christian concern about international relations was directly attributable to his influence.[69] Gulick was appreciative but rejected Cavert's offer of assistance to enable them to retire in New York. His increasing deafness had cut him off too much from "swiftly moving events and the ideas of the leaders," he said. Both his age and the financial condition of the council made retirement a necessity, and he tendered his resignation effective July 1.[70]

On April 10, Gulick's seventy-fourth birthday, the Federal Council held a testimonial dinner for him. Nearly three hundred letters honored his service, and an additional number came from Japan. Those honoring him included former Secretary of State Stimson, ABCFM Secretary James Barton, Norman Vincent Peale, Kenneth Scott Latourette, Carrie Chapman Catt, George Wickersham, Philip C. Jessup, and Foreign Affairs Minister Hirota Kōki. Ambassador Saitō Hiroshi spoke words of tribute, as did Federal Council officials. Saitō took the opportunity to urge admission of Japanese immigrants on a quota basis, and he praised Gulick's work, especially the doll messenger campaign. In his response, Gulick endorsed Roosevelt's Good Neighbor Policy, and called for the United States to take the lead in the movement for world peace.[71] In September the Japanese emperor conferred on him the Third Class Order of the Sacred Treasure in recognition of his service in promoting Japanese-American friendship.[72]

Gulick ended his public career with an action that expressed his continued interest in peace. On May 21 he and Cara participated in a New York peace parade together with ten thousand other enthusiasts. It was a fitting symbol of a dedication to peace that marked the interwar years. The First World War had transformed the missionary into a crusader for peace.[73]

11

GULICK AND JAPAN

RETURN TO THE BEGINNING—JAPAN:

Gulick's decade-long involvement in the peace movement inevitably brought him back to a consideration of relations between the United States and Japan. The deteriorating relations between the two nations formed the subject matter of his last book, *Toward Understanding Japan* (1934). The relationship had occupied a major portion of several of his previous books as throughout the twenties Gulick had praised Japan's progress toward democracy, welcomed signs that its aggressiveness toward China had diminished, and looked forward to the day when America would moderate its opposition to Asian immigration and the two nations could establish a firm friendship. The Manchurian crisis alarmed him, but he still was unwilling to abandon his faith in Japan. His writings in the thirties illustrate his slow realization that the two nations were indeed heading toward war. It was an intellectual awareness that caused him pain, yet even as war came he remained optimistic that out of the devastation would come a new Japan, purged of militarism, and a new America ready to abandon its racist discrimination against Asians. Eventually peace with equity and justice would be realized between the two nations he loved.

WALKING THE LINE:

Gulick claimed he "held no brief for Japan,"[1] yet in his writings prior to 1937 he walked a fine line between promoting under-

189

standing and tolerance for Japanese actions and apologizing for Japanese militarism. Even as early as the Twenty-one Demands of 1915 he could write, "I feel confident that Japan is not so black as she has been painted."[2] He had always tried to convince the world that the Japanese were not a brutal people, although as a missionary he sometimes deplored their values. Sometimes this necessitated withholding information about their actions until such time as they could be explained and coupled with assurances that such behavior had ceased. Such, for example, was the case in his reaction to the abortive movement in 1919 for Korean independence from Japanese rule.

Gulick sought to alert the Japanese to the damage the repression of the Koreans was doing to their cause in the United States, and to publicize the most promising aspects of Japan's response to the rebellion in order to lessen the negative impact. He wrote the Japanese consul general that the news of Japan's behavior, especially charges of wholesale brutality, was disturbing to its friends. After Japan suppressed the Korean rebellion he wrote Henry Atkinson of the Church Peace Union that "at no time has U.S. feeling been so bitter, and Japan is largely to blame due to the Korean situation and Siberia and Shantung."[3] (This statement, which does not accord with the image of Gulick as an agent of Japan, was apparently never read by Military Intelligence.)

Although Gulick's public announcements about Korea were optimistic, they tended to belie his own deep concern. In an unpublished manuscript dated 1920 he admitted that reports had alarmed him, too. Tales of "torture, floggings, the burning of churches and villages and a whole system of terrorization of an unarmed people have produced a deep revulsion against Japanese rule." If Japan wished to recover esteem in America, it had to reform its administrative practices thoroughly and promptly and establish true local self-government.[4] In public, however, he announced only that administrative reforms were likely, that the Japanese leadership had admitted the military government of Korea was a disaster and had recognized the harm that repression was doing to its world image.[5]

Gulick worked to improve relations after the disputes following the end of World War I—Shantung, the racial equality clause, and the naval race. In *American-Japanese Relations, 1916-1920: A Retrospect* (1921), the quadrennial report of the Council on Relations with the Orient, Gulick, in surveying America's Japanese problem, enumerated actions that had aroused hostility toward that nation. He stressed that the occupation of Shantung had been the most damaging. Despite rumors of war, he felt there were some grounds for optimism. Anti-Japanese sentiments had actually ebbed during the World War, and many sympathetic publications and the agreements achieved at the Washington Arms Conference had helped moderate public opinion.[6] Despite his guarded optimism, he recognized that it would require a bold diplomatic initiative to get Japanese-American relations back onto a positive course. In 1923 Gulick published *Winning the Far East*. Based on his personal experiences during his 1921 trip to East Asia, the book expressed the optimism that he held about relations between the two nations despite the storm warnings of the 1920s. He celebrated the effects of the Washington treaties and praised Japan's turn toward democratic government. Japan's aggressive and militaristic policy toward China had ceased, he believed; that nation's presence in Manchuria existed solely for fear of Soviet aims there. Japan's increasing prosperity would ultimately solve its food and population problems, and the country would have no reason for further aggression.[7]

Gulick emphasized in this book Japan's unease about American actions. The development of the naval base at Pearl Harbor and the expanding of ROTC programs in colleges seemed evidence to him—and to Japan—that the nation was becoming increasingly militaristic.[8] In addition, America's racist policies continued to hurt relations. Even though Gulick was somewhat contemptuous of the Chinese, whose failure to modernize contrasted so sharply with Japan's achievements, he recognized that all Asia was awakening and could not be ignored.[9] Asians certainly did not want conflict with the United States, and war with its major trading partner would be absolutely suicidal for Japan. Gulick deplored American military maneuvers in the Pacific, which were a "drive on the federal treasury" designed only to demonstrate America's fighting strength.[10]

China's reunification under Chiang Kai-shek, completed in

1927, which would ultimately lead to conflict with Japan in Manchuria, initially evoked Gulick's support. He recognized that China was "putting its house in order . . . emerging as a self respecting nation." He approved of America's noninvolvement in the Chinese revolution, concurring with the Federal Council that the American government should not intervene to protect missionaries threatened by the Northern Expedition, the countrywide sweep of the Nationalist army to unify China. Even the Nanking incident, in which Western-owned buildings were plundered, and a Japanese naval officer, the American vice-president of the University of Nanking, and several British subjects were killed by Nationalist soldiers, did not provoke council officials to change their position.[11] "We are today China's real, honest friend," Gulick claimed, basing his statement on America's history of sympathetic and unselfish dealing with that nation dating from the turn of the century. Since the overthrow of the Manchus, the United States had viewed China's struggles with friendly concern, and Gulick urged Americans to distinguish between the radicals and Chinese moderates, both of whom sought to end the unequal treaties and force foreigners out of their land. However, the moderates would achieve this goal legally and fairly if unprovoked. He advised missionaries and merchants to avoid the army's path and to declare their support for China's awakening.[12]

However, Gulick became more concerned in the spring of 1928 when the Nationalists began the second phase of the Northern Expedition, directed at Peking and the seizure of Manchuria. Chiang tried to avoid another antiforeign outbreak like the Nanking incident, particularly as his troops approached the Shantung peninsula. Five thousand Japanese soldiers had been sent to Tsinan to protect their nationals and property. When they clashed with Nationalist troops in May, fighting spread quickly throughout the city, continuing despite a temporary truce. For over a year after the Tsinan incident the Japanese ruled the city, imposing a reign of terror on its Chinese population.[13]

Gulick learned more of the incident through American Board missionary to China, Robert Whitaker, whose wife was Gulick's cousin, the daughter of his uncle, John T. Gulick. He transmitted to the State Department a copy of Whitaker's letter to the board describing Japanese atrocities at Tsinan. Whitaker pointedly commented that he didn't intend his information as anti-Japanese propaganda, and stressed that his sympathies and those of his wife were with Japan. Gulick forwarded the letter without comment, for it undoubtedly echoed his own feelings—that it was important to withhold judgment and give Japan the benefit of the doubt.[14] The State Department shared his opinion and supported Japan.

The Tsinan incident marked the breakdown of goodwill between China and Japan and was a prelude to the Manchurian crisis. Events followed in rapid succession. When Japanese troops arranged the murder of Chang Tso-lin, warlord of Manchuria, America initially maintained an attitude of aloof detachment; it did, however, move quickly to recognize the new Nationalist government of China.

But the effects of the Depression in East Asia made the maintenance of peace a very fragile thing. Japan suffered early and long from the economic crisis because its prosperity was inextricably tied to trade with America and China and the exploitation of resources in Manchuria. The Depression brought the collapse of the American market and a drop in the China trade. Akira Iriye has noted that "the failure to achieve any degree of constructive cooperation with the powers in China all meant the removal of the basic rationale for Japan's economic diplomacy."[15] It appeared that only the military had a plan for economic recovery. Although the civilian government did not condone this unauthorized aggression, the governmental system established under the Meiji constitution gave the military leadership direct access to the emperor and enabled it to pull down cabinets when its wishes were frustrated. Hence the Kwantung Army, stationed in Manchuria to guard Japan's economic interests, felt no compunctions about acting on its own despite the civilian government's concern. Relations between China and Japan were further strained by two minor events in Manchuria, the Wanpaoshan incident and the murder of Captain Nakamura, and, on September 18, 1931, conflict erupted when a Japanese army officer blew up a section of the South Manchurian railroad. The army rapidly moved to take control of the city of Mukden, and then broadened its activities throughout the land.

The American government responded cautiously to the outbreak of aggression, uncertain who was responsible. Gulick also sought an explanation for the fighting. He wrote Japan's consul general in New York inquiring about information he received regarding attempts of the Chinese and Japanese to settle their differences peacefully prior to the Manchurian incident. He met Viscount Ishii Kikujirō in June of 1933 to discuss the episode, and Ishii convinced him of the correctness of Japan's position and mentioned in passing the possible use of the World Court to resolve the differences of the two nations.[16]

Unlike Gulick, the State Department ultimately concluded that Japan was indeed to blame. Secretary Stimson explored ways of making his disapproval known without taking leadership from the League of Nations, and he finally issued the doctrine bearing his name which denied recognition to Manchukuo, the puppet state created by Japan.

The Manchurian crisis shattered the euphoria engendered in the peace movement by the Pact of Paris, for it demonstrated all too well that only the declaration of war by aggressors had been outlawed. "Chasing bandits" and "restoring order" did not count. Gulick agreed with the peace groups that Japan should be called on to stop fighting, but when that failed, they divided over what next to advocate. The government's feeble cooperation with the League of Nations pleased those groups wanting closer ties with it but there was much dispute over the proper response to take if the league called for sanctions against Japan. Many agreed with Gulick that sanctions were themselves an act of war. Twenty-eight different organizations joined together in April of 1931 to establish a nonsectarian Interorganizational Council on Disarmament. The body, which included the Federal Council of Churches, sent petitions to Washington and began discussions of the Manchurian question in late September. However, the Interorganizational Council was unable to achieve a consensus on sanctions and disintegrated in early 1933. The Emergency Peace Committee, a more radical peace group, could not agree on a program either, and was succeeded by the National Peace Conference, directed by Walter M. Van Kirk, Gulick's successor-apparent at the Federal Council. The executive secretary of the Women's International League for Peace and Freedom, Dorothy Detzer, pressed incessantly for a hard line against Japan. She and Mildred Olmsted were in favor of strong action, and Olmsted wrote supporter Emily Balch that "without waiting any longer for dear old souls like Dr. Gulick who think that all is well because peace sentiment in this country is growing, the Women's International League should take the lead" in demanding that the president use "vigorous and unqualified measures against Japan." The peace groups, however, could only agree on an end to military spending and the end of Asian discrimination in the nation's immigration policy.[17] In any case, Stimson could not persuade the president to go beyond a moral sanction against Japan's actions.

Gulick opposed punitive measures against Japan. Although he initially supported that nation and urged impartiality, he sought some way to halt the conflict until guilt was affixed. On January 19, 1932, he wrote CIJG members asking if they would favor the use of economic sanctions as a way of putting some force in the Pact of Paris. Would they support a multilateral treaty imposing sanctions on both sides in a war? "Once a conflict begins it is hard to tell who started it and the immediate need is to stop the fighting and then assess responsibility."[18] But his proposal quickly encountered opposition, for sanctions bitterly divided the peace advocates.

A moderate article Gulick wrote on the Manchurian crisis even provoked his son. Asked to critique it, Sidney, Jr., advised his father to consider modifying his conclusions because of Japan's senseless and brutal bombing of the defenseless city of Shanghai. The January 1932 attack came only three weeks after the announcement of the Stimson Doctrine, and it thoroughly outraged Western statesmen. Sidney, Jr., expressed an almost universal sentiment when he advised his father that "the Japanese are responsible for terrible wrongdoing and she [sic] should recognize she has antagonized the whole world."[19] The elder Gulick held to his position, although he did condemn Japan for the attack on Shanghai. He wrote an editorial for the *Bulletin* of the Federal Council, stating "Japan's best American friends are amazed, dismayed, and sorrowful. The Japan now carrying on the conflict in Shanghai is not the Japan they have known and loved."[20]

Gulick finished a new book on the Far East crisis, *Toward*

Understanding Japan, before he retired from the Federal Council in 1934, and it was published the following year. The book's purpose was revealed by its subtitle, *Constructive Proposals for Removing the Menace of War*, but its thesis reflected the author's Christian perspective as well as his sympathies. Arguing that Americans seeking to understand Japan should attempt to see the world from the Japanese perspective, he traced the history of Japan's international relations, explaining the underlying motivations and mitigating circumstances which would clarify the reasons for its actions. To his sympathetic mind, Japan only sought to "set a good example of law and prosperous rule in Manchuria so China might do likewise."[21]

Japan's actions had to be understood in the context of its domestic problems and in comparison to the actions of other nations, particularly the United States, according to Gulick. Japan had an enormous population problem and faced a serious economic plight, and it harbored strong resentment of the United States because of its exclusionist immigration policy and high tariffs. The United States should recognize its own imperialist heritage before condemning Japan, Gulick urged. Recent actions of the United States had done little to reassure the Japanese, particularly American recognition of the Soviet Union and sale of planes to Nationalist China. The situation in Japan seemed to be improving. Its population was stabilizing, food production increasing, and civilians seemed to be regaining power in the government. Gulick feared the possible communist domination of China and its conspiring with Russia against Japan.[22] Communism in East Asia now seemed to him a greater threat than Japanese militarism, but he may have been grasping at straws in his attempts to downplay the significance of Japanese aggression.

Gulick traced Japanese-American relations from the turn of the century, in this study stressing Japan's often-fearful response to American actions. He regretted that Japan's recent behavior had demonstrated the impotence of the league, the Paris Peace Pact, and the Nine Power Treaty—a tremendous blow to the world's peace machinery.[23] Recognizing the extensive harm done by the exclusion clause, Gulick regretted that his efforts to prevent that legislation had failed; he once again called for inclusion of Japan in the quota system.

Gulick urged Americans to use restraint in judging Japan and advocated that the English-speaking nations assist in reopening trade markets. "If the West desires peace in the Far East it must help Japan's people to make a living and be secure without violence and war. . . . The time has come for the West to give Japan respect, help, and the honorable treatment which her culture and achievements merit," he wrote. He still seemed, at least publicly, to discount the possibility of war between America and Japan, particularly one initiated by Tokyo; only an actual attack on Hawaii or the Pacific Coast would warrant American naval and military resistance.[24]

Gulick's outline for a constructive policy toward Japan offered no new insights. He also advocated changes in America to solve tensions that might lead to war—state planning, a more equitable distribution of income, and renunciation of the use of force to aid business and finance abroad—indicative of a belief system that supported the more radical social ideals of the New Deal, although not Roosevelt's foreign policy. Sounding like some of the disillusioned progressives, he called for expanded trade and the abolition of all offensive weapons. The naval ratio should be changed to give Japan parity with the United States and Great Britain, and then even further reduced, he felt. Independence for the Philippines was essential, as was abolition of Japanese exclusion and recognition of the government of Manchukuo. The case of Japan's mandated Pacific islands should go to the World Court. Gulick called for a nonaggression pact and a security agreement between the United States and Japan, and he supported Japan's rejoining the League of Nations. (He did not discuss American membership, however.) He concluded the work with a rhetorical question: "Do we regard the Open Door and the territorial integrity of China as worth a war? This is the fundamental question."[25] To him the answer was clearly no.

Toward Understanding Japan was received with moderate enthusiasm. No one questioned the author's credentials, but one reviewer noted that past injustices perpetrated by the Europeans in Asia scarcely justified Japan's present actions. Stanford historian Payson J. Treat, himself identified as a Japanophile by the Bureau of Investigation, pointed out that Gulick's constructive proposals were "reasonable enough, but, like the immigration quota which Gulick proposed in 1914, they seem far removed from the realities of American statesmanship."[26] Another critic called the book the "best apology for Japan's aggressive policy" that he had read,[27] and that was the lasting impression the book made as the two nations drifted closer to war. Gulick had tried to walk a fine line between apologizing for Japanese militarism and seeking to explain the reasons why that nation might feel aggrieved enough to embark on such a course. But when Japan seized Manchuria such rationalizations paled before its naked aggression. Gulick, whose response to American armaments was virtually pacifist, came too close to condoning militarism abroad. His son Sidney warned him that unless the book clearly called for Japan to cooperate with the United States, readers might feel that he had been duped by astute Japanese military propaganda.[28] But, like the wing of the peace movement that rejected the notion of sanctions, he concluded that the lesson of Manchuria had to be a firm determination to keep the United States at peace at all costs.[29] Denouncing uninformed jingoist rhetoric, he believed war could be prevented if the antagonists tried to understand each other. He sought to bring that about, but in vain.

An interesting postscript to *Toward Understanding Japan* appeared after Pearl Harbor in an article written by Harold A. Larrabee. Larrabee sought to analyze the manner in which American writers had assessed the dangers from Japan, and he noted that Gulick and Oswald Garrison Villard, who wrote a similarly-intentioned work about the same time, were both "mistaken seers" who bent over backward to try to show how unlikely it was that war would come. He blamed Gulick's misjudgment on his reforming zeal. "Gulick, the Christian apostle of peace, so detested the thought of war between this country and Japan that he greatly exaggerated the potency of the forces acting to prevent it, and saw in the realistic cautions of his opponents only the warmongering of 'unscrupulous agitators.' " Noting correctly that Gulick's intention was to shape public opinion to a more favorable attitude toward Japan, he alleged that in so doing, Gulick had ignored the facts. "Special pleading is no less special pleading and no less disastrous to human destiny because its motives are so exalted," he concluded.[30]

Of Gulick's critics Larrabee was the most perceptive. Gulick was no apologist, but he was a special pleader, and despite his motives one must conclude that by the mid-1930s he had been forced to overlook and condone much in order to deny that Japan's course was aggressive or imperialistic.

THE DRIFT TOWARD WAR IN THE PACIFIC:

Sidney and Cara planned to visit their children for the next three months following his 1934 retirement; then Sidney was to go to Honolulu to visit his sister Fanny Jewett, while Cara went to Ashland, Oregon, to have medical treatments for arthritis. Sidney stayed in Honolulu for seven months, as his sister was ill, and then returned to Ashland, where he and Cara resided until March 1, 1936, when he returned to Honolulu. Fanny sold him her home on Manoa Road, and Cara joined him in the summer. Honolulu, where his elderly aunts Julia and Annie Gulick also resided until their deaths, would be their retirement home.[31]

When Sidney first arrived in Hawaii he began to write his reminiscences, intending them for his children and grandchildren. Like many elderly people he found that he could recall events early in his life with greater clarity than those of the last twenty years. He also gave many sermons and talks in Ashland on world events in 1935 and 1936. A frequent topic was, "Is War Between the United States and Japan Likely?" He always concluded in the negative and apparently believed it. The possibility of forming a committee on peace in the Pacific that would support the Kellogg-Briand Pact but avoid endorsing "Japan's militaristic aggressions in China"[32] intrigued him, but he decided against such an activist course.

However, the breakdown of the Tangku truce and Japan's conquest of north China in 1936 disturbed Gulick for two reasons. One was the damaging effects of these events on what he saw as a movement in Congress to include Japan in the quota system. As he wrote Count Kaneko Kentarō, Japanese aggression destroyed the opportunity to end Japanese exclusion in the United States. He was also beginning to recognize Japan's aggression for what it was. In *Toward Understanding Japan* he had tried to make Americans see the Manchurian crisis from Japan's perspective, but he now admitted to Kaneko that "the efforts of American friends of Japan have again been largely nullified by what is happening in China proper." The expansion of Japan's arena of conquest was particularly hard for him to accept. He wrote, "I must confess that I find it more difficult to understand and explain Japan's recent procedures in China than I did those in Manchuria." To him Japan's behavior now seemed clearly immoral. Gulick wished to attribute its brutal actions, which seemed designed to totally demoralize the Chinese, to "certain traders and business interests" rather than to the Japanese government, but he found it difficult. If Kaneko could only persuade the government to denounce the lawless behavior of the military, this action could change anti-Japanese sentiment in America to a semblance of sympathy and goodwill.[33] Although he wished to persuade himself that the government was ignorant of the actions of its runaway military, he now sought proof before further condoning Japan's actions.

Gulick began work on a new book, *Mixing the Races in Hawaii* (1937), an attempt to promote racial harmony in the islands and to use that experience as a lesson for the mainland.[34] But even as he turned to an academic topic he found himself drawn back to the ongoing Far East crisis. The National Peace Council sent him a questionnaire which became the inspiration for another analysis and set of recommendations on America's East Asian policy. He sent his reply to officials in Japan in addition to publishing it in the *Honolulu Star-Bulletin* in August 1936. He wrote that the idea of the United States as a good neighbor to all the Pacific powers was still attractive to him. America should cease trying to compel Japan to follow its wishes in China, should abandon the 5:5:3 naval ratio of the Five Power Treaty, should stop fortifying its insular possessions in the Western Pacific, and should under no circumstances use sanctions against Japan. Since the West had denied Japan the ability to "earn an honest living" through the export of its manufactured goods, it had no right to complain if that nation expanded into China, he claimed. Only Asians could solve Asia's problems. Japan "must learn the excessive costs of militarism," but from China, not America. If they abandoned the civil war against the Communists, the Nationalists could eventually exhaust the Japanese, and if they failed they should be abandoned to their fate. "We can't force Japan to give up the fruits of her aggression—hence we should accept it," he wrote.[35] In his opinion, America's protests only strengthened the militarists. He also wrote the newspaper opposing the Navy League's plan to maintain a permanent naval base in the Philippines. A staunch isolationist when it came to Asia, Gulick now believed America should only defend the homeland and not imitate the "imperialistic policies of decadent Europe."[36]

Gulick was ambivalent. He was disturbed by Japan's renewed aggression, yet he could not bring himself to condemn them categorically. He refused to blame Japan after fighting broke out at the Marco Polo bridge July 7, 1937. In a letter to the *Star-Bulletin* he asked people to withhold judgement on the causes of the conflict: "An impartial study of all the facts would result in a judgement less harsh on Japan than is now generally held."[37] Even when Japan sank the American gunboat *Panay* on December 12, 1937, he sought to find some extenuating circumstances. The *Panay* had been anchored upriver from Nanking near three Standard Oil tankers, and had evacuated American embassy personnel as the fighting between Chinese and Japanese troops approached the city. Japanese military officials knew its whereabouts. The clearly marked ship was bombed and sunk; two men were killed, about thirty wounded, and those attempting to escape were reportedly machine-gunned. A sharp American protest brought profuse apologies from Ambassador Saitō and Foreign Minister Hirota. Although the American government was outraged when it learned all the facts, it did not consider fighting over the incident. Instead, the episode so galvanized the antiwar sentiment in Congress that the House seriously considered the famous Ludlow amendment, which would have necessitated a nationwide referendum on the question of going to war.[38]

Gulick, similarly anxious to avoid a break over the incident, wrote the *Honolulu Advertiser* during the height of the crisis. His assessment of the *Panay* incident was steeped in isolationism. Both the Japanese and the American embassy had warned foreigners to leave the war zone, he remarked, and thus those who remained had done so at their own risk and had forfeited all claims on either government. He speculated that the gunboat might well have been on the Yangtze to protect the Standard Oil tankers that were delivering gasoline to Chinese warplanes, and if this were the case it had lost all claim to neutral status. The regrettable incident could be attributed to "stupid blunders" by both Americans and Japanese. Although the *Advertiser* published Gulick's letter, which supported the noninterventionist consensus so powerful on the mainland, it so offended the editor that he drafted an editorial of refutation. The passengers did include embassy personnel ordered to remain at their posts as well as newsmen, he pointed out, and he concluded, "Any self-respecting nation has the right to protect its citizens."[39]

Gulick recognized that whatever effect he had had in promoting international understanding and goodwill toward Japan had ended, the result of his advancing age and his unpopular point of view. But although he had lost his influence he still did what he could for peace. In April 1938, in an answer to a letter from the president of the Rotary Club in Matsuyama, Japan, Gulick expressed his concern with the turn of events in East Asia and his continued support for Japan. Although he recognized that the Sino-Japanese War was the fault of both nations as well as the Western nations' historic "predatory policies," he now found it difficult to convince his friends that Japan was not solely to blame. Japan's rhetoric offended even him. The constant reiteration of its desire to make China friendly and cooperative while at the same time bombing and killing thousands of its innocent civilians seemed duplicitous. If Japan were honest about its grievances against China over Manchuria the American public might be more understanding, even able to see the Japanese as more than irrational hypocrites, he wrote.[40]

Gulick was appalled by news of the atrocities committed by Japanese soldiers sacking Nanking. Yearning for some evidence that their commanders had punished those who had acted so barbarously, or at least that the senior military were unaware of the behavior of the troops, he requested friends in Tokyo to send him proof.[41] But he declined to edit a book of statements by Japanese leaders on the nation's problems. He recognized that the Japanese government was clearly dominated by the military and unless things changed markedly, "the less said the better." No attempt at interpreting the Far East situation could at that point make the West sympathetic to Japan. He reluctantly recognized Japan's culpability but still urged that accounts be impartial and fair.[42]

Despite his advancing years Gulick kept up with events. The consul general of Japan supplied him with Japanese periodicals; although he was no longer able to read the language, a Japanese American minister translated for him. He also subscribed to various English-language journals from Japan, as well as *Amerasia* and *Far Eastern Survey*. He read the output of such writers as Thomas A. Bisson and the notorious Kawakami, as well as publications of the Foreign Policy Association and popular news magazines. He was absorbed by the crisis and sought to understand each new event.[43]

His Japanese friends continued to solicit Gulick's sympathetic opinions. The consul general in Honolulu asked his reaction to a book by Kawai Tatsuo entitled *The Goal of Japanese Expansion*, published by the Hokuseido Press in Tokyo in 1938, an enthusiastic endorsement of the idealistic pan-Asianist rhetoric of the militarists. While Gulick did not openly contradict the Japanese author, he noted that the work's tone sounded very similar to America's "crusade for democracy" rhetoric of World War I. Each belligerent found it necessary to put a "moral halo" around its purposes and to condemn its opponents. He pointed out that Western readers, whose attention was fixed on news of the attacks on Nanking and Shanghai, would be offended by the book's tone. Gulick insisted that his criticisms stemmed only from his love for Japan and his desire to see its case put effectively before the American people, but he doubted that that would occur before peace was concluded in China.[44]

The situation in East Asia became more desperate; the war with China settled into a stalemate and discussions with the United States were frustrated by differences over Japan's China policy. Gulick attempted to alert individuals to the dangers the crisis posed for the United States. He wrote his successor at the Federal Council of Churches, Walter W. Van Kirk, in response to a message from the FCCCA's national study conference on the world situation. The piece was accurate, he said, but it did not

discuss Japan's intense fear of communism, which was critical to
an understanding of the situation. When Chiang Kai-shek formed
the United Front with the Communists in 1936, Japan decided for
war; the conflict had all the hallmarks of a holy war against
communism. Gulick had found in communism the extenuating
circumstances he sought as he attempted to exculpate Japan for
the Sino-Japanese conflict. He also advised Van Kirk that the
United States was making a mistake in not recognizing Manchukuo.
"Secretary [Cordell] Hull would, I think, get further with his program for maintaining American rights in China if he would recognize this new order and that . . . the old order will not and cannot return."[45]

In March of 1940 Gulick made a last effort to alert the State
Department. He warned Hull that, "If and when Japanese military leaders begin to see the collapse of their military program in
China, it would not be all strange were they to precipitate war
with the U.S. in order to be able to claim that their defeat was not
due to China. They would prefer to perish fighting a giant, than to
be driven out of China by a foe whom they had stigmatized as
puny and contemptible." He urged Hull to remember this when
he contemplated embargoing war material to Japan. If such an
action effectively hampered military operations in China "it
would be in keeping with the Japanese spirit to retaliate on the
U.S. in such ways as to bring on war." That this would be suicidal
for Japan would be irrelevant, for inevitable defeat would not
deter the Japanese. He believed the State Department should
have invoked the Neutrality Act against both China and Japan at
the beginning of their conflict, for he believed China had deliberately extended the war to Shanghai and south of the Yellow River
in an attempt to force Western intervention. Gulick was willing
that his prophecy be made public, but he asked Hull and the editors of *Christian Century*, to whom he also sent it, not to publish it
under his name.[46] But in fact both recipients ignored it. Lingering
suspicions of his affiliation with Japan had negated his influence,
and this vital message, which displayed his perceptive understanding of the Japanese mind, fell on deaf ears.

Other developments also evoked his interest and demonstrated how one-sided his isolationism really was. After 1936 Gu-

lick supported aid to the democracies resisting Hitler. The German leader was, to him, cruel, pagan and deceitful; he concurred in aiding England as much as possible, but thought Germany should take the initiative in declaring war on the United States.[47] He accepted America's preparations for war, recognizing its likelihood and believing in the need for self-defense. When the Hawaiian Japanese petitioned the State Department, asking Hull to help simplify the process by which they could renounce their dual Japanese citizenship, Gulick was pleased. The Niseis' willingness, even enthusiasm, to be drafted encouraged him to believe their show of patriotism might warrant reopening the issue of Japanese exclusion and naturalization.[48]

But Gulick's deafness and age ruled out his participation. In June 1941 his beloved Cara died of pneumonia, and he spent the last months of that year tilling his garden and working on his research and writing.

JAPAN IN WAR AND PEACE:

When the bombs fell on Pearl Harbor Gulick was not surprised, for he had foreseen it. He wrote his children the next day, "I reckon the Japanese are desperate and prefer to be beaten by the U.S.A. than by China. When beaten she'll get better terms from us than from any other power." He doubted Japan would be able to attack Honolulu again, and he prepared to spend the war there, renting rooms in his home to war workers.[49]

The plight of Hawaii's Japanese Americans was acute after the attack on Pearl Harbor. Their physical similarity to the hated enemy brought out all the old racial animosity and led to cries for their removal, and Gulick was quick to react to the local situation. He drafted an article about the proposed evacuation of one hundred thousand Nisei from the islands. It was absurd, unconstitional, un-Christian, and unnecessary, he stated. They were loyal and patriotic and had responded enthusiastically to wartime measures. Japanese language schools had totally failed to convert them to Tokyo's militarism. However, he supported the detention of suspicious individuals, but only after careful investigation.[50] He testified as a character witness for some of his Japanese American friends and visited a few who were interned, but his deafness prevented him from doing more.

The relocation of the mainland Japanese Americans did not affect him directly. He applauded the attempts to prevent it made by his brother-in-law, Galen Fisher, a prominent California Congregationalist who had worked for the YMCA in Japan. Gulick, observing from a distance, accepted the specious rationalization that it was a military necessity. He was gratified that they accepted their fate passively and cooperated with the authorities. The Japanese militarists had completely failed to indoctrinate the Nisei, whose patriotic behavior before and after Pearl Harbor and acceptance of relocation was ample proof of that. Gulick hoped that the American government would be as noble in its ultimate treatment of them. "Should not those individual Japanese who suffered great financial loss of personal property honestly acquired be financially reimbursed and put on their financial feet?" he asked rhetorically.[51] He did not live to see their long struggle for justice or their evolution into America's so-called "model minority." He would certainly have supported their fight for redress.

Gulick, who had long denied that war would ever come between Japan and America, recognized by 1940 that it was inevitable. He now welcomed the opportunity it offered to purge Japan of militarism, but was very concerned that America devise a wise policy for its dismantling after the war. Reviewing an article by Nathaniel Peffer, "A Dangerous Myth about Japan," Gulick criticized the noted scholar's evaluation of Japanese militarism. Peffer maintained that it had evolved over the centuries rather than resulting from a military coup d'état. Gulick's analysis of the abortive military coup on February 26, 1936, demonstrated his thorough knowledge of Japan's recent history. The West had so deeply influenced Japan that the Japanese military had to resort to assassinations to uproot democracy and crush liberalism. Gulick believed that one could not understand the Japanese people's acceptance of militarism unless one recognized the devastating impact of America's tariff and immigration policies. Given military censorship and thought control, it was not surprising that most of the population approved the militarists' acts, but he con-

tended that many Japanese did not support the policies of
General Tōjō Hideki, the prime minister. Once Japan had suffered drastic defeat and the militarists had been overthrown, the
people would discover how they had been misled and the emperor made a puppet. Then the nation would reject militarism.
Retaining the emperor was essential to ensure Japan's compliance; he believed, incorrectly, that Hirohito had been deceived
by the military and kept ignorant of the plans for attacking Pearl
Harbor.[52] Gulick's remarks again demonstrated his perceptiveness and foresight as well as his tendency toward apologetics.

The Pacific War was a life and death struggle in the sense that
the outcome would deeply affect the future of the world. Gulick
devoted much consideration to the manner in which America
should treat postwar Japan. He concluded that the West had to
inflict a crushing military defeat to destroy any possible belief
that Japan had been "stabbed in the back." The Japanese then
would reject the notion that they were a divine race with a pre-
ordained mandate to conquer the world. Participation in the
postwar government should be restricted to those who had opposed militarism, "sane civilian elements who have not bowed the
knee to Baal." He cautioned against a desire for revenge and
warned America not to become self-righteous in victory. America
must be ready to forgive and welcome a peace-loving Japan back
into the family of nations.[53]

When Gulick was interviewed by the *Honolulu Star-Bulletin*
about the treatment of postwar Japan he elaborated on those recommendations. Japan's forces should be withdrawn to the home
islands, the army demobilized, and all its war materiel confis-
cated, he said. The present political structure should be maintained with minor changes to eliminate the army and navy ministers from the cabinet. It was essential to retain the emperor, whom
Gulick absolved from guilt in the nation's militaristic binge, because that ruler embodied the spirit of the nation, but nonetheless
he wished to see compulsory emperor worship ended. All militarist societies must be disbanded, and freedom of the press,
speech, and assembly provided for the people. He advocated giving Japan equal access to world trade to enable it to develop a
sound economy. The schools must be purged of militaristic indoc-

trination and the real history of Japan's past taught to combat superstition. He did not think a prolonged military occupation would be necessary, nor did he think the American people would condone it. Japan should be assured that it would eventually be permitted to take its "honorable place among nations."[54]

Gulick hoped for changes in America, too. Although during the war was scarcely the time to end Japanese exclusion, he rejoiced that anti-Chinese legislation was being repealed, and he expected that after the war Japan too would be included in a quota.[55] He never ceased to believe that ultimately justice would be done.

Gulick's analysis of the needs of postwar Japan were farsighted and realistic. General Douglas MacArthur's eventual program bore many similarities to Gulick's proposals, but Gulick was not there to see them. In late 1944 he suffered a recurrence of the cancer that had troubled him thirty years earlier. He flew back to the mainland to stay with his daughter Sue Davis in Boise, Idaho, for treatment. Even during this final illness his mind remained alert, but he did not comment on the atomic bombs or Japan's surrender. He spent his days reflecting on his philosophy of life and the troubling questions raised by twentieth-century wars.[56] Consoled by his abiding Christian faith, he died on December 24, 1945, in his eighty-sixth year.

EPILOGUE:

SIDNEY GULICK AND THE SEARCH FOR PEACE

IN RETROSPECT:

Gulick's career involved four interrelated and overlapping subjects: missionary work in Japan, international peace and disarmament, the immigration controversy, and the promotion of sympathetic understanding between the United States and Japan. Disparate as these endeavors may have seemed at times, the binding adhesive was Japan. That country and its people, wherever they resided, provoked such feelings of love and empathy that he devoted half his life to seeking justice for them and peace between them and the United States. His basic concern never wavered, though his reaction to particular actions varied as his hatred and fear of militarism grew. Suffused with Christian optimism, he never abandoned hope for an eventual just and peaceful outcome even as the world was enveloped in war.

The missionary years were both a prelude and an education. He learned that a fundamentalist approach to Christianity had limited appeal to the Japanese, particularly after the initial phase of enthusiasm for the faith as a Western innovation diminished. His more liberal interpretation of Protestantism met with better success, as did his attempt to promote modern science and the theory of evolution as not incompatible with Christian beliefs. The Japanese came to respect him as a man of conviction and integrity, and he was thus able to interpret their needs to the United States. Japan was, for Gulick, at first an alien and uncomfortable land, but he soon found it challenging and stimulating. He respected the Japanese for their intellectual curiosity, their willingness to borrow and adapt, and their ability to modernize. Studying Japanese history and applying the concept of social evolution to Japanese society, he recognized that Japan's authoritarian system was deeply rooted in its paternalistic culture. Although he loved democracy, he believed that the Japanese political system suited that nation. He probably misjudged the depth of the warrior tradition and underestimated the pervasive grip on government that the Meiji constitution had given the military establishment. Imperialism was a natural phenomenon in a sense, yet he was more willing to concede Japan a right to "maintain order" over its weaker neighbors, Korea and China, than he was his own country with respect to Mexico. Japan's expansionism became truly repellant only when it produced barbaric behavior. The rape of Nanking was inexcusable even though Gulick could accept Tokyo's reasons for invading Manchuria. Yet in the Meiji years he found no contradictions, for Japan's foreign relations then posed no such ambiguities. The diplomacy of imperialism as Japan learned it was acceptable, certainly when played out against such an unsavory nation as Czarist Russia, and even the conquest of Korea occasioned very few doubts. Gulick's missionary years predisposed him to understand and justify Japan's subsequent foreign policy. He did indeed "put himself in their shoes" and from that vantage point he accepted the logic of Japan's actions.

The Japanese character he likewise found comprehensible and in many aspects laudable. While his Protestant mores made him condemn what he perceived as their vices—drinking, immorality, and their discriminatory treatment of women—he found little that Christianity could not cure. The Japanese were hardworking, ambitious, perhaps a trifle arrogant, but quick to learn and persevering. He appreciated their curiosity about science and modern technology. Although he recognized a dark side to their nature as evidenced by a certain tendency to lie and deceive, he did not believe subterfuge was their basic characteristic. That they would react violently, even suicidally, when cornered and presented with ultimatums amounting to an intolerable loss of face was quite understandable, and the vaunted notion of oriental "inscrutability" was meaningless to him. The Japanese were a resource-poor people who had been mistreated in their dealings with the West; if the West would only accept them as equals and not discriminate against them, they would meet any behavioral standards those nations might erect. In many ways it appears that he understood Japan better than he understood America.

Much of Gulick's missionary experience and his reflections on the meaning of his career in Japan found expression in a book he worked on during the last decade of his life. It was a philosophical treatise entitled *The East and the West: A Study of Their Psychic and Cultural Characteristics* (1962).[1] The work, a product of his lifelong interest in the East, was based on the extensive reading in history, religion, and philosophy to which he had devoted himself after his retirement. It was a massive undertaking, and unfinished when he died, but his family felt a commitment to complete it. In a forward his friend and fellow scholar Ariga Tetsutaro described Gulick as a "Christian missionary who persistently and consistently worked for world peace with an ardor seldom excelled,"[2]— an excellent commentary on Gulick's life.

The work reflected Gulick's Western Christian perspective, yet he tried as a scholar to rise above that to view the cultures broadly and objectively. Acknowledging certain similarities as well as basic differences between East and West, he sought to outline these as they pertained to art, religion, and philosophy.

The study began with an analysis of geographic and climatic effects on culture. He found that although a fundamental difference in cultures was the Western concern with moral character, an internal trait, and the Eastern with outward form, such as courtesy, basically the West was open and active, the East passive and formal. He disapproved of Eastern family patterns; he saw their concept of marriage and the family system as paternalistic, authoritarian, and frequently polygamous, and preferred the West, with its monogamous system. The Orient was submissive to authority and extremely conscious of the unequal nature of relationships, especially between men and women, while the Occident was gregarious and individualistic. The patriarchial family where concubinage was condoned led the East into authoritarianism and a fundamental pessimism. On the other hand, the West's monogamous family system, although it too was frequently patriarchial, instilled in its members a sense of optimism. Western individualism and rational thinking made that culture life-affirming, while the East's was life-negating. While the East overemphasized introspective thinking and abstraction, the West stressed the visible world and hence excelled at science. Somehow Asia's achievements in philosophy could not, in the mid-twentieth century, compare.

Gulick then compared Buddhism and Christianity in his book. Treating Buddhism analytically, he displayed none of the contempt for that non-Christian belief that missionaries were so wont to do, but he was less sympathetic to other Eastern beliefs, which he characterized as animistic, polytheistic, pantheistic, and monistic. Eastern ethics were more social custom than religion, and they did not value the individual. Eastern mysticism stressed abstract universals and absolutes while the extroverted Westerners emphasized concrete, verifiable experience. He then analyzed religious art, finding in its religious symbols a correlation with the psychic nature of the people—in the East, passive quietism, in the West, active achievement.[3] The East denied that man is the measure of all things; it minimized personality, which was the only key that could unlock the nature of Ultimate Reality. The fundamental tragedy of the East, he concluded, was that it did not know Christ, and without Him could not construct a thoroughly rational and intelligible universe.

Gulick's conclusions betrayed his view of traditional society as a static system. The West's history was turbulent, the product of its ideas about God, the world, and man. The authoritarianism of the East, its rejection of individualism, its mysticism and lack of intellectualism made it rigid. He praised Western rationalism because it valued persuasion rather than force, promoted individualism, and stressed compromise. These principles together with modern science had brought the West social progress and the hope of ending poverty and disease. On this idealistic note the book concluded.

Gulick's final book demonstrated his own optimism and religious faith. In retrospect, it seemed somewhat out of place in mid-twentieth century literature since it made no mention of communism or fascism, and its belief in progress rang somewhat hollow in the light of the Holocaust and two world wars. He provided a solid comparative analysis of some of the major religious traditions of the East and the West, and he had amassed and synthesized a vast body of knowledge and fitted it into a Christian framework. Yet the total effect was startlingly like a nineteenth-century work.

The renowned historian Arnold J. Toynbee reviewed the book for *Pacific Affairs*, in an insightful analysis that sheds further light on Gulick the missionary. He praised the book's subject matter and the author's "attractive personality," but he saw it as an historic document, a statement really expressive of the conflict within the ranks of Protestant missionaries of Gulick's generation over the relative merits of traditional Asian civilization and Christianity. The struggle was between the missionary and the reconciler, Toynbee wrote, between those who wished to convert and those who sought to give proper value to all the contributions made by mankind to the human experience. Gulick first attempted to view this conflict impartially, but by the end of the book "the missionary drives the reconciler off the field." What new insights Gulick's many years of experience had given him were finally overwhelmed by his traditional Christian approach. Toynbee found it regrettable that Gulick did not value more the East's search for peace and serenity, and that he seemed to applaud Western "aggressiveness." While Toynbee recognized that the word in the American context connoted outgoingness, even salesmanship, as a European he found it had a particularly unpleasant ring. Gulick also condemned facets of the Eastern experience while praising the same traits in the West. Toynbee concluded that the sensitive-minded reconciler was clearly present in Gulick, as well as the "blinkered and 'aggressive' missionary"; had he been born a generation later, the reconciler in him might have prevailed.[4]

Toynbee identified both the strengths and weaknesses in Gulick's approach to Japan. While he always sought to convert, to bring that land to Christianity, at the same time it was those facets of Japan which appeared most "Western" that won his greatest approval. Gulick praised Japanese intellectual curiosity, dynamism and lack of passivity. Although he valued peace as a world goal, he always admired Japan's spunkiness. The fact that Japan was no longer a traditional Asian civilization he found most appealing. Much of his criticisms of the East were really of Hindu India, and when he spoke of traditional society he usually did not have Japan in mind. Toynbee recognized that Gulick's praise of "aggressiveness" was typically Western. He did not perceive that it was also strikingly uncharacteristic of missionaries. In the 1930s most members of the Japan missionary contingent remained silent about Japan's aggression, but out of fear for their own safety, not because they approved.[5] Only the total pacifists rejected any attempt to deter Tokyo. Gulick may have remained a missionary at heart, but his goal was the reconciling of Japan and America at any cost, and appeasement coupled with excuses for Japanese militarism did not find universal acceptance among the missionary community to which he had once belonged.

However, Gulick was a missionary on the subject of the Japanese in America. Although he recognized that the Issei were from the middle and lower classes and often poorly educated, he believed that their hard work, thrift, and devotion to duty would eventually make their descendants outstanding citizens, and he sought to convince America of this. That they would become America's "model minority" would not have surprised him at all. If a "Japanese problem" existed, it was of America's making, for some Americans had encouraged the immigration of cheap labor and then sought to make it into a permanent inferior class, ineligible for citizenship. Racism pure and simple had inspired the demand for Japanese exclusion, Gulick believed, and he had little sympathy or understanding for those who portrayed the Japanese as an unassimilable yellow peril. He saw a need to limit immigration but could not condone the Californians' antipathy toward Orientals nor their discriminatory behavior.

The universal quota system that Gulick promoted would have been an eminently fair and reasonable solution to the problem of admitting immigrants, and the tragedy was that Congress might well have accepted that solution if it had not been for the Hanihara letter. Its distortion by Senator Lodge enabled the exclusionists to achieve their major goal. Denying the Japanese a quota was disastrous for Japanese-American relations, more so than Gulick recognized at the time. It was an overtly racist act, an egregious insult, and clearly discriminatory. Although a quota alone would not have prevented Pearl Harbor, it would have deprived the Japanese military of a potent weapon in their efforts to portray the United States as the nation's natural enemy. Gulick's plan was farsighted and humane, and he came very close to convincing the American Congress that his quota system including Japan was the most equitable and workable solution to the immigration question. California's exclusionists hated him for this, but the very strength of their venomous attack is testimony to the determination of his effort. He was a tireless and courageous advocate of justice.

Gulick was also perceptive in his recognition of the link between domestic policy and foreign relations. As New Left historians have observed in another context, what a nation does at home has a direct bearing on its foreign policy. One can trace economic motivation as a thread connecting such disparate elements as immigration, expansion, and war. At the roots of the exclusion policy was racism and a fear of economic competition from Japanese laborers. Ironically, the only long-term foundation of peace between America and Japan lay in the latter nation's willingness to pursue economic diplomacy, foregoing short-term gains for the promise of prosperity through trade. That trade, however, became the victim of America's high tariff policy during the twenties, while racism led to Japanese exclusion. The tariff and the immigration laws poisoned relations during the one decade when peace had a chance. Japan based its diplomacy during that decade on its economic well-being, of which overseas emigration was a vital part. The rejection of the racial equality clause in the Covenant of the League of Nations and the racist actions of the American Senate led to the formation of a number of right-wing anti-American associations to protest the government's policy, and demands for continental expansion reemerged. As Akira Iriye has written, "America's racism seemed to call for a pan-Asianist response." Racial equality was the key to the world's acceptance of a new order based on economic interdependence among nations. To Japan that included the right to resettle its surplus population.[6]

The issue was symbolic as much as it was real. Gulick recognized that exclusion was a deep affront to Japan, causing it serious loss of face. Theodore Roosevelt had sensed that too, in 1907 and 1908, and he had worked out a compromise in the Gentlemen's Agreement to accomplish America's objectives without insulting Japan. America's leaders seemed to have lost that ability in 1924. Gulick knew the importance of maintaining appearances as much as he understood the need to curtail immigration. His greatest contribution was to instruct America in the need to be sensitive to other nations' needs. Postwar immigration policy reflects his message: that while other reasons may be valid causes of restriction, race alone cannot be a justification for exclusion.

Gulick was an important minor figure in the internationalist movement of the interwar years. He believed in a harmonious world order based on reason and the Christian spirit, but World War I taught him that such a goal could not be achieved through war, and his views on conflict changed dramatically as he became a fervent apostle of peace. Like so many of his fellow clerics in 1914 he thought that the European war was a necessary fight of the forces of good against evil. Believing fervently in nonintervention, he subscribed to the crusade to make the world safe for democracy only after Wilson's efforts to mediate had failed and the German U-boat brought war to America. He then joined the ranks of Wilsonian internationalists. Disillusioned with the war's outcome, he did not break faith with the dream of collective security; he saw the League of Nations as a major avenue to prevent the recurrence of such a cataclysm, and, like the World Court, a worthy goal. Never a total pacifist, he believed in the historic concept of a "just war," but he worked with determination in the Federal Council of Churches to prevent another conflict, particularly in Asia. Like so many others, he championed the causes espoused by the religious wing of the peace movement. He became an advocate of arms limitation, the World Court, and the outlawry of war movement. Recognizing that a defenseless America was unacceptable, he advocated instead drastic multinational arms reductions and urged the nation to lead the way. Arms expenditures and buildups were mere steps along the road to war, as was universal military training, he felt. When the outlawry movement replaced the league and court as an even more attractive solution to war, he helped persuade the churches to endorse it. He fervently supported the Kellogg-Briand Peace Pact but he recognized that the nations had to be committed to the cause of peace before the pact would be effective. Gulick shared many of the weaknesses of the peace movement of which he was a part: he was visionary, idealistic and reluctant to endorse sanctions or any use of force to compel compliance. His immigration plan was based on a realistic assessment of the situation—the need to control numbers and, at the same time, not to affront a powerful nation—yet his plans for peace underestimated the dangers to American security posed by the Axis powers. He did not understand the devastating implications for peace of the world-wide economic depression, and he came more to believe that only Asians could solve Asia's problems in the years just before the war.

Gulick was most concerned about Japan. He recognized the need to reduce friction and prevent the possibility of a trans-Pacific conflict. He believed if he presented Americans with a more sympathetic and accurate picture of Japan that he might convert them to his position. The China missionaries did this very successfully for the nation they championed, but Gulick worked virtually alone in his attempts to make a case for Japan. He was hampered by a lack of support from fellow missionaries or even much encouragement from the Federal Council of Churches. Although he could understand the reasons for Japan's takeover of Manchuria, few Christian internationalists could condone this use of force, and Gulick himself had doubts when Japanese militarism showed no signs of abating. He could not assume a previous positive image of Japan on which to construct his case, for since the turn of the century America had mistrusted that land. Yet he recognized the dangers of war if America did not change its non-recognition policy—which he disapproved of as unnecessary and erroneous—and in that he was correct. As the thirties passed and the Japanese moved steadily against China, he saw the futility of "sticking pins in tigers," of irritating Japan by opposing its expansion without moving effectively to stop it or help it solve its economic problems. He opposed economic sanctions even after the outbreak of war in 1937, for he feared they would only cause Japan to turn on America. He believed Japan was acting out of fear of communist aggression in Asia rather than from a desire to seize territory for its own sake, and there he touched on an issue the United States would not recognize until the late 1940s. China's resistance should not be aided by American arms either, he felt; the Neutrality Acts prohibiting the sale of weapons to either side in a conflict should have been applied. Yet he favored letting the East Asians settle the issue themselves, and he seemed to hope the Chinese could ultimately defeat Japanese militarism. Japan's brutal warfare finally raised questions in his mind about a military solution, but he felt America should stay out of the conflict. War would come, he warned Secretary Hull in 1940, if America's policy of unyielding opposition to Japanese expansionism did not change. He was right. He had, after a life of study, come to understand the Japanese mind all too well. His failure was in his inability to convince influential Americans of the truth of his observations.

Gulick believed in international justice and goodwill. The creation of a Christian internationalism was the necessary work of the churches if the Western nations were to be reformed—a task he considered as important as the conversion of the East. He blamed organized religion for its failure to prevent conflict in 1914, and one could draw the same conclusions from the failure of the peace movement in the 1920s. A Christian approach to international relations did not fail; it had never been tried. Each president from Wilson to Roosevelt conceived of diplomacy in realistic terms and sought to achieve his goals through manipulation since he had no force to use. Neither the presidents nor the Christian internationalists were imaginative enough to devise a way to stop Hitler; but perhaps only force could have done that.

Gulick was a man of God who sought peace in a hostile world, a Wilsonian and a Christian statesman who believed in the liberal solutions—collective security, free trade, and the democratic world order, within a Christian context. It was both ironic and unfair that he should have run afoul of the nascent security state of the 1920s. The record does not reveal who wanted Gulick's reputation smeared, or why. Certainly the China missionaries did not encounter such harrassment. While exclusionist leaders in California like McClatchy and Phelan disliked Gulick, it seems unlikely that they would have alerted not one but three intelligence operations to keep him under surveillance. It appears that Gulick's affinity for Japan was the key. While other ethnic groups were unpopular in America, in the years immediately following World War I no other foreign nation seemed to pose such a threat to America's security. The navy did, after all, begin to play war games in 1924 assuming Japan would be the eventual enemy. The persecution of Gulick stems from that same climate of fear, and such a sentiment explains why Gulick would have such poor success in convincing his countrymen that Japan was a reasonable, nonaggressive nation. The belief that Japan would ultimately be our opponent in war must have affected far more than just the navy.

Gulick died as the atomic age opened and thus did not have to deal with its challenge to the world view he held dear. As Stanley Hoffmann has written of that world-shattering transformation:

One could no longer vacillate from insulation to world utopias. One had to say goodby to Briand-Kellogg Pacts that excommunicate war, to policies of non-recognition without sanctions, to bills and resolutions that try to build safe walls for isolation in the hope that evil would not seep through. One had to say goodby to foolish illusions about the rule of trust among the Great Powers, or the rule of law among states through the ministry of a world organization; but one also had to give up the dream of the universal triumph of democratic ideals through an armed crusade, through "just war." In the atomic age, this would put an end to history itself.[7]

For Hoffmann the answer was national security: one wonders what Sidney Gulick would have chosen since his world view was based on the unchanging bedrock of Christendom. The Christian internationalist approach to peace in the 1920s and 1930s could not meet the challenge of global war and the opening of the atomic age. The solutions of the twenties had proven inadequate to maintain peace, but was that the result of the failure of their basic premise? Gulick would have denied that, and a resurgence

of the peace movement in the 1980s testifies to the persistence of
his dream. To him the search for peace, equity, justice, and a way
to translate universal brotherhood into reality was a timeless and
immortal quest. At his death he did not believe he had failed. To
fight the good fight for a cause in which one believed was justification enough. He was certain one day America would end Asian
exclusion and treat its citizens of Japanese origin with dignity and
respect, and he was right. America and Japan did become allies,
and peace in the Pacific is preserved by their friendship. Gulick's
goals may have been premature, but history has vindicated him.

NOTES

1. A MISSIONARY CHILD

1. Henry O. Dwight, H. Allen Tupper, and Edwin M. Bliss, eds., *Encyclopedia of Missions* (New York: Funk and Wagnalls, 1904), 281; Rufus Anderson, *History of the Mission of the American Board of Foreign Missions to the Sandwich Islands*, 3d ed. (Boston: Congregational Publishing Board, 1872); Ann Eliza Gulick and Mrs. Orramel H. Gulick, *The Pilgrims of Hawaii* (New York: Fleming H. Revell Co., 1918), 312–13.

2. Sidney L. Gulick, "A Sketch of My Life," m.s., circa 1904, papers of Sidney L. Gulick, Jr. (hereafter cited as SLG, Jr. Papers). Sidney will hereafter be referred to as SLG when citing correspondences, or otherwise as Gulick.

3. Ibid.

4. Ibid.

5. Alan F. Perry, "The American Board of Commissioners for Foreign Missions and the London Missionary Society in the Nineteenth Century: A Study of Ideas"; Fred Field Goodsell, *You Shall Be My Witnesses*.

6. R. Pierce Beaver, "North American Thought on the Fundamental Principles of Missions During the Nineteenth Century: A Survey Article," *Church History* 21 (December 1952):347.

7. Jane Hunter, *The Gospel of Gentility: American Women Missionaries in Turn-of-the-Century China* (New Haven: Yale Univ. Press, 1984), 11. The quotation is from R. Pierce Beaver, *All Loves Excelling: American Protestant Women in World Mission*, 51–52.

8. See Sandra C. Taylor, "The Sisterhood of Salvation and the Sunrise Kingdom: Congregational Women Missionaries in Meiji Japan," *Pacific Historical Review* 47 (February 1979): 27–45, and Beaver, *All Loves Excelling*, 50–53.

9. Barbara Welter, "The Cult of True Womanhood: 1820–1860," *American Quarterly* 18 (Summer 1966), 151–74.

10. Taylor, "Sisterhood of Salvation," 27–45; Beaver, *All Loves Excelling*, 50–53.

11. The sources for these years of Gulick's life are "A Sketch of My Life," "Chronology," written August 16, 1933, in the author's possession, and the journal he kept sporadically from age ten on, in the family papers at Houghton Library, Harvard (hereafter cited as GFP for Gulick family papers, followed by a number designating box number in which the manuscript may be found). The family maintained a voluminous correspondence, most of which is included in the papers. Information on Ollie is from Frances Gulick Jewett, *Luther Halsey*

Gulick (Boston: Congregational Sunday School and Publishing Society, 1895), 248–49, 264–65.

12. "A Sketch of My Life."

13. Ibid.

14. SLG to Cara Fisher, Dec. 23, 1879, GFP 10.

15. SLG to his children, Aug. 30, 1942, Honolulu, SLG, Jr. Papers.

16. Journal, Dec. 21, 1877, GFP 10.

17. "A Sketch of My Life."

18. Ibid.

19. Journal, July 29, 1880–Jan. 1882; SLG to Louisa Gulick, Apr. 4, 1880, GFP 10.

20. Journal, Oct. 3, 1880, GFP 10.

21. Ibid., and "A Sketch of My Life."

22. "A Sketch of My Life."

23. Hattie Gulick to Luther H. Gulick, Sr., Feb. 20, 1882, GFP 10.

24. SLG to Cara, n.d. 1870; also May 14 and Aug. 20, 1882, Mar. 13, and Mar. 27, 1883, GFP 10.

25. SLG to children, Aug. 30, 1942, SLG, Jr. Papers.

26. "A Sketch of My Life."

27. Ibid.

28. Ibid.

29. Journal, Jan.–May 1884; SLG to Cara, Sept. 2, Sept. 18, Sept. 28, Oct. 31, and Nov. 4, 1884; Cara to SLG, Dec. 22, 1884, GFP 10.

30. Journal, n.d. 1885, GFP 10.

31. "Chronology" and "A Sketch of My Life"; Luther H. Gulick, Sr., to SLG, July 7, 1885; SLG to Luther, Sr., Aug. 24, 1885; SLG to Cara, n.d. 1886, GFP 10.

32. SLG to Rev. Judson Smith, ABCFM, Boston, Jan. 1, Mar. 3, Mar. 28, and Apr. 5, 1886, ABCFM, Japan Letters, vol. 10; Journal, Jan. 3–Sept. 1886.

33. Cara to SLG, Sept. 22 and Oct. 28, 1886; Hattie Gulick to SLG, Oct. 29, 1886; SLG to Cara, Nov. 5, 1886; Cara to SLG, Jan. 1, 1887, GFP 11.

34. SLG to Cara, Jan. 11, 1887, GFP 11.

35. Cara to SLG, Jan. 19, 1887, GFP 11.

36. SLG to Rev. N. G. Clark and D. D. Reid, Boston, Mar. 7, 1887; SLG to Rev. Smith, Mar. 10, 1887, ABCFM, Japan Letters, vol. 10.

37. SLG to Cara, Jan. 29, 1887, GFP 11; interview with Sidney L. Gulick, Jr., San Diego, Calif., Jan. 24, 1980.

38. SLG to the ABCFM, Feb. 18, 1887, GFP 11, and ABCFM, Card Files, Box 34, Houghton Library.

39. Cara to SLG, Feb. 13, 1887; SLG to Cara, Feb. 26, 1887, GFP 11.

40. "A Sketch of My Life" and "Chronology."

41. "Reminiscences," Oct. 1, 1934, GFP 20, and "Chronology." Sidney wrote a series of sketches after his retirement, which he titled "Reminiscences." Many had specific titles, which are indicated in subsequent notes.

2. THE MAKING OF A MISSIONARY

1. Histories of the first period of Christianity in Japan include: G. B. Sansom, *The Western World and Japan: A Study in the Interaction of European and Asiatic Cultures* (New York: Vintage, 1949), chapter 6; Otis Cary, *Roman Catholic and Greek Orthodox Missions*, vol. 1 of *A History of Christianity in Japan*, chapters 1–7; Kenneth Scott Latourette, *The Great Century: Northern Africa and Asia*, vol. 6 of *A History of the Expansion of Christianity*; George Elison, *Deus Destroyed: The Image of Christianity in Early Modern Japan* (Cambridge, Mass.: Harvard Univ. Press, 1973); C. R. Boxer, *The Christian Century in Japan: 1549–1650* (Berkeley: Univ. of California Press, 1951).

2. Histories of the Protestant missions in Japan include: Latourette, *The Great Century*; Evarts B. Greene, *A New Englander in Japan: Daniel Crosby Greene* (Boston: Houghton Mifflin Co., 1927); John Hyde DeForest, *Sunrise in the Sunrise Kingdom* (New York: The Young People's Missionary Movement, 1904); Winburn T. Thomas, *Protestant Beginnings in Japan*; H. Ritter, *A History of Protestant Missions in Japan*; M. L. Gordon, *Thirty Eventful Years: The Story of the American Board's Mission in Japan, 1869-1899*; Gladys Eugenia Bryant, "American Congregational Missionaries and Social Reform in Meiji Japan (1870–1900)" (Ph.D. diss., Vanderbilt Univ., 1971); Cary, *Protestant Missions*, vol. 2 of *History of Christianity*.

3. Gordon, *Thirty Eventful Years*, 5–13; Bryant, "American Congregational Missionaries," 364–68, 404.

4. Greene, *A New Englander in Japan*, 1–20; Gordon, *Thirty Eventful Years*, 6–8.

5. Thomas, *Protestant Beginnings*, 71–72.

6. Sansom, *Western World*, chapters 11–12; Edwin O. Reischauer, *The United States and Japan* (Cambridge, Mass.: Harvard Univ. Press, 1957), 328.

7. Sansom, *Western World*, 468–71; Hugh Borton, *Japan's Modern Century: From Perry to 1970* (New York: Ronald Press, 1970), chapter 5.

8. Kishimoto Hideo, *Japanese Religion in the Meiji Era*, 52–54.

9. Gordon, *Thirty Eventful Years*, 11–13; Ernest E. Best, *Christian Faith and Cultural Crisis: The Japanese Case*, 70–77; Cary, *History of Christianity* 2:73–81; Kishimoto, *Japanese Religion*, 69.

10. Cary, *History of Christianity* 2:77–82; Best, *Christian Faith*, 7; Kishimoto, *Japanese Religion*, 17–18.

11. Kishimoto, *Japanese Religion*, 48.

12. Cary, *Japan and Its Regeneration* (New York: Student Volunteer Movement for Foreign Missions, 1899), 101–7; Taylor, "Sisterhood of Salvation," 32.

13. Cary, *Japan and Its Regeneration*, 122–23.

14. Orramel Gulick to the ABCFM, Kobe, Dec. 16, 1871, ABCFM, Japan Letters, vol. 1.

15. Masao Takenaka, *Reconciliation and Renewal in Japan* (New York: Student Volunteer Movement for Christian Missions and Friendship Press, 1957), 15–16; George E. Moore, "Samurai Conversion: The Case of Kumamoto," 40–48.

16. Takenaka, *Reconciliation and Renewal*, 18–19. On the reasons for conversion, see Irwin Scheiner, *Christian Converts and Social Protest in Meiji Japan*, chapters 3 and 4; Kishimoto, *Japanese Religion*, 179; John Howes, "Japanese Christians and American Missionaries," in Marius B. Jansen, ed., *Changing Japanese Attitudes Toward Modernization*, 344–56; Amakawa Junjiro, "An Aspect of the Adaptation of 'The Protestant Ethics' to Meiji Japan," *Kwansei Gakuin University Annual Studies* 24(December 1975): 51–53.

17. Sansom, *Western World*, 473; Cary, *History of Christianity* 2:123; Mutsui Hisashi, "Dōshisha and the Kumamoto Band," *Japan Christian Quarterly* 25(April 1956):112; Howes, "Japanese Christians," 340–44; Moore, "Samurai Conversion," 40–48; Scheiner, *Christian Converts*, 76–95. The two best-known future leaders from this group of converts were Ebina Danjō and Tokutomi Soho. See also Amakawa, "Aspect of the Adaptation," 52.

18. Kishimoto, *Japanese Religion*, 18–22.

19. Cary, *History of Christianity* 2: 114–19; Gordon, *Thirty Eventful Years*, 21–23. On Niijima's life, see Jerome D. Davis, *A Sketch of the Life of Rev. Joseph Hardy Neesima* (Tokyo: Z. P. Maruya, 1890).

20. Mutsui, "Dōshisha and the Kumamoto Band," 112.

21. Yamamori Tetsunao, *Church Growth in Japan: A Study in the Development of Eight Denominations, 1859–1939*, 27–31; and Thomas, *Protestant Beginnings*, 70–74.

22. Yamamori, *Church Growth*, 54–56; Best, *Christian Faith*, 84–90; Howes, "Japanese Christians," 366–68.

23. M. L. Gordon, *An American Missionary in Japan*, 8–9.

24. George W. Knox, "Japan and Foreign Missions," *Missionary Review* 11(1888):92.

25. W. C. Kitchin, "Christianity as a Factor in Japanese Politics," *Chautauquan* 18(1891):346–49.

26. James H. Pettee, "A New Peril in Japan," *Missionary Herald* 82(1886): 174–75.

27. Dwight Learned, "A Plea for New Missionaries," *Missionary Herald* 82(1886):179–80.

28. *The Outlook* 52(1895):836. See also Knox, "Japan and Foreign Missions," 92–94, and "A General View of Missions—Japan," *Andover Review* 8(1887): 202–10; and Gordon, *American Missionary*, 74–79.

29. Pettee, "Reasons for Converting Japan Now," *Missionary Herald* 82(1886):263–64.

30. Gordon, *Thirty Eventful Years*, 83–88.

31. SLG to Rev. N. G. Clark, Aug. 26 and Oct. 26, 1889, ABCFM, Japan Letters, vol. 10; and SLG to Dr. Davis, Jan. 4, 1890, GFP 11.

32. SLG to friends, June 14 and June 18, 1890, GFP 11.

33. "Reminiscences: The Church Union Movement, 1888," Aug. 15, 1935, GFP 20; and Cary, *History of Christianity* 2:193–95.

34. Yamamori, *Church Growth*, 54–56.

35. Julia Gulick to the ABCFM, n.d. 1892, ABCFM, Japan Letters, vol. 4.

36. SLG letters of Sept. 12 and Oct. 10, 1890, Nov. 7, 1891, Oct. 11, 1892, Letterbook 1890–95, GFP 12.

37. SLG to the ABCFM, Apr. 4, 1891, ABCFM, Japan Letters, vol. 21.

38. Newsletter (to family and friends), Jan. 10, 1892, GFP 12.

39. "Reminiscences: Kumamoto," Sept. 17, 1934, GFP 21.

40. Borton, *Japan's Modern Century*, chapter 8.

41. Michio Nagai, "Westernization and Japanization: The Early Meiji Transformation of Education," in Donald Shively, ed., *Tradition and Modernization in Japanese Culture*, 35–42.

42. Sansom, *Western World*, 463–67; Shively, "The Japanization of the Middle Meiji," in *Tradition and Modernization*, 88–89; Robert S. Schwantes, *Japanese and Americans: A Century of Cultural Relations*, 167; Nagai, "Westernization and Japanization," 75; Kenneth Pyle, *The New Generation in Meiji Japan: Problems of Cultural Identity, 1885–1895* (Stanford, Calif.: Stanford Univ. Press, 1969), 120–22.

43. Cary, *History of Christianity* 2:221–27.

44. Shively, "Japanization," 97–103.

45. Thomas, *Protestant Beginnings*, 186–90; Robert E. Speer, *Missions and Modern History: A Study of the Missionary Aspects of Some Great Movements of the Nineteenth Century* (New York: Fleming H. Revell Co., 1904), 2:412–13.

46. Kishimoto, *Japanese Religion*, 26–29.

47. As cited in Cary, *History of Christianity* 2:143.

48. Schwantes, "Christianity versus Science: A Conflict of Ideas in Meiji Japan," 128–31; Cary, *History of Christianity* 2:148; Latourette, *The Great Century*, 396–98.

49. Daniel Crosby Greene, "The Period of 'Trial' of Christianity—The 1890s," in Ritter, *History of Protestant Missions*, 274.

50. George M. Rowland, "The Modern Japanese Christian Church," in George Blakeslee, *Japan and Japanese-American Relations* (New York: G. E. Stechert, 1912), 183–84.

51. Cary, *History of Christianity* 2:218–19.

52. Best, *Christian Faith*, 150.

53. Howes, "Japanese Christians," 349–56.

54. Best, *Christian Faith*, 240–41. See also "The Present Religious Crisis in Japan," *Andover Review* 15 (1891): 598–613; and George W. Knox, "The Year 1890 in Japan," *Missionary Review* 14(1891):643–47.

55. Pettee, "Japanese Desire for Self-Government," *Missionary Herald* 89(1893):363.

56. Best, *Christian Faith*, 148–50.

57. Cary, *History of Christianity* 2:244.

58. Kishimoto, *Japanese Religion*, 273–76.

59. SLG to Schuyler S. White, Mar. 1, 1890, GFP 11; SLG to the ABCFM, Mar. 14, 1892, Feb. 24, 1893, May 14, 1895, ABCFM, Japan Letters, vol. 21.

60. SLG to James Barton, May 14, 1895, ABCFM, Japan Letters, vol. 21.

61. SLG to Rev. Clark, Oct. 24, 1893, GFP 21.

62. SLG to the ABCFM, May 14, 1885, ABCFM, Japan Letters, vol. 21.

63. SLG to the ABCFM, Apr. 1, 1894, and Feb. 12, 1895, ABCFM, Japan Letters, vol. 21.

64. SLG to friends, Jan. 6, 1898; SLG to the ABCFM, Jan. 22, 1894, ABCFM, Japan Letters, vol. 21.

65. On the Dōshisha controversy, see Cary, *History of Christianity* 2:255–58; William Ellsworth Strong, *The Story of the American Board: An Account of the First Hundred Years of the American Board of Commissioners for Foreign Missions*, 358–62.

66. SLG to the ABCFM, Dec. 2, 1894, ABCFM, Japan Letters, vol. 21.

67. SLG to friends, Jan. 6, 1898, ABCFM, Japan Letters, vol. 21.

68. SLG to Cara, Dec. 15, 1895, GFP 15.

69. SLG to the ABCFM, Mar. 3, 1895, ABCFM, Japan Letters, vol. 21.

70. SLG to the ABCFM, Mar. 28, 1893, ABCFM, Japan Letters, vol. 21.

3. THE MAKING OF A JAPAN EXPERT

1. SLG to family, Jan. 12, 1896; SLG to Cara, Jan. 22, 1896, GFP 13.

2. SLG to the ABCFM, July 14, 1896, ABCFM, Japan Letters, vol. 21.

3. See Robert T. Handy, ed., *The Social Gospel in America, 1870–1920* (New York: Oxford Univ. Press, 1966), 25.

4. Gulick, *The Growth of the Kingdom of God*, 190–91.

5. Ibid., 309–10.

6. SLG to Cara, June 1897, and to brothers and sisters, Mar. 9 and Apr. 5, 1897, GFP 14.

7. SLG to the ABCFM, Nov. 18, 1897, ABCFM, Japan Letters, vol. 21.

8. "Reminiscences: Matsuyama, 1896–1904," Sept. 17, 1936, GFP 20.

9. Addison Gulick, *Evolutionist and Missionary, John Thomas Gulick Portrayed Through Documents and Discussions* (Chicago: Univ. of Chicago Press, 1932), 383. See also C. M. Severance, *Sketches of Missionaries in the 1890s*, Frank and Otis Cary, eds., Dōshisha University (Kyoto), Moonlight Series No. 8 (February 1979).

10. Addison Gulick, *Evolutionist*, 398, 505–6.

11. From the manuscript of a novel, "An Italian Tale of Love," which Sidney Gulick described as a "sermonic story" embodying his idea of "evolutionary theism," c. 1896, GFP 13.

12. Interview with Luther H. Gulick, Mar. 16, 1980, New York City; telephone conversation with Sidney L. Gulick, Jr., Nov. 18, 1981. The board papers do not mention this episode.

13. Schwantes, "Christianity versus Science." On Fenellosa see Lawrence W. Chisolm, *Fenellosa: The Far East and American Culture* (New Haven: Yale Univ. Press, 1963).

14. SLG to Prof. D. C. Wells, Dartmouth, Jan. 7, 1900, GFP 14.

15. SLG to the ABCFM, Feb. 9 and Apr. 27, 1898, ABCFM, Japan Letters, vol. 21.

16. SLG to the ABCFM, Sept. 7, 1898, ABCFM, Japan Letters, vol. 21.

17. "Reminiscences: Kumamoto," Sept. 18, 1936, GFP 20.

18. Gulick, *Evolution of the Japanese*, v–vi.

19. Ibid., 27, 77.

20. Ibid., 289.

21. Ibid., 337–38, 438–48.

22. See Lafcadio Hearn, *Japan: An Attempt at Interpretation* (New York: MacMillan, 1904), and Percival Lowell, *Occult Japan, or the Way of the Gods: An Esoteric Study of Japanese Personality and Possession* (Boston and New York: Houghton Mifflin, 1895). The best biography of Hearn is Elizabeth Stevenson, *Lafcadio Hearn* (New York: MacMillan, 1961).

23. *The Nation*, 77, Dec. 10, 1903; *New York Times*, July 18, 1903; *The Outlook*, Mar. 12, 1904; *American Journal of Sociology*, n.d. (clippings from GFP 15).

24. William James to SLG, Aug. 2, 1904, GFP 15.

25. SLG to the ABCFM, Apr. 21, 1904, ABCFM, Japan Letters, vol. 31.

26. SLG to the ABCFM, June 10, 1904, ABCFM, Japan Letters, vol. 31.

27. "Reminiscences," Sept. 18, 1936, GFP 20.

28. Thomas, *Protestant Beginnings*, 58–60.

29. SLG to a Mr. Sturges, Jan. 30, 1903, GFP 15.

30. SLG to the ABCFM, May 10 and Nov. 5, 1903, ABCFM, Japan Letters, vol. 31; to Edward Gulick, May 3, 1903; and to John T. Gulick, Oct. 9, 1903, GFP 15. Gulick's book, published in Japanese but titled in English *Evolution*, was published in Japan in 1910 and revised as *Evolution of the Human Race* in 1913.

31. SLG to Jerome Davis, Jan. 31, 1904; to George Albrecht, Feb. 3, 1904; to Dwight Learned, Feb. 3, 1904; to Daniel Crosby Greene, Feb. 16, 1904; to Learned, Feb. 19, 1904, GFP 15; and to the ABCFM, Apr. 12, 1904, ABCFM, Japan Letters, vol. 31.

32. SLG to Julia Gulick, Mar. 20, 1904, GFP 15.

33. SLG to Orramel Gulick, Apr. 19, 1904; to the ABCFM, May 21 and June 10, 1904, GFP 15.

34. Cara to SLG, Oct. 10, 1934, GFP 20.

35. "Reminiscences: Cara," Sept. 14, 1934, GFP 20.

36. SLG to Cara, n.d. 1879, GFP 20.

37. SLG to the ABCFM, Mar. 3, 1895, ABCFM, Japan Letters, vol. 21. The Gulicks ultimately had five children: Susan Fisher (born 1889), Luther Halsey (1892), Leeds (1894), Ethel (1899), and Sidney Lewis, Jr. (1903).

38. SLG to Cara, Jan. 1897, GFP 14.

39. According to reports, people so "possessed" became hysteric, acting out

the characteristics of a fox. Gulick observed many cases of this and attempted to analyze it. On spirit possession, see Winston Davis, *Dojo: Magic and Exorcism in Modern Japan* (Stanford, Calif.: Stanford Univ. Press, 1980), and Carmen Blacker, *The Catalpa Bow: A Study of Shamanistic Practices in Japan* (London: Allen and Unwin, 1975).

40. Interview with Luther Gulick, Mar. 16, 1980, New York City.

41. Ibid.

42. "Reminiscences: Our Children," Sept. 15, 1934, GFP 20.

43. "Reminscences: Cara," Sept. 14, 1934, GFP 20.

44. Gulick, "The Modern Conception of Foreign Missions," *The Outlook* 81 (1905): 563–67.

4. FROM MISSIONARY TO THEOLOGIAN

1. SLG to Cara, Jan. 3, Feb. 11, Feb. 28, Mar. 27, Apr. 1, Apr. 16, May 3, Aug. 15, 1905, GFP 15; and SLG to the ABCFM, Mar. 30 and June 26, 1905, ABCFM, Japan Letters, vol. 31.

2. "Chronology."

3. Cara to SLG, Sept. 14, 1905; SLG to Otto Hassenpflug, Apr. 22, 1906, GFP 15.

4. "Chronology."

5. "Chronology," and SLG to friends, n.d. 1907, GFP 15.

6. See Akira Iriye, *Pacific Estrangement: Japanese and American Expansion, 1897–1911.*

7. *Missionary Herald* 80(1884):304–6; Greene, *A New Englander in Japan*, 178–79, 214–16; William Neumann, *America Encounters Japan*, 68.

8. Sandra C. Thomson (now Taylor), "Meiji Japan Through Missionary Eyes: the American Protestant Experience," *The Journal of Religious History* 7(Spring 1973):255.

9. Payson J. Treat, *Diplomatic Relations Between the United States and Japan* 2:1876–1895, 436–37; and Cary, *History of Christianity* 2:253.

10. Treat, *Diplomatic Relations* 3:1895–1905, 3:79–80.

11. *Growth of the Kingdom of God*, 220.

12. "Reminiscences: Volunteer for China," Oct. 1, 1934, GFP 20.

13. SLG to friends, Mar. 16, 1904, GFP 15.

14. Gulick, "Japanese Progress and Purpose," *Missionary Review* 28(1905): 182.

15. Anon., *Missionary Review* 27(1904):569.

16. William E. Griffis, "Past and Present Christian Work for Japan," *Missionary Review* 28(1905):183–84. See also H. Loomis, "Christian Work among Japanese Soldiers," *Missionary Review* 28(1905): 119–25.

17. Elting Eliot Morison, ed., *The Letters of Theodore Roosevelt* 4:724, as cited in Charles E. Neu, *Troubled Encounter: The United States and Japan*, 41–42.

18. SLG to Edward Gulick, Dec. 8, 1904; SLG to Cara, Dec. 14, 1904, GFP 15.

19. Gulick, *The White Peril in the Far East*, 17–18, 33–34, 48, 55.

20. Ibid., 59–71.

21. Ibid., 153, 105–9, 118–22.

22. Ibid., 154–62.

23. Ibid., 164–69.

24. Eleanor Tupper and George McReynolds, *Japan in American Public Opinion* (New York: MacMillan, 1937), 6–16.

25. Iriye, *Pacific Estrangement*, 127–28.

26. Strong, *Story of the American Board*, 365–67.

27. Howes, "Japanese Christians," 360–61.

28. A. Whitney Griswold, *The Far Eastern Policy of the United States*, 104–5.

29. Schwantes, *Japanese and Americans*, 167; SLG to the ABCFM, Dec. 7, 1907, ABCFM, Japan Letters, vol. 31.

30. SLG to the ABCFM, Dec. 1, 1908 and Dec. 19, 1910, ABCFM, Japan Letters, vol. 31 and 38.

31. "Chronology" and SLG to Cara, Aug. 31, 1910, GFP 16.

32. Gilbert Bowles to a Mr. Root of the Northern California Peace Society; Bowles to SLG, Nov. 13, 1913; John Lincoln Dearig, ed., *The Christian Movement in Japan including Korea and Formosa: A Yearbook from 1914* (Yokohama: Conference of Federated Missions, 1914), 12:54–59, 155–59; Ernest W. Clement, ed., *The Christian Movement in Japan* (Tokyo: The Standing Committee of Co-operating Christian Missions, 1908), 76–77. See also Nobuya Banda and John F. Howes, eds., *Pacifism in Japan: The Christian and Socialist Tradition* (Vancouver, B.C.: Univ. of British Columbia Press, 1978).

33. SLG to Hamilton Holt, Oct. 30 and Nov. 3, 1911, GFP 16; Warren F. Kuehl, *Hamilton Holt: Journalist, Internationalist, Educator*, 101–2.

34. Iriye, *Pacific Estrangement*, 127–38; Iriye, "Japan as a Competitor, 1895–1917," in Iriye, ed., *Mutual Images: Essays in American-Japanese Relations*, 81–82; Roger Daniels, "Japanese Immigrants on a Western Frontier: The Issei in California, 1890–1940," in F. Hilary Conroy and T. Scott Miyakawa, *East Across the Pacific: Historical and Sociological Studies of Japanese Immigration and Assimilation*, 76–91.

35. Neu, *Troubled Encounter*, 55–65; Daniels, *Politics of Prejudice*, 11–45; Iriye, *Pacific Estrangement*, 157–66.

36. "Will There Be War in the Far East?" *The Outlook* 85(1910):258–60.

37. "Peace Resolution of the American Board's Japan Mission," 1911, ABCFM, Japan Letters, vol. 38.

38. SLG to editor, *Denver Post*, July 14, 1911, GFP 16.

39. SLG to Nitobe Inazō, July 20, 1911; to James Brown Scott, May 22, 1912; to Frederick Lynch, July 2, 1912, GFP 16.

40. Neu, *Troubled Encounter*, 47. See also Sandra C. Taylor, "The Ineffectual Voice: Japan Missionaries and American Foreign Policy, 1870–1914," *Pacific Historical Review* 53(Winter 1984): 20–38.

41. Arthur Diosy, *The New Far East* (New York: G. P. Putnam's Sons, 1899), 19–20.

42. Gulick, "Personal and Confidential," 1915, GFP 16.

43. James E. Reed, "American Foreign Policy and Missions," *Church History* 41(1972):232–33; Paul Varg, *Missionaries, Chinese, and Diplomats: The American Protestant Missionary Movement in China, 1890–1952* (Princeton: Princeton Univ. Press, 1958), 52; and Robert F. McClellan, "Missionary Influences on American Attitudes toward China at the Turn of this Century," *Church History* 38 (1969): 475–85.

44. James E. Reed, *The Missionary Mind and American East Asia Policy 1911–1915* (Cambridge, Mass.: Harvard Univ. Press, 1983), 24–36.

45. See Edward R. Beauchamp, *An American Teacher in Early Meiji Japan* (Honolulu: Univ. of Hawaii Press, 1976).

46. SLG to Rev. L. T. Chamberlain, July 26, 1911; to C. L. Severance, July 30, 1911, GFP 11.

47. Gulick, *Working Women of Japan*, 158.

48. Iriye, *Across the Pacific: An Inner History of American East Asian Relations*, 79.

49. "Chronology"; SLG to J. L. Barton, Feb. 1, 1913, GFP 17; to the ABCFM, June 29, 1913, ABCFM, Japan Letters, vol. 38.

50. "Chronology."

51. SLG to Prof. W. Ukita, Tokyo, Apr. 16, 1913, GFP 17.

52. SLG to G. P. Flint, Apr. 22, 1913, GFP 17.

53. SLG to James L. Barton, Apr. 27, 1913, GFP 17.

54. SLG to the ABCFM, Feb. 1, 1913, ABCFM, Japan Letters, vol. 38.

55. SLG to Shailer Mathews, Federal Council of Churches, June 10, 1913, ABCFM, Japan Letters, vol. 38.

56. SLG to the ABCFM, July 17 and Aug. 15, 1913, ABCFM, Japan Letters, vol. 38.

57. Federal Council *Bulletin*, No. 67, Jan. 1914, 4–5.

58. SLG to Barton, May 5, 1917, ABCFM, Japan Letters, vol. 38.

5. IN TRANSITION

1. SLG to Cara, Aug. 2, 1913; to Hatti, Aug. 26, 1913; to his children, Oct. 19, 1913; to Cara, Nov. 21, 1913, GFP 17; to the ABCFM, Aug. 21, 1913, ABCFM, Japan Letters, vol. 38.

2. Daniels, "Japanese Immigrants," 78–79, and "The Japanese," in John Higham, *Ethnic Leadership in America*, 36–63; Daniels, *Polictics of Prejudice*, 1–2.

3. Daniels, *Politics of Prejudice*, 44–48.

4. Ibid., 49–64.

5. Carey McWilliams, *Prejudice: Japanese-Americans, Symbol of Racial Intolerance*, 7, 298.

6. Gulick, *The American Japanese Problem: A Study in the Racial Relations of the East and the West*, 187.

7. See Yuji Ichioka, "Japanese Associations and the Japanese Government: A Special Relationship, 1909–1926," *Pacific Historical Review* 46 (1977):409–37.

8. Gulick, *American Japanese Problem*, 144.

9. He returned to the subject twenty years later in *Mixing the Races in Hawaii: A Study of the Coming Neo-Hawaiian American Race* (1937). The book, basically a study of the Japanese subculture in the Hawaiian Islands and the effects of intermarriage, marked a final rejection of his earlier objections to race mixing.

10. Gulick, *American Japanese Problem*, 153.

11. Ibid., 274–80.

12. Ibid., 284–95.

13. U. S. Senate, Reports of the Immigration Commission, 66th Cong., 3d sess., S. Doc. 747, Abstracts of Reports 1:47.

14. Daniels, *Politics of Prejudice*, 80.

15. *Book Review Digest, 1914* (New York: H. W. Wilson Co., 1915), 229.

16. Daniels, *Politics of Prejudice*, 79.

17. SLG to Cara, Nov. 21, 1913, GFP 17.

18. Charles Macfarland to SLG, Sept. 12, 1913; SLG to Rev. Shailer Mathews, June 3, 1913; to Hattie, Dec. 7, 1913; and Robert E. Speer, Report to the Commission on Foreign Missions of the FCCCA, 1913, GFP 17.

19. C. Roland Marchand, *The American Peace Movement and Social Reform, 1898–1918*, 333, 343–46; Charles H. Hopkins, *The Rise of the Social Gospel in America Protestantism, 1865–1915* (New Haven: Yale Univ. Press, 1940), 306.

20. Marchand, *Peace Movement*, 339–41; 346.

21. Ibid., 346.

22. Charles Macfarland, *Pioneers for Peace Through Religion* (New York: Fleming H. Revell Co., 1946), 39–40.

23. Gulick, "Resolution to the Japan Mission of the American Board in Respect to the Relations of the U.S. and Japan," June 3, 1913, GFP 17.

24. Barton to SLG, Feb. 18, 1914; SLG to Barton, Feb. 19 and Feb. 25, 1914, ABCFM, Japan Letters, vol. 38; Frederick Lynch to SLG, Feb. 24, 1914, Church Peace Union Papers, Council on Religion in International Affairs Collection, Butler Library, Columbia University, box 216, (hereafter cited as CRIA, followed by a number designating box number).

25. SLG to Hattie, Dec. 7, 1913; to Cara, Feb. 1 to 8, and Feb. 15, 1914, GFP 17; Daniels, "American Historians and East Asian Immigrants," 460–61.

26. Daniels, *Politics of Prejudice*, 79.

27. SLG to Barton, May 5, 1917, ABCFM, Japan Letters, vol. 38.

28. Iriye, "Japan as a Competitor," 76.

29. SLG to Stanley K. Hornbeck, May 3, 1917; Kenneth S. Latourette to SLG, May 8, 1917, CRIA 220.

30. Emmeline G. H. Condict to Secretary Charles Evans Hughes, Nov. 28,

1924. General Records of the Department of State, RG 59, File 771.945/1235. National Archives, Washington, D.C. Microcopy 423, Roll 8 (hereafter cited by decimal file number only).

31. See chapter eight.

6. THE FEDERAL COUNCIL OF CHURCHES, THE PEACE ORGANIZATION, AND THE WORLD WAR

1. David S. Patterson, *Toward a Warless World: The Travail of the American Peace Movement, 1887–1914*, 213–14; Marchand, *Peace Movement*, 351–55; Gulick, "Reminiscences: At the Outbreak of the World War," Aug. 16, 1934, GFP 20; Robert Lester, *Forty Years of Carnegie Giving: A Summary of the Benefactions of Andrew Carnegie and of the Work of the Philanthropic Trusts Which He Created* (New York: Charles Scribner's Sons, 1941), 78; quotation from Charles DeBenedetti, *The Peace Reform in American History*, 10.

2. Frederick Lynch to Charles Jefferson, July 14, 1914, CRIA 216. Lynch noted Gulick's services "are increasingly valuable (no other address aroused such enthusiasm . . . as his did) and he is having great influence with the press . . . ." See also Marchand, *Peace Movement*, 356–59; and Lester, *Forty Years*, 70.

3. Frederick Lynch, *Through Europe on the Eve of War* (New York: Church Peace Union, 1914; rpt. New York: Garland, 1971), 10.

4. Ibid., 40; and "Report of Delegates from FCCCA at Church Peace Conference at Constance, Germany, and London, Aug. 2–5, 1914," CRIA 216.

5. "Reminiscences: At the Outbreak of the World War," Aug. 16, 1934, GFP 20; SLG to children, Aug. 6, 1914, GFP 17.

6. Gulick, Appendix II, p. 114, in Lynch, *Through Europe*.

7. Ibid., 114–20.

8. David S. Patterson, introd. in Lynch, *Through Europe*, 10–12.

9. Gulick and Macfarland, *The Church and International Relations* (New York: Missionary Education Movement for the Federal Council of Churches of Christ in America, 1916), pt. 1, pp. 1–8.

10. DeBenedetti, *Origins of the Modern American Peace Movement, 1915–1929*, 99–100.

11. Gulick and Macfarland, *International Relations*, pt. 2, pp. 50–51.

12. Ray H. Abrams, *Preachers Present Arms* (New York: Round Table Press, 1933; rev. ed., Scottdale, Pa.: Herald Press, 1969), 23.

13. Gulick and Macfarland, *International Relations*, pt. 3, pp. 160–93.

14. Darrell E. Bigham, "War as Obligation in the Thought of American Christians, 1898–1920," 49–50, 45–53.

15. SLG to his sons, Aug. 11, 1914, GFP 17.

16. *New York Times*, Sept. 28, 1914.

17. Gulick and Macfarland, *International Relations*, pt. 2, pp. 54–60.

18. "Reminiscences: At the Outbreak of the World War," Aug. 16, 1934, GFP 20.

19. "Reminiscences: The World Alliance," Aug. 17, 1934, GFP 20.

20. Gulick and Macfarland, *International Relations*, pt. 3, pp. 30–37.

21. Gulick, *The Fight for Peace: An Aggressive Campaign for American Churches*, 43–54.

22. Ibid., 62–73.

23. Ibid., 130–67.

24. Ibid., 172–73.

25. *Book Review Digest, 1916* (New York: H. W. Wilson Co., 1917), citing *New York Times*, July 4, 1915; *The Independent* 82 (May 17, 1915): 296; *The Outlook* 110 (June 23, 1915): 475.

26. Gulick and Macfarland, *International Relations*, pt. 1, pp. 84–86; SLG to Barton, Mar. 2, 1916, ABCFM, Japan Letters, vol. 38; Marchand, *Peace Movement*, 361–62.

27. "Reminiscences: The World Alliance," May 17, 1934, GFP 20; Macfarland, *Pioneers for Peace*, 113–14; Gulick and Macfarland, *International Relations*, pt. 1, p. 171.

28. As cited in Marchand, *Peace Movement*, 356.

29. SLG to WAIFTC members, July 14, 1916, WAIFTC Papers, Swarthmore College Peace Collection, Haverford, Pa. (hereafter cited as SCPC).

30. SLG to Macfarland, Dec. 6, 1915, CRIA 370.

31. Marchand, *Peace Movement*, 356–59, 361–62; SLG correspondence, June 6, 1917, CRIA 220.

32. Memo, July 1, 1916, CRIA 219.

33. Gulick and Macfarland, *International Relations*, pt. 2, pp. 104–20, 143.

34. Gulick to Lynch, June 16, 1916, CRIA 370.

35. WAIFTC to members, American Branch, June 28, 1916, CRIA 370.

36. SLG to Cara, May 5, 1917; to Otis Cary, May 5, 1917; to Barton, May 5, 1917, GFP 18.

37. Family papers, May–June 1917, July 11, 1917, and Oct.–Dec. 1917; SLG to family, Sept. 23, 1917, GFP 18; announcement, June 20, 1917, CRIA 220.

38. Abrams, *Preachers Present Arms*, 80.

39. Gulick, "The Duty of the Church in This Hour of National Need," GFP 18.

40. "Reminiscences: The World Alliance," Aug. 17, 1934, GFP 20; Gulick and Macfarland, *International Relations*, pt. 2, pp. 62–66; "National Committee on the Churches and the Moral Aims of War," folder, 1917, CRIA 221; Macfarland, *Pioneers for Peace*, 64–65; Kuehl, *Hamilton Holt*, 131–32.

41. WAIFTC Report, Apr. 4, 1918, CRIA 370.

42. Bigham, "War as Obligation," 50–53; Cushing Strout, *The New Heavens and New Earth: Political Religion in America* (New York: Harper and Row, 1974), 249.

43. John A. Hutchinson, *We Are Not Divided*, 181–82. See Abrams, *Preachers Present Arms*, 79–86, for a more critical judgment.

44. "Chronology."

45. Kuehl, *Hamilton Holt*, 131–32; Macfarland, *Pioneers for Peace*, 67–76.

46. Samuel M. Cavert, *The Churches Allied for Common Tasks* (Federal Council of Churches of Christ in America, 1921), 73, as cited in Abrams, *Preachers Present Arms*, 146.

47. SLG to Cara, May 1, 1918, GFP 18; Federal Council *Bulletin*, 1, No. 6 (June 1918): 15; No. 7 (July 1918): 7; and No. 9 (October 1918): 15–16.

48. SLG to Cara, Dec. 15 and 22, 1918; Atkinson to SLG, Jan. 9, 1918, GFP 18.

49. *New York Times*, Mar. 23 and 29, 1919; "Report to WAIFTC, CPU, and FCCCA, 1919," GFP 18.

50. "Chronology," and Journal to family, Feb. 12 to 21, 1919, GFP 18.

51. Journal, Feb. 12 to 21, 1919, GFP 18.

52. Robert M. Miller, "Attitudes of the Major Protestant Churches in America Toward War and Peace, 1919–1929," 15.

53. DeBenedetti, *Origins*, 99.

54. Marchand, *Peace Movement*, 365.

55. "Reminiscences: The World Alliance," Aug. 17, 1934, GFP 20. The CPU actually funded the FCCCA rather well over the years, but not so handsomely as the WAIFTC. In 1940 the totals spent on the different organizations were the following:

National Committee on the Moral Aims of War	$119,470.00
WAIFTC (foreign branches)	606,888.13
WAIFTC (American Council)	580,823.00
FCCCA	277,308.99
The total spent by the CPU to 1940 was	$2,275,317.16

as cited in Lester, *Forty Years*, 79.

56. SLG to Macfarland, Dec. 6, 1915, CRIA 370.

57. DeBenedetti, *Origins*, 100.

7. CRUSADING FOR IMMIGRATION REFORM

1. Gulick, "Outlines of a New American-Oriental Policy," *The California Outlook* (October 11, 1913): 6–8; SLG to V. S. McClatchy, June 27, 1919, GFP 17.

2. Senator Dillingham to SLG, Jan. 19, 1914 (misdated 1913), GFP 17; *New York Times*, Feb. 3, 1914.

3. Decimal file number 811.52/230, and 811.52/233, RG 59, National Archives; SLG to S. E. Hilles, Mar. 14, 1917, CRIA 220.

4. *New York Times*, Mar. 1 and June 21, 1914; Frederick Lynch to a Mr. Phillips, Apr. 13, 1914; Commission on Relations with Japan, minutes, May 20, 1914, CRIA 216; Federal Council *Bulletin*, No. 11, Mar. 1, 1914, Bancroft Library, Univ. of California (hereafter cited as Bancroft), and Federal Council *Bulletin*, No. 56, Oct. 15, 1914, SCPC.

5. SLG to executive committee, FCCCA, Oct. 5, 1914; Commission on Relations with Japan, minutes, Oct. 9, 1914; SLG to President Wilson, Oct. 9, 1914, CRIA 216.

6. SLG to Samuel Gompers, Oct. 16, 1914, CRIA 216.

7. Commission on Peace and Arbitration to Frederick Lynch, Jan. 8, 1915, CRIA 215; Report of the Christian Embassy to Japan, Apr. 1915, Commission on Relations with Japan, folder, FCCCA papers, SCPC; *New York Times*, Jan. 29 and 30, and Feb. 28, 1915; Shailer Mathews, *New Faith for Old: An Autobiography* (New York: MacMillan, 1936), 198–203.

8. SLG to Chester Rowell, Jan. 9, 1915, Rowell Papers, Bancroft.

9. "A Church Mission to Japan," *Literary Digest* 50 (March 27, 1915): 693.

10. Harry A. Millis, *The Japanese Problem in the United States: An Investigation for the Committee on Relations with Japan Appointed by the Federal Council of Churches of Christ in America* (New York: MacMillan, 1915), vii, viii, ix; *The Report of the Christian Embassy to Japan* (New York: Federal Council of Churches, 1915), 41–44.

11. Gulick, *The Pacific Coast and the New Oriental Policy: A Report to the Commission on Relations with Japan of the Federal Council of Churches of Christ in America* (New York: Federal Council of Churches, 1916); Millis, *Japanese Problem*, 298–99.

12. Montaville Flowers to Chester Rowell, Apr. 16, 1914, Rowell Papers, Bancroft; Daniels, *Politics of Prejudice*, 81.

13. Rowell to Flowers, Apr. 27, 1915, Rowell Papers, Bancroft.

14. Montaville Flowers, *The Japanese Conquest of American Public Opinion* (New York: George H. Doran, 1917).

15. E. M. Blanford, report in FBI files, Oct. 21, 1915, RG 65, 12E Box 4A/OG 55, National Archives. Additional information was acquired through a Freedom of Information Act request. (Information so obtained will henceforth be cited FOIA.)

16. Varg, *Missionaries, Chinese, and Diplomats*, 143–45; and Neu, *Troubled Encounter*, 85–90. Varg refers to Gulick as "in the employ of the Japanese government as an advisor and propagandist," 144. His source was Bishop Bashford's diary.

17. SLG to Sen. James Phelan, Mar. 18, 1914, Phelan Papers, Bancroft; SLG to Phelan, Nov. 4, 1915; Flowers to Holt, Dec. 14, 1915; Holt to Flowers, Dec. 31, 1915, CRIA 218.

18. *The Journal and Messenger* (Cincinnati), Oct. 8, 1914, GFP 17.

19. SLG to Prof. Millis, Dec. 23, 1914, CRIA 216; letter to author, May 10, 1982, from James K. Hall, Chief, Freedom of Information-Privacy Acts Section, Records Management Division, Federal Bureau of Investigation.

20. Gulick, "New Oriental Policy," *Asia* 17(1917):720–21; *Immigration Journal* reprints dated June 8, 1916, in CRIA 218.

21. Gulick, *America and the Orient*, 13–27, 43–48.

22. *Independent* 88 (October 2, 1916):30, as cited in *Book Review Digest, 1916* (New York, 1917): 233.

23. SLG to Sen. John Downey Works, July 26, 1916, Works Papers, Bancroft.

24. Sen. Benjamin F. Welty to SLG, Dec. 23, 1916, CRIA 220.

25. Daniels, *Politics of Prejudice*, 98.

26. SLG to Doremus Scudder, Feb. 15, 1916, CRIA 218.

27. SLG to K. Kanzaki, Feb. 15, 1916, CRIA 218.

28. Flowers, *Japanese Conquest*, 59–62, 79–88, 89–100.

29. Daniels, *Politics of Prejudice*, 81.

30. Harvey H. Guy to SLG, Apr. 7 and 12, 1916, and Feb. 21, 1917; SLG to Guy, Apr. 13, 1916, CRIA 218 and 220.

31. *American Democracy and Asiatic Citizenship*, 105, 257, ix.

32. *Book Review Digest* (New York, 1918): 193.

33. 39 Stat. 874.

34. Elizabeth J. Harper and Roland F. Chase, *Immigration Laws of the United States*, 10; Frank F. Chuman, *The Bamboo People: The Law and Japanese Americans* (Del Mar, Calif.: Publishers Inc., 1976), 94–95.

35. SLG to family, July 1917, GFP 18.

36. SLG to Cara, Oct. 17, 1918, GFP 18; SLG to Pres. Ray Lyman Wilbur, Oct. 14 and Nov. 8, 1918, Wilbur Papers, Hoover Institution of War, Revolution and Peace, Stanford University (hereafter cited as Hoover).

37. John Higham, *Strangers in the Land* (New Brunswick, N.J.: Rutgers Univ. Press, 1955), 302–3; SLG to Luther Gulick, May 10, 1917, GFP 18, and an undated memo, GFP 3.

38. SLG to NCCIL members, Apr. 1919, GFP 18; SLG to H. A. Atkinson, Mar. 17 and 24, 1919, CRIA 370.

39. "Report of Progress," n.d., 1919, NCCIL folder, SCPC.

40. "Report of Progress #2," n.d., 1919, Wilbur Papers, Hoover.

41. "Report of Progress #3," Aug. 25, 1919, CRIA 370.

42. SLG to Wilbur, Aug. 26, 1919, Wilbur Papers, Hoover.

43. "Report of Progress #5" Jan. 20, 1920, NCCIL folder, SCPC.

44. SLG to NCCIL members, Mar. 5, June 15 and 18, 1920, CRIA 373.

8. THE EXCLUSIONISTS COUNTERATTACK

1. Peter H. Wang, *Legislating Normalcy: The Immigration Act of 1924* (San Francisco: R. and E. Research Associates, 1975), 72–74; Tupper and McReynolds, *Japan in American Public Opinion*, 177.

2. Fred High to SLG, May 17, 1916; SLG to High, June 23, 1916; Flowers to SLG, June 30, 1916; SLG to Flowers, July 1, 1916; Macfarland to High, July 18, 1916, CRIA 218.

3. Edward F. Morse, report of Oct. 30, 1920, RG 65/12E/Box 211B/OG 311343.

4. Memorandum on Sidney L. Gulick, May 20, 1921, Dept. of Justice, FOIA.

5. Chuman, *Bamboo People*, 75.

6. Daniels, *Politics of Prejudice*, 81–91; Dorothy Kaucher, *James Duval Phelan: A Portrait, 1861–1930* (Saratoga, Calif.: Gallery Committee of the Montalvo Assoc., 1965), 23–24.

7. SLG to Sen. Phelan, Feb. 28, 1920, Phelan Papers, Bancroft.

8. Congressional Directory, 66th Cong., 3d sess., Dec. 1920, p. 9; and John

E. Reinecke, *Feigned Necessity: Hawaii's Attempt to Obtain Chinese Contract Labor, 1921–1923* (San Francisco: Chinese Materials Center, 1979), 205.

9. SLG to family, June 20, 1919, GFP 18; testimony of Sidney L. Gulick, House Committee on Immigration, June 8, 1919, HR 67A-F18.3. The Bureau of Investigation later prepared a detailed memorandum on the subject of Gulick's financial support, basically supporting Gulick's contentions except for occasional allegations about mysterious sources of funds from the Japanese government to the FCCCA to underwrite Gulick's work; Dept. of Justice, file submitted by J. E. Hoover, May 20, 1921, FOIA.

10. "Reminiscences: Personal Slanderous Attacks," July 26, 1934, GFP 20.

11. Gulick testimony and Macfarland testimony, House Committee on Immigration, June 13 and 18, 1919, HR 67A-F18.3.

12. Macfarland, *Across the Years* (New York: MacMillan, 1936), *Pioneers for Peace*, and *Christian Unity in the Making: The First Twenty-five Years of the Federal Council of Churches of Christ in America* (New York: Federal Council of Churches of Christ in America, 1948).

13. SLG to family, June 20, 1919, GFP 18.

14. Daniels, *Politics of Prejudice*, 91.

15. V. S. McClatchy testimony, House Immigration and Naturalization Committee, HR 67A-F18.3.

16. McClatchy, "The Germany of Asia," a pamphlet cited in Tupper and McReynolds, *Japan in American Public Opinion*, 170.

17. Gulick to McClatchy, June 27, 1919, Papers of the National Council of Churches, Presbyterian Historical Society, Philadelphia.

18. Replies to SLG circular letter July 1919 from David Starr Jordan, July 15, 1919, from J. F. C. Hagen, July 18, 1919, from R. N. Lynch, July 25, 1919, GFP 18.

19. The *Sacramento Bee* published "Japan's Peaceful Penetration," June 1919, "Our New Racial Problem," "Japanese Immigration and Its Menace," and "The Birthrate as an Agency for Colonization," in November 1920, and "Japanese-American Relations" and "Causes which Produce Friction and the Obvious Remedies," n.d. All are by McClatchy and are in GFP 18. See also SLG to McClatchy, June 27 and Aug. 13, 1919, GFP 18.

20. *San Francisco Examiner*, Aug. 15, 1919.

21. *New York Times*, Mar. 21, 1921 and Apr. 8 and 11, 1920; Macfarland, *Christian Unity in the Making*, 163–64, and CRO minutes, Sept. 8, 1919, CRIA 370.

22. Gulick, *Japan and the Gentleman's Agreement* (New York: Commission on Relations with the Orient of the FCCCA, 1920).

23. James D. Phelan, *Travel and Comment* (San Francisco: A.M. Robertson, 1923), 8.

24. Gulick testimony, "The Modified Percentage Plan for Restriction of Immigration," House Committee on Immigration and Naturalization, hearings May 22, 1920, HR 66th Cong., 2d sess.

25. "Reminiscences: Personal Slanderous Attacks," July 25 and 26, 1934, GFP 20.

26. Frank J. Donner, *The Age of Surveillance: The Aims and Methods of America's Political Intelligence System* (New York: Alfred A. Knopf, 1980), 3–6.

27. Reports of July 18 and 23, Aug. 2 and 17, 1918, Dept. of Justice, FOIA.

28. Gulick did meet with a special agent of the Bureau of Investigation on Apr. 12, 1921, after he had learned of their concerns. The agent denied the investigation was of him personally and claimed it only involved the activities of the NCCIL (a clear falsehood). Gulick denied he was a Japanese agent and gave the agent copies of his recent writings. Bureau Report, Apr. 15, 1921 (name of agent deleted), Dept. of Justice records, FOIA.

29. SLG to Numano, Y., June 5, 1916, CRIA 218.

30. Interview with Sidney Gulick, Jr., Jan. 24, 1980.

31. See, for example, K. K. Kawakami to SLG, Dec. 30, probably 1917, GFP 18.

32. Reports dated Mar. 25, 1919, Apr. 3 and 10, 1919, Counsellor Files, Dept. of State, Decimal File 894.0–41 and May 5, 1919, 894–74. (Hereafter cited as Counsellor Files.)

33. F. W. Wilson, report of July 7, 1919, Counsellor Files, 894.0–41.

34. Wilson, report of Aug. 28, 1919, Counsellor Files, 894/117. This file was marked "investigative, confidential, and F.B.I."

35. Wilson, report, "Japanese Activities in the U.S." labeled "Confidential," Counsellor Files, 894.0–41.

36. Counsellor Files, 894.0–41.

37. Letter from John Lord O'Brian, Special Assistant to the Attorney General for War Work, to Brig. Gen. M. Churchill, director of Military Intelligence, War Dept., Oct. 7, 1918, RG 65, Box 2876, File 195892.

38. K. K. Kawakami, *Senator Phelan, Dr. Gulick and I* (San Francisco, privately published, 1920); John P. Irish, *The Stolen Letters of Senator Phelan: How Did He Get Them?* (Oakland, privately published, 1920), SCPC.

39. Edward P. Morse, report of Nov. 6, 1920, RG 65/OG 55.

40. Morse, report, week of Oct. 23, 1920, RG 65/12E/Box 211B/OG 311343. See also report of Oct. 9 and Oct. 16, 1920, RG 65/12E/Box 3A/OG 55.

41. Morse, report, week of Oct. 30, 1920, RG 65/12E/Box 211B/OG 311343.

42. David Williams, "The Bureau of Investigation and Its Critics, 1919–1921: The Origins of Federal Political Surveillance," *Journal of American History* 68 (December 1981): 576–77.

43. H. D. Kirk, report of Nov. 13, 1920, RG 65/12E/Box 211B/OG 311343.

44. Report of Nov. 20, 1920, RG 65/12E/Box 4A/OG 55.

45. Report of Dec. 1, 1920, RG 65/12C/Box 69/BS 204048–21.

46. Report of Dec. 4, 1920, RG 65/12E/Box 4A/OG 55.

47. Reports of Apr. 18, May 17 and 20, Aug. 2, 1921, and July 15, 1922. The report noting the charge was unsubstantiated is dated Aug. 11, 1926. The Bureau of Investigation apparently believed for a while Flowers's allegation that Gulick had been sent here by the Japanese government, which promised to subsidize all his work on their behalf. Memorandum of May 20, 1921, Dept. of Justice files, FOIA. Also located in Counsellor Files, 894–240.

48. Williams, "The Bureau of Investigation," 576–77. See also Robert K. Murray, *Red Scare: A Study of National Hysteria, 1919–1920* (New York: McGraw-Hill, 1955), 193–94.

49. Weekly Intelligence Report, Jan. 22, 1921, RG 65/12C/Box 47/BS 202600-6.

50. Ibid.

51. Ibid.

52. Report of Feb. 7, 1921, Dept. of Justice files, FOIA.

53. Report on National Committee on American-Japanese Relations, Jan. 10, 1922, Dept. of Justice files, FOIA.

54. Report of Apr. 18, 1924, Dept. of Justice files, FOIA.

55. File of Sept. 24, 1942, on American Friends Service Committee; file of May 23, 1943, on the Nomonhan Incident mentions Gulick but is totally censored. File of Apr. 28, 1952, on Sidney L. Gulick, Jr., Dept. of Justice, FOIA.

56. Letter to author, May 10, 1982, from James K. Hall, FBI.

57. "Reminiscences: Personal Slanderous Attacks," July 25, 1934.

58. "Reminiscences: Bishop Bashford," July 23, 1934, GFP 20.

59. SLG to Attorney General Harry M. Daugherty, Mar. 3, 1921, RG 65/Box 3057/File 202600-989.

60. *New York Times*, June 21, 22, and 25, 1924. Macfarland also refuted the charges in *Across the Years*, 209–14.

61. Mrs. Emmeline Grace H. Condict to Secretary Charles Evans Hughes, Nov. 28, 1924, M 423, Roll 8, 711.925/1235.

62. See the report of the New York (State) Legislature, Joint Committee Investigating Seditious Activities (the Lusk Committee), *Revolutionary Radicalism: Its History, Purpose and Tactics*, 4 vols. (Albany, N.Y.: J. B. Lyon Co., 1920).

63. Attaché's report, on Dr. Sidney M. [*sic*] Gulick, Office of Naval Intelligence, Dec. 18, 1922, FOIA.

9. THE EXCLUSIONISTS TRIUMPH

1. Richard D. Glasow, "A Second Nathaneal: Sidney Lewis Gulick and the Campaign against Japanese Immigration Exclusion, 1913–1924," graduate paper, University of Santa Clara, Jan. 1971, 4–13, 4–14. The author wishes to thank Mr. Glasow for this paper, his note files, and his interview tapes with Leeds and Sidney L. Gulick, Jr., done in 1970.

2. Ibid., 4–16, 4–17.

3. U.S. Congress, Senate Report 789, *Emergency Immigration Legislation*, to accompany H.R. 14461, 66th Cong., 3d sess., No. 7774, Cal. No. 756, 1921, p. 1.

4. *New York Times*, Dec. 10, 1920.

5. Daniels, *Politics of Prejudice*, 95; Wang, *Legislating Normalcy*, 17–19. The bill was 42 Stat. 5.

6. Gulick, "Japanese in California," *Annals of the American Academy of Political and Social Science* 43 (January 1921), 55–69.

7. SLG to members of the National Committee on Immigration Legislation, Jan. 15, Mar. 24, and June 6, 1921, CRIA 222; and Gulick, *A Permanent Immigration Policy* (New York: The National Committee for Constructive Immigration Legislation, 1921), SCPC.

8. Senate Committee on Immigration, *Japanese Immigration Legislation,* hearings before the committee, S. 2576, 68th Cong., 1st sess., 1924, 97–127.

9. American Committee of Justice, *Japanese Immigration and Colonization,* 1922.

10. Federal Council *Bulletin* (1921): 85–95.

11. Gulick's minutes of the meeting of the Committee on Right Relations with Japan, Feb. 18, 1921, CRIA 224.

12. Ibid., Mar. 7, 1921, CRIA 224.

13. Ibid., June 16, 1921, Jane Addams Papers, SCPC.

14. Letter from the committee to H. A. Atkinson, May 31, 1921, CRIA 224.

15. SLG, for the FCCCA, to Ray Lyman Wilbur, July 19, 1921, Wilbur Papers, Hoover.

16. Gulick's report, meeting of the National Committee on American-Japanese Relations, Oct. 17, 1921, CRIA, 224.

17. SLG to Pres. Warren G. Harding, RG 59, 811.5294/361; National Committee on American-Japanese Relations, Apr. 7 and May 23, 1922, CRIA 226.

18. Daniels, *Politics of Prejudice,* 96–98; Harper, *Immigration Laws,* 11; Wang, *Legislating Normalcy,* 17–19.

19. SLG to family, Aug. 3 and 30, Sept. 13, Oct. 8 and 22, Dec. 25, 1922, GFP 18.

20. SLG to family, Dec. 13, 1922, GFP 18.

21. SLG to family, Sept. 13 and Oct. 22, 1922, GFP 18.

22. Gulick, *The Winning of the Far East: A Study of the Christian Movement in China, Korea, and Japan,* 52–54; Macfarland, *Pioneers for Peace,* 130–31.

23. SLG to family, Oct. 8, 1922, GFP 18.

24. SLG to family, Oct. 8, 1922, and Feb. 10, 1923, GFP 18; Gulick, "New Light on American-Japanese Question," Federal Council *Bulletin,* vol. 6 (April-May 1923): 11.

25. Lt. R. E. Webb, report to Naval Intelligence, Aug. 27, 1923, FOIA.

26. L. McNamee, report of Jan. 22, 1923, FOIA.

27. Maj. P. H. Bagby, report to N. A. Armour, Office of Undersecretary of State, July 23, 1923, 894–240, Counsellor Files.

28. Gulick, *Winning of the Far East,* 55–60.

29. George Wickersham to Jane Addams, Feb. 2, 1924, Jane Addams Papers, SCPC; National Committee on American-Japanese Relations, minutes, Feb. 2, 1924, CRIA 236.

30. Daniels, *Politics of Prejudice,* 98; Rodman W. Paul, *The Abrogation of the Gentlemen's Agreement* (Cambridge, Mass.: Harvard Univ. Press, 1936), 14–17.

31. Press release, Feb. 26, 1924, issued by Arthur Hungerford, National

Committee on American-Japanese Relations; SLG to Jane Addams, Feb. 8, 1924, Jane Addams Papers, SCPC.

32. Senate Committee on Japanese Immigration Hearings, 68th Cong., 1st sess., 1924, p. 34, as cited in Daniels, *Politics of Prejudice*, 99.

33. Japanese Immigration Hearings, 104–5, 165–66.

34. Ibid., 60–80.

35. Congressional Record, 68th Cong., 2d sess., pp. 5415, 5475, 5741, as cited in Daniels, *Politics of Prejudice*, 99–100.

36. Dept. of State, *Foreign Relations of the United States*, 1924 (Washington, 1939), 338, 372–73.

37. *Congressional Record*, 68th Cong., 2d sess., p. 6305, and Daniels, *Politics of Prejudice*, 102–3.

38. George Wickersham and Sidney L. Gulick, *Should Congress Enact the Japanese Exclusion Section?* (New York: The National Committee on American-Japanese Relations, 1924), CRIA 236; letter to members, "Declaration and Appeal," National Committee on American-Japanese Relations, Apr. 24, 1924, Evarts B. Greene Papers, Butler Library, Columbia University.

39. Daniels, *Politics of Prejudice*, 104.

40. National Committee on American-Japanese Relations, minutes, May 22 and June 13, 1924, CRIA 236.

41. As cited in Audrie Girdner and Anne Loftis, *The Great Betrayal: The Evacuation of Japanese Americans During World War II* (New York: MacMillan, 1936), 67–68.

42. *New York Times*, Apr. 19, 1924.

43. Gulick, *Toward Understanding Japan: Constructive Proposals for Removing the Menace of War*, 103.

44. *New York Times*, May 27, 1924.

45. As cited in Raymond L. Buell, *Japanese Immigration* (Boston: World Peace Foundation, 1924), 316.

46. Macfarland, *Pioneers of Peace*, 13; Buell, *Japanese Immigration*, 316–17.

47. *Federal Council Report*, 1924, p. 137.

48. Y. Ichihashi, *Japanese in the United States: A Critical Study of the Problems of the Japanese Immigrants and Their Children* (Palo Alto: Stanford Univ. Press, 1932), 317.

49. *New York Times*, Mar. 1, 1924.

50. SLG to Sidney, Jr., May 23, 1924, GFP 19.

51. SLG to Leeds, May 25, 1924, GFP 19.

52. William Axling, *Japan Wonders Why?* (New York: Commission on International Justice and Goodwill, 1924), FCCCA Papers, SCPC.

53. SLG to Wilbur, July 30, 1924, Wilbur Papers, Hoover.

54. Gulick, *Reestablishment on Right Relations Between America and Japan* (New York: Commission on Relations with the Orient, 1924), reprinted in Julia E. Johnsen, comp., *Japanese Immigration* (New York: H. W. Wilson Co., 1925), 83.

55. Gulick, "What Can I Do to Help Reestablish Right Relations with Ja-

pan?" brochure, (New York: National Committee on American-Japanese Relations, 1926), SCPC; see also Buell, *Japanese Immigration.*

56. "Japanese on the Pacific Coast: A Report to the Commission on Relations with the Orient by Sidney L. Gulick," 1927, Samuel McCune Lindsay Papers, Box 9, Butler Library, Columbia University.

57. Ibid.

58. Ibid.

59. Gulick, "Less Anti-Japan Feeling in the Western United States," *Trans-Pacific* 15 (November 5, 1927):13.

10. CHRISTIAN INTERNATIONALISM IN THE TWENTIES

1. DeBenedetti, *The Peace Reform*, chapter 6.

2. Hutchinson, *We Are Not Divided*, 196; CPU files, memo, Dec. 21, 1921, and *CIJG Annual Report, 1921*, CRIA 222; Robert Miller, "Attitudes of the Major Protestant Churches," 30–33; A. Whitney Griswold, *The Far Eastern Policy of the United States*, 293–98.

3. *CIJG Annual Report, 1921*, CRIA 222; DeBenedetti, *Origins*, 102–3.

4. Memo, probably authored by Gulick, n.d., FCCCA Papers, CIJG folder, SCPC.

5. DeBenedetti, *Origins*, 103; *Achievements of the Conference as Steps Toward a Warless World* (New York: CIJG pamphlet, 1922); *Working for a Warless World* (New York: CIJG pamphlet, 1921), FCCCA Papers, SCPC.

6. *New York Times*, Mar. 6, 1922; Gulick, *CIJG Annual Report, 1922*, FCCCA Papers, SCPC.

7. "Chronology."

8. Gulick, *Christian Crusade for a Warless World*, 38–39.

9. Hutchinson, *We Are Not Divided*, 199–200.

10. Maj. W. H. Cowles to W. L. Hurley, State Dept., Nov. 5, 1921, Counsellor Files, 894–560. See also Robert H. Ferrell, *Peace in Their Time: The Origins of the Kellogg-Briand Pact* (New Haven: Yale Univ. Press, 1952; reprint, New York: Norton, 1969), 26.

11. Press release dated Nov. 2, 1922, Counsellor Files, 800.30/3.

12. Secretary Edwin Denby to Secretary Charles Evans Hughes, copy sent to Charles Macfarland, Nov. 4, 1921, Counsellor Files, 800.30/3.

13. Hughes to Macfarland, Nov. 4, 1921; Macfarland to Hughes, Nov. 7, 1921; Counsellor Files, 800.30/3; Gulick, *Far Eastern Problems and the Conference on Limitation of Armaments* (New York: CIJG pamphlet, n.d. [1921?]).

14. Dec. 12, 1921, Counsellor Files, 894–822.

15. As reported to his family, Aug. 7, 1925, GFP 19.

16. SLG to family, Aug. 25 and Sept. 19, 1925, GFP 19.

17. Miller, "Attitudes of the Major Protestant Churches," 24–25.

18. CIJG minutes, Sept. 10, Oct. 20, Nov. 26, 1923, CRIA 230; minutes of

Nexus Committee, Jan. 28, 1924, WAIFTC Papers, SCPC; Memorials to the Senate, May 1924, 500 C 114/172 and 500 C 114/358.

19. DeBenedetti, *Origins*, 103–4; and Selig Adler, *The Uncertain Giant, 1921–1941: American Foreign Policy Between the Wars* (New York: MacMillan, 1965), 85.

20. SLG to Ethel, Nov. 24, 1924, GFP 19; *New York Times*, Jan. 28, 1925; WAIFTC minutes, Jan. 23, 1925, CRIA 241.

21. Adler, *Uncertain Giant*, 86–87.

22. DeBenedetti, *Origins*, 100; Adler, *Uncertain Giant*, 88–89; Hutchinson, *We Are Not Divided*, 202.

23. Federal Council Declaration, Dec. 16, 1921, to Secretary Charles Evans Pughes and President Warren G. Harding, 500 A 4/P 81/260 and 500 A 4/P 81/277.

24. Minutes of the CIJG, Oct. 27, 1924, CRIA 236; minutes of Nexus Committee, Oct. 31, 1924, CRIA 238; "A Call to the Churches to Mobilize for World Justice and World Peace," Nov. 1924, CRIA 236; *The Churches of America Mobilizing for World Justice and World Peace* (New York: FCCCA pamphlet, 1924), FCCCA Papers, SCPC.

25. SLG to Leeds, Nov. 30, 1924, GFP 19.

26. Minutes of Nexus Committee, May 26, 1926; and SLG to editor, *Christian Century*, Nov. 25, 1926, GFP 19.

27. Adler, *Uncertain Giant*, 89; Ferrell, *Peace in Their Time*, 72–81.

28. Confidential document, "The Churches of America and Armistice Week," Apr. 24, 1927, FCCCA Papers, SCPC; Selig Adler, *The Isolationist Impulse: Its Twentieth Century Reaction* (New York: Abelard-Schuman, 1957), 230–31.

29. *New York Times*, Nov. 11, 1927, as cited in Ferrell, *Peace in Their Time*, 129–30.

30. Gulick, *Shall the U.S. Unite With the Major Nations in Renouncing War and in Adopting Constructive Measures for Peace?* (New York: FCCCA pamphlet, 1928), FCCCA Papers, SCPC; DeBenedetti, *Origins*, 186–93; Macfarland, *Christian Unity*, 294.

31. Gulick, "The Proposal to Renounce War: A Four Weeks Study Course" (New York: CIJG, August 1928), FCCCA Papers, SCPC.

32. Miller, "Attitudes of the Major Protestant Churches," 28; "The Proposal to Renounce War"; Ferrell, *Peace in Their Time*, 243–44.

33. Gulick, "The Meaning of the Peace Pact," *National Education Association Journal* 17 (November 1928), 253.

34. Federal Council of Churches, *1929 Report*, 45, as cited in Hutchinson, *We Are Not Divided*, 203.

35. Adler, *Isolationist Impulse*, 235–38.

36. Folder, "Committee on World Friendship Among Children," FCCCA Papers, SCPC; SLG to members, Mar. 27, 1933, CRIA 245.

37. "Doll Campaign," 1926, CRIA 241.

38. Folder, "Committee on World Friendship Among Children," FCCCA Papers, SCPC; "Committee on World Friendship Among Children," 1928, CRIA 243.

39. Hutchinson, *We Are Not Divided*, 203–4.

40. Henry A. Atkinson to SLG, June 19, 1926, CRIA 241.

41. Author's personal conversation with Prof. Akira Iriye, Apr. 7, 1983.

42. "Chronology"; Gulick, for the Committee on World Friendship Among Children, *Dolls of Friendship*; pamphlets, *Adventures in World Friendship* and *Creating a World of Friendly Children* (New York: FCCCA, probably 1926).

43. Gulick, *International Relations of the United States: Brief Summaries for Busy Men and Women*, No. 2, *China* (New York: Commission on International Justice and Goodwill, June 1927), SCPC. (Hereafter cited by specific subject and date only.)

44. Gulick, *The New Prospect for Lasting Peace* (n.d., probably 1929), SLG, Jr., Papers. (All succeeding issues are from this source.)

45. Gulick, *New Plans for Disarmament*, No. 4 (n.d., probably 1929).

46. Gulick, *Working for World Peace*, No. 6 (n.d., probably 1929).

47. Gulick, *Shall the United States Join the World Court?* (n.d., probably 1930).

48. Gulick, *Why the United States Should Join the World Court* (n.d., probably 1931).

49. Hutchinson, *We Are Not Divided*, 204.

50. Gulick, *The London Naval Conference*, No. 8 (n.d., probably 1930); Adler, *The Uncertain Giant*, 129.

51. Gulick, *The London Naval Conference*.

52. SLG to Henry Stimson, Mar. 3, 1931, RG 59, 500 A 15 A 4/69.

53. Robert H. Ferrell, *American Diplomacy in the Great Depression: Hoover-Stimson Foreign Policy, 1929–1933* (New Haven: Yale Univ. Press, 1957; reprint, New York: Norton, 1970), 104–5.

54. Gulick, *The World Disarmament Conference*, No. 9 (n.d., probably 1931).

55. SLG to Stimson, May 15, 1931, RG 59, 500 A 15 A 4/144.

56. Gulick, *Coming to Grips with the War System*, No. 10 (n.d., probably 1931); SLG to Pierre Boal, State Dept., Oct. 28, 1931, RG 59, 500 A 14 A 4/538; Gulick, *How to Work for World Peace*, No. 11 (n.d., probably 1931).

57. Samuel McCrae Cavert to Hoover and Stimson, Jan. 26, 1932, RG 59, 500 A 15 A 4/781.

58. Gulick, *Mary Quizzes John About Reparations and Debts*, No. 13 (n.d., probably 1932).

59. Gulick, *Harry and Jack Discuss the American Navy*, No. 14 (n.d., probably 1932).

60. Gulick, *Mrs. Jones and Prof. Smith Discuss Disarmament*, No. 15 (n.d., probably 1933). The Federal Council was accused of being under communist influence at least as early as 1927; Francis Ralston Welsh to Secretary Kellogg,

Jan. 24, 1927, RG 59, 811.00 B/670; and Harry Curran Wilbur to Kellogg, Apr. 11, 1927, 811.00 B/696.

61. Minutes of World Court Committee, Dec. 23, 1930, Jan. 26, Feb. 10 and 20, Mar. 17, June 9, Oct. 14, 1931, CRIA 245; *New York Times,* Mar. 21, 1931.

62. Gulick, *Mrs. Jones and Mary Discuss the World Court,* No. 17 (September 1932); *Coming to Grips with the War System,* No. 19 (September 1932); Gulick and Walter W. Van Kirk, *Mary and Prof. Smith Discuss Sanctions,* No. 21 (September 1932); Gulick and Van Kirk, *David and the R.O.T.C.,* No. 23 (January 1933); Gulick, *Mary Answers Questions about the League of Nations,* No. 2 (n.d., probably 1932); SLG to the ABCFM, Jan. 19, 1931, GFP 19.

63. SLG to President Roosevelt, June 1, 1933, RG 59 811.113/320; Hutchinson, *We Are Not Divided,* pp. 204–8.

64. Gulick, "The Price of World Peace," ms. dated 1934 (?), in folder, "Addresses 1931–38," GFP 20.

65. "A Program for World Peace," Executive Committee of the FCCCA, Apr. 27, 1934, GFP 20.

66. Cara to family, June 27, 1930, GFP 19.

67. SLG to Cara, Jan. 3, 1932; Galen Fisher to SLG, May 13, 1933, GFP 19.

68. Gulick, "Report of China Famine Relief, USA, Inc.," Apr. 3, 1934, GFP 20.

69. Cavert to SLG, Jan. 3, 1934, GFP 30.

70. SLG to Cavert. Jan. 6 and 24, 1934, GFP 20.

71. Notes on retirement dinner by Galen Fisher, Apr. 10, 1934, GFP 20; *New York Times,* Apr. 11, 1934.

72. Sawada Renzo to SLG, Oct. 9, 1934, GFP 20.

73. SLG to Fanny, Mar. 1 and May 21, 1934; SLG to Cara, Oct. 25, 1934, GFP 20.

11. GULICK AND JAPAN

1. Gulick, *Anti-Japanese War Scare Stories,* 6.

2. SLG to the ABCFM, June 15, 1915, ABCFM, Japan Letters, vol. 38.

3. SLG to Atkinson, Dec. 23, 1919, CRIA 370.

4. Gulick, "American-Japanese Relations," ms. 1920, GFP 3.

5. *New York Times,* Aug. 18, 1920.

6. Gulick, *American-Japanese Relations, 1916–1920: A Retrospect* (New York: Quadrennial Report, Commission on Relations with the Orient, 1921).

7. Gulick, *Winning the Far East,* 122–27.

8. Ibid., 130.

9. Gulick, "China's Failure to Advance Laid to Lack of Leadership," *Trans-Pacific* 9(May 19, 1923):19. Like all "Asia hands," he played favorites.

10. *Detroit Free Press,* Nov. 10, 1925, in GFP 19.

11. Minutes, joint meeting of executive committee, National Committee on American-Japanese Relations and Commission on the Orient of the Commission

on International Justice and Goodwill, May 23, 1927, FCCCA Papers, SCPC; Akira Iriye, *After Imperialism: The Search for a New Order in the Far East, 1921–1931*(Cambridge, Mass.: Harvard Univ. Press, 1965), 125–30.

12. Gulick, "Friendship of the United States for China," *Annals of the American Academy of Political and Social Science* 132(July 1927):102–7.

13. Iriye, *After Imperialism*, 193–205.

14. SLG to Asst. Secretary Nelson Johnson, Oct. 1, 1928, RG 59, 893.00 Tsinan/111, M 329, Roll 85; Iriye, *After Imperialism*, 218.

15. Iriye, *After Imperialism*, 283.

16. K. Horinouchi to SLG, Apr. 10, 1933; SLG to Viscount Ishii, June 1, 1933, National Council of Churches Papers, Presbyterian Historical Society, Philadelphia.

17. Mildred Olmsted to Emily Balch, Dec. 31, 1931, Women's International League for Peace and Freedom Papers, SCPC, as cited in Warren I. Cohen, "The Role of Private Groups in the United States," in Dorothy Borg and Shumpei Okamoto, eds., *Pearl Harbor as History: Japanese-American Relations, 1931–1941*, 421–29, quotation from p. 424.

18. SLG to members, CIJG, Jan. 19, 1932, Nicholas Murray Butler Papers, Butler Library, Columbia University.

19. SLG, Jr., to SLG, n.d., 1932, GFP 19; the article is "Toward an Understanding of Japan," *Women and Missions* (journal published by the Presbyterian Church and the USA Board of Missionaries), 179–82, located in folder, "SLG Addresses," GFP 20. See also Ferrell, *American Diplomacy in the Great Depression: Hoover-Stimson Foreign Policy, 1929–1933* (New Haven: Yale Univ. Press, 1957), 170, and Dorothy Borg, *The United States and the Far Eastern Crisis of 1933–1938* (Cambridge, Mass.: Harvard Univ. Press, 1964), 8–19.

20. Editorial, reprinted from the Federal Council *Bulletin*, Mar. 1932, SLG, Jr., Papers.

21. Gulick, *Toward Understanding Japan*, 22–23.

22. Ibid., 23, 55–58.

23. Ibid., 90–91.

24. Ibid., 170–72.

25. Ibid., 210–60.

26. Book review, *New York Times*, Apr. 1935, and review by Payson J. Treat, *Annals of the American Academy of Political and Social Science* 180 (July 1935):236.

27. Review by C. H. Peake, *Social Studies* 27(January 1936):62.

28. SLG, Jr., to SLG, Jan. 14, 1934, GFP 20.

29. Cohen, "Role of Private Groups," 428–29.

30. Harold A. Larrabee, "Pacific Prophets," *Public Opinion Quarterly* 6(Fall 1942):461–62.

31. SLG to Fanny Jewett, Mar. 1, 1934; SLG to Cara, Oct. 25, 1934, Mar. 13 and 18, 1936, GFP 20.

32. SLG notes and papers, 1934–1935, GFP 20.

33. SLG to Count Kaneko Kentarō, Dec. 11, 1935, GFP 20.

34. See the review by Frank H. Hawkins, *American Sociological Review* 3 (1938):279.

35. Gulick, "Suggestions for a Realistic Far Eastern-American Policy," Aug. 11, 1936, GFP 3.

36. *Honolulu Advertiser*, Apr. 7, 1937, GFP 20.

37. *Honolulu Star-Bulletin*, Jan. 21, 1938.

38. Borg, *Far Eastern Crisis*, 486–503.

39. "Gulick Discusses Panay Case," Dec. 30, 1937, and editorial, *Honolulu Advertiser*, n.d., clippings in GFP 3.

40. SLG to Inouye Kaname, Apr. 11, 1938, GFP 20.

41. SLG to Paul Tajima, June 30 and Sept. 17, 1938, GFP 20.

42. Gulick, "Japan in China" written for the *New York Times*, Aug. 20, 1938, GFP 20. It was published in the Federal Council *Bulletin*, Nov. 1938.

43. SLG to Galen Fisher, Dec. 24, 1938.

44. SLG to Hon. Kudo Banjiro, Dec. 30, 1939 (?), GFP 20.

45. SLG to Walter Van Kirk, n.d. 1940, GFP 20.

46. SLG to Cordell Hull and editors of *Christian Century*, Mar. 11, 1940, GFP 20.

47. SLG to Fisher, Dec. 29, 1940, GFP 20.

48. SLG to editors, *Christian Century* and *Star-Bulletin*, Jan. 1, 1941, GFP 20.

49. SLG to children, Dec. 8, 1941, GFP 20.

50. Gulick, "Shall Hawaii Evacuate 100,000 Nisei?" ms., GFP 20.

51. SLG to editor, *Oakland Tribune*, Oct. 31, 1942, GFP 20.

52. Gulick, "The Alleged 'Dangerous Myth' About Japan," ms. Nov. 27, 1942, GFP 20.

53. Gulick, "Post-War Japan and Our Treatment of Her," ms. May 1943, GFP 20.

54. Gulick, "Treatment of Postwar Japan," notes for an interview with *Honolulu Star-Bulletin* reporter, May 24, 1944, GFP 20.

55. SLG to Luther, Sept. 5, 1943, GFP 20.

56. "At Four Score Years and Five: My Philosophy of Life as I Grow Old," SLG to his children, Apr. 10, 1945, SLG, Jr., Papers.

EPILOGUE

1. Gulick, *The East and the West: A Study of Their Psychic and Cultural Characteristics*, 25, 28.

2. Ibid., 28.

3. Ibid., 281. See Taylor, "The Ineffectual Voice," 29–36.

4. Arnold J. Toynbee, review of *The East and the West: A Study of Their Psychic and Cultural Characteristics*, by Sidney L. Gulick, *Pacific Affairs* 37(1964):197.

5. Taylor, "The Ineffectual Voice," 30.

6. Akira Iriye, "The Failure of Economic Expansion: 1918–1931," in Ber-

nard S. Silberman and H. D. Harootunian, eds., *Japan in Crisis: Essays on Taisho Democracy* (Princeton: Princeton Univ. Press, 1974), 259.

7. Stanley Hoffmann, *Primacy or World Order: American Foreign Policy Since the Cold War* (New York: McGraw-Hill, 1978), 17–18.

A NOTE ON SOURCES

PRIMARY SOURCES

Papers relating to the life and work of Sidney Gulick are to be found in several places. The family papers are in Houghton Library at Harvard University. They comprise some thirty-three file boxes, and were catalogued by year by Gulick's son-in-law John Barrow. Sidney's papers are in boxes 3 and 8 through 21. Letters from the Gulick family during the missionary years can also be found at Houghton in the papers of the American Board of Commissioners for Foreign Missions, the Japan Letter volumes and the Vinton Book, volume 2. Much of Gulick's work with the Federal Council of Churches is documented in the collections entitled "The Council on Religion and International Affairs" and the "World Alliance for International Friendship through the Churches," located at Butler Library, Columbia University. Letters from him are also to be found in the manuscript collections of Lincoln Steffans, Samuel McCune Lindsay, Evarts B. Greene, and Nicholas Murray Butler. A smaller number of papers on his work are to be found in the Federal Council Papers, and the Jane Addams Collection in the Swarthmore College Peace Collection, Swarthmore, Pennsylvania. The papers of Hamilton Holt at Rollins College, Florida, also contain a few of Gulick's letters and the Presbyterian Historical Society, Philadelphia, also has some. There are also a few Gulick materials at the Bancroft Library at the University of California in the papers of Senator James D. Phelan, Chester Rowell, Senator John D. Works, and Benjamin Ide Wheeler. The Hoover Institution on War, Revolution, and Peace contains some of his pamphlets, and the name file in the National Archives produced the letters he wrote to the Department of State and to various presidents. Some of the intelligence material on Gulick is to be found in the Department of Justice files at the Archives and in the diplomatic division; most, however, is the result of a Freedom of Information Act request. I obtained most of his published pamphlet material, some family letters, and the "Chronology" and "A Sketch of My Life," from his son, Sidney L. Gulick, Jr., of La Mesa, California. Additional family information came from long conversations with Sidney, Jr., and with Gulick's oldest son, Luther H. Gulick of New York City. The pictures were supplied by Mrs. Ethel Gulick Barrow of Austin, Texas.

Gulick was a prolific writer, as this work has demonstrated. Ariga Tetsutaro in the preface to Gulick's last book, *The East and the West*, noted that he had published thirty-five works, fourteen of them in English. Some of these, however, included pamphlets, and others were works translated from English to Japanese. The major works he published in Japanese (with the assistance of his aid Tomita-san) were entitled (in English) *A Sketch of the History of German Theology* (1909); *Evolution: Cosmic, Terrestrial, Biological* (1910); *Evolution of the Human Race* (1913); and *General Cyclopedia, with Classification of Human Knowledge* (1914). These were privately printed in Japan at Dōshisha University and are not available in the United States.

Gulick's works in English are the following: *The Growth of the Kingdom of God* (New York: Fleming H. Revell Co., 1896); *Evolution of the Japanese: A Study of Their Characteristics in Relation to the Principles of Social and Psychic Development* (New York: Fleming H. Revell Co., 1903); *The White Peril in the Far East: An Interpretation of the Significance of the Russo-Japanese War* (New York: Fleming H. Revell Co., 1905); *The American Japanese Problem: A Study of the Racial Relations of the East and West* (New York: Charles Scribner's Sons, 1914); *The Fight for Peace: An Aggressive Campaign for American Churches* (New York: Fleming H. Revell Co., 1915); *Working Women of Japan* (New York: Missionary Education Movement of the U.S. and Canada, 1915); *America and the Orient: Outlines of a Constructive Policy* (New York: Missionary Education Movement of the U.S. and Canada, 1916); *American Democracy and Asiatic Citizenship* (New York: Charles Scribner's Sons, 1918); *The Christian Crusade for a Warless World* (New York: MacMillan, 1923); *The Winning of the Far East: A Study of the Christian Movement in China, Korea, and Japan* (New York: George H. Doran, 1923); *Dolls of Friendship* (New York: Friendship Press, 1929); *Toward Understanding Japan: Constructive Proposals for Removing the Menace of War* (New York: MacMillan, 1935); *Mixing the Races in Hawaii: A Study of the Coming Neo-Hawaiian American Race* (Honolulu: The Hawaiian Board Book Rooms, 1937); *The East and the West: A Study of Their Psychic and Cultural Characteristics* (Rutland, Vt.: Charles E. Tuttle, 1962). In addition, Gulick published numerous pamphlets and articles which are cited in the text or endnotes.

SECONDARY SOURCES

Missionaries to Japan

The history of Protestant Christianity in Japan has been recounted in some basic works. Otis Cary, *A History of Christianity in Japan*, 2 vols. (London and New York: Student Volunteer Movement for Foreign Missions, 1899; reprint Rutland, Vt.: Charles E. Tuttle, 1976), and H. Ritter, *A History of Protestant Missions in Japan*, translated by George A. Albrecht (Tokyo: Methodist Publishing House, 1898), are still useful. Kenneth Scott Latourette, *The Great Century: Northern Africa and Asia*, vol. 6, *A History of the Expansion of Christianity* (New York: Harper and Bros., 1944) is a classic. Two more recent works are especially useful: Winburn T. Thomas, *Protestant Beginnings in Japan* (Rutland, Vt.: Charles E. Tuttle, 1959), and Charles W. Iglehart, *A Century of Protestant Christianity in Japan* (Rutland, Vt.: Charles E. Tuttle, 1960). Also helpful were Ernest E. Best, *Christian Faith and Cultural Crisis: The Japanese Case* (Leiden: E. J. Brill, 1966), and Yamamori Tetsunao, *Church Growth in Japan: A Study in the Development of Eight Denominations, 1859–1939* (South Pasadena, Calif.: Wm. Carey Library, 1974). Of the many books written by and about Congregational missionaries in Japan, the most useful for this study were the two books by M. L. Gordon: *An American Missionary in Japan* (Boston: Houghton Mifflin, 1892), and *Thirty Eventful Years: The Story of the American Board's Mission in Japan, 1869–1899* (Boston: Congregational House, 1901).

There have been several important analyses of the role of Protestant missionaries, among which John Edwin Smylie, "Protestant Clergymen and American Destiny: II, Prelude to Imperialism, 1865–1900," *Harvard Theological Review* 56 (October 1963): 297–311; and Paul Varg, "Motives of Protestant Missionaries, 1890–1917," *Church History* 23 (1954), 68–82, were stimulating and insightful. James E. Reed, *The Missionary Mind and American East Asia Policy, 1911–1915* (Cambridge, Mass.: Council on East Asian Studies for Harvard Univ. Press, 1983) is very provocative.

The best works on the American Board itself are: William Ellsworth Strong, *The Story of the American Board: An Account of the First Hundred Years of the American Board of Commissioners for Foreign Missions* (Boston: Pilgrim Press, 1910; reprint New York: Arno Press and the *New York Times*, 1969); Clifton J. Phillips, *Protestant America and the Pagan World: The First Half Century of the American Board of Commissioners for Foreign Missions, 1810–1860* (Cambridge, Mass.: Harvard Univ. Press, 1969); and Alan F. Perry, "The American Board of Commissioners for Foreign Missions and the London Missionary Society in the Nineteenth Century: A Study of Ideas," unpublished Ph.D. dissertation, Washington University, 1974. Also useful are Fred Field Goodsell, *You Shall Be My Witness* (Boston: American Board of Commissioners for Foreign Missions, 1959), and R. Pierce Beaver, *All Loves Excelling: American Protestant Women in World Mission* (Grand Rapids, Mich.: Wm. Eerdmans, 1968), written more from a missionary perspective.

For a study of the Japanese response to the missionary appeal, one must begin with Robert S. Schwantes's useful work, *Japanese and Americans: A Century of Cultural Relations* (New York: published by Harper for the Council on Foreign Relations, 1955), and his "Christianity versus Science: A Conflict of Ideas in Meiji Japan," *Far Eastern Quarterly* 12 (November 1952): 123–32. *Japanese Religion in the Meiji Era* (Tokyo: Obunsha, 1956), compiled by Kishimoto Hideo and translated by John F. Howes, provides helpful background information. Most useful on the Japanese Christians are Irwin Scheiner, *Christian Converts and Social Protest in Meiji Japan* (Berkeley: Univ. of California Press, 1970), and the different interpretation presented by George E. Moore, "Samurai Conversion: The Case of Kumamoto," *Asian Studies*, University of the Philippines, 4 (April 1966): 40–48. John F. Howes, "Japanese Christians and American Missionaries," in Marius B. Jansen, ed., *Changing Japanese Attitudes Toward Modernization* (Princeton: Princeton Univ. Press, 1963) is invaluable for an understanding of the subject. Two essays in Donald H. Shively, ed., *Tradition and Modernization in Japanese Culture* (Princeton: Princeton Univ. Press, 1971), are important: Michio Nagai, "Westernization and Japanization: The Early Meiji Transformation of Education" (pp. 35–76), and Donald H. Shively, "The Japanization of Middle Meiji" (pp. 77–119).

The Peace Movement

There are three books basic to an understanding of the peace movement during the time Gulick was active in it: David S. Patterson, *Toward a Warless World: The Travail of the American Peace Movement, 1887–1914* Bloomington: Univ. of Indiana Press, 1976); C. Roland Marchand, *The American Peace Movement and Social Reform, 1898–1918* (Princeton: Princeton Univ. Press, 1972); and Charles DeBenedetti, *Origins of the Modern American Peace Movement, 1915–1929* (Millwood, N.J.: KTO Press, 1978). To that list I would add the following as useful for this work: DeBenedetti's *The Peace Reform in American History* (Bloomington: Univ. of Indiana Press, 1980), and Warren F. Kuehl, *Hamilton Holt: Journalist, Internationalist, Educator* (Gainesville, Fla.: Univ. of

Florida Press, 1960). John A. Hutchinson's *We Are Not Divided* (New York: Round Table Press, 1941), is the only overview of the Federal Council available. Two very useful articles on the Protestants and World War I are Darrell E. Bigham, "War as Obligation in the Thought of American Christians, 1898–1920," *Peace and Change* 7 (Winter 1981): 45–57; and Robert M. Miller, "The Attitudes of the Major Protestant Churches in America Toward War and Peace, 1919–1929," *The Historian* 19 (1956): 13–38.

The Immigration Controversy

The essential works for an understanding of a history of Japanese Americans are those by Roger Daniels. Fundamental to this period is *The Politics of Prejudice: The Anti-Japanese Movement in California and the Struggle for Japanese Exclusion* (Berkeley: Univ. of California Press, 1962; reprint Gloucester, Mass.: Peter Smith, 1966), a careful analysis of California politics and the Japanese question. Further information can be gained from "American Historians and East Asian Immigrants," *Pacific Historical Review* 43 (1974): 460–61; "Japanese Immigrants on a Western Frontier: The Issei in California, 1890–1940," in F. Hilary Conroy and T. Scott Miyakawa, *East Across the Pacific: Historical and Sociological Studies of Japanese Immigration and Assimilation* (Santa Barbara: ABC-Clio, 1972); and "The Japanese," in John Higham, ed., *Ethnic Leadership in America* (Baltimore: Johns Hopkins Univ. Press, 1978), all by Daniels. Carey McWilliams, *Prejudice: Japanese-Americans, Symbol of Racial Intolerance* (Boston: Little, Brown, 1944), is older and dated. Akira Iriye has some important insights into Japan's reasons for encouraging emigration in his essay, "Japan as a Competitor, 1895–1917," in Iriye, ed., *Mutual Images: Essays in America-Japanese Relations* (Cambridge, Mass.: Harvard Univ. Press, 1975). The laws relating to Japanese immigration can be found in Elizabeth J. Harper and Roland F. Chase, *Immigration Laws of the United States* (Indianapolis: Bobbs-Merrill, 1975).

General Works on American-Japanese Relations

Although studies of American diplomacy with Japan have dated from the pioneering efforts of Tyler Dennett, *Americans in Eastern Asia* (New York: MacMillan, 1922); Payson J. Treat, *Diplomatic Relations Between the United States and Japan*, 3 vols. (Stanford: Stanford Univ. Press, 1932 and 1938, reprint Gloucester, Mass.: Peter Smith, 1963); and A. Whitney Griswold, *The Far Eastern Policy of the United States* (New Haven: Yale Univ. Press, 1938), the most outstanding work in the field has been done by Akira Iriye. The books, *Across the Pacific: An Inner History of American East Asian Relations* (New York: Harcourt, Brace and World, 1967), and *Pacific Estrangement: Japanese and American Expansion, 1897–1911* (Cambridge, Mass.: Harvard Univ. Press, 1972) were essential. Also helpful were William Neumann, *America Encounters Japan: From Perry to MacArthur* (Baltimore: Johns Hopkins Univ. Press, 1963), and Charles E. Neu, *The Troubled Encounter: The United States and Japan* (New York: Wiley, 1975). The essay by Warren I. Cohen, "The Role of Private Groups in the United States," in Dorothy Borg and Shumpei Okamoto, eds., *Pearl Harbor as History: Japanese-American Relations 1931–1941* (New York: Columbia Univ. Press, 1973), was also useful.

INDEX